THE SOVIET UNION UNDER GORBACHEV:
Prospects for Reform

Edited by David A. Dyker

CROOM HELM
London • New York • Sydney

© 1987 David A. Dyker
Croom Helm Ltd, Provident House, Burrell Row,
Beckenham, Kent, BR3 1AT
Croom Helm Australia, 44-50 Waterloo Road,
North Ryde, 2113, New South Wales

British Library Cataloguing in Publication Data

The Soviet Union under Gorbachev: prospects for reform.
    1. Soviet Union — Social Conditions — 1970-
    I. Dyker, David A.
    947.085′4   HN523.5
    ISBN 0-7099-4519-1

Published in the USA by
Croom Helm
in association with Methuen, Inc.
29 West 35th Street
New York, NY 10001

Library of Congress Cataloging-in-Publication Data

The Soviet Union under Gorbachev.

    Bibliography: p.
    Includes index.
    1. Soviet Union—Economic policy—1981-
2. Soviet Union—Politics and government—1982-
I. Dyker, David A.
HC336.25.S685 1987   338.947   87-15432
ISBN 0-7099-4519-1

Filmset by Mayhew Typesetting, Bristol, England
Printed and bound in Great Britain
by Billing & Sons Limited, Worcester.

Contents

Contents

Preface

This book represents the fruits of an informal study group, centred on the School of European Studies, University of Sussex, which met through the summer of 1986. Our aim was to bring together the experience — practical as well as academic — of a small group of Soviet specialists with contrasting expertises, and see how close we could come in our assessments of the likely future of Gorbachev's Soviet Union. Without any undue prompting from the editor, a remarkably high degree of consensus was achieved, and the result is a tolerably clear prognostication. How correct it is events alone can show. Our thanks are due to David R. Jones, editor of *Soviet Armed Forces Review Annual*, for permission to use the material presented in Tables 6.1 and 6.2. We must also record our appreciation of the help we received from the staff of the School of European Studies in the preparations of the typescript.

David A. Dyker,
School of European Studies, University of Sussex

Notes on Contributors

David A. Dyker was born in Aberdeen in 1944 and educated at the University of Glasgow and the Institute of National Economy, Tashkent, USSR. He is the author of *The Soviet Economy* (Crosby Lockwood Staples, London, 1976), *The Process of Investment in the Soviet Union* (Cambridge University Press, Cambridge, 1983) and *The Future of the Soviet Economic Planning System* (Croom Helm, London, 1985). He lectures in Economics in the School of European Studies, University of Sussex.

Iain Elliot was born in Kilmarnock, Scotland, in 1943. Educated at the Universities of Glasgow and Leningrad, he currently holds the position of senior lecturer in Russian Studies at Brighton Polytechnic. Dr Elliot's publications include *The Soviet Energy Balance* (Praeger, New York, Washington and London, 1974). He is editor of the fortnightly newsletter *Soviet Analyst*.

Zdeněk Kavan, born in London in 1947 and educated in Prague, has made his home in Britain since 1968. He is the author of 'Human Rights and International Community', in James Mayall, (ed.) *The Community of States* (Allen and Unwin, London, 1982). Zdeněk Kavan is lecturer in International Relations in the School of European Studies, University of Sussex.

Alan H. Smith was born in 1944 in London, and educated at the University of Birmingham. His published works include *The Planned Economies of Eastern Europe* (Croom Helm, London, 1983). After varied experience working in the oil industry and teaching business studies, he joined the School of Slavonic and East European Studies, University of London, where he holds the position of lecturer in Economics.

1

Introduction

David A. Dyker

In the period since the 1985 change in the Soviet leadership there has been, understandably, a good deal of emphasis on Gorbachev the personality. In terms of self-projection, handling of the media, and presentation of policy departures, the new General Secretary has undoubtedly struck a new note, set a new style. The aim of the present work is to try to get beyond the stage management, to peel off the packaging, and evaluate the policy departures on their own merits. In so doing we have not lacked for formal pronouncements to serve as a starting point. With planning experiments, agricultural reorganisations and arms reduction proposals, not to mention intra-Comecon vicissitudes and ubiquitous personnel changes, our problem in the present context was rather one of selection. The principle we chose emerges directly from our title. We are interested in *prospects for reform*. That is why we have not devoted special chapters to, for instance, nationality relations, religion and political dissent. In terms of evaluation of likely secular trends in Soviet polity and society, those and other dimensions may be as important as any. But it is very improbable that they will be the subject of specific, major legislation or negotiation this year or next. That is why we have concentrated on Gorbachev's internal politics, Soviet foreign policy in all its ramifications, and economic reform. Other issues are introduced to the extent that they shed light on these, our central concerns. They are, needless to say, intertwining themes. We have tried to point up the linkages as we go along, and to pull together as many threads as possible in our Conclusion. Certainly the full pattern has not yet been revealed to us, and in the last analysis this must remain a provisional assessment. But, of course, 'il n'y a rien qui dure que le provisoire'.

David A. Dyker

What do we mean by 'reform'?

Why has 'reform' been such a dominant theme in the Soviet Union, and in Soviet studies, for over a quarter of a century now? Other countries, it seems, can get by without reforms, so why not the Soviet Union? The simplest answer is that in a system so highly centralised, so heavily based on the military principle of command, very little can change without express permission from Party and government. In our search for a workable definition, then, we begin by contrasting 'reform' to 'evolution'.

There can be no doubt, however, that in the Soviet Union itself, under Brezhnev, 'reform', like 'experiment', became a weasel word. In practice, through a period of overwhelming inertia in policy-making, reforms and experiments served as *substitutes* for policies, rather than their foundations. After the emasculation of the 1965 industrial planning reform (see below) for example, the principle was established that nothing that changed anything should ever be generalised to the level of the economic system as a whole. That is why Gorbachev talks of the need for 'radical reform' — not to imply necessarily that he wants to turn the whole system upside down, but simply to indicate that he means business in a way that Brezhnev did not. In our treatment we also proceed on the basis of a concept of radical reform. By 'reform' we imply 'a policy of social and economic reforms by gradual stages rather than by revolutionary change' (Bullock and Stallybrass, 1977, p. 532). Our understanding of 'radical' does not pre-empt the discussion — which indeed forms the main part of this book — of just how far Gorbachev needs to go. But it certainly implies that he will have to go very much further than any of his predecessors have gone. Agnes Heller writes that 'the absolute and necessary precondition of genuine reform is at present totally absent from the Soviet scene. This precondition is a thoroughgoing structural critique of the past: one that is not limited to vague references in misty party documents, but goes on in open public debate' (Heller, 1985, p. 26). We may baulk a little at the strength of the conclusion, but can hardly dispute the rightness of the emphasis on the assessment of the past, on that which is structural/systemic, and on the importance of open discussion.

Background: the roots of the economic problem

It is in the economic sphere that the leitmotif of reform has recurred most frequently since the death of Stalin, and this has reflected an extreme tension between the pressures of economic development and the forms of economic administration. For however sharp may be the underlying technological or social pressures, they cannot get through to the socio-economic system without the consent of the authorities. *Pace* Galbraith, there can be no technological imperatives in the Soviet system, only political ones. At the same time Party and government are constrained in their freedom to respond or not respond to pressures by the need to survive. This is where the theme of *dirigisme* becomes more complex and interesting, for it is precisely the principle of centralisation which stands in greatest need of reform *from the point of view of planning and management itself.*

The Soviet planning system developed at a time, and in circumstances, unique in Soviet, and indeed world experience. Under the leadership of Joseph Stalin, a man obsessed with the role of political control, and in the context of severe economic backwardness, the Soviets developed an approach which attacked the economic development problem through an essentially political process of *mobilisation*. It was within that framework that a high degree of centralisation was seen as essential, that the principle of command was purposefully extended through the whole of the Soviet economy, starting with collectivisation of agriculture by force in 1930–2. For rapidly growing Soviet industry that meant the imposition of a hierarchical system of planning, running from the State Planning Commission (Gosplan) at the centre, down through a number of industrial-sectoral ministries to the enterprise at the bottom of the ladder. Every enterprise was set an obligatory production target, and bonuses, promotion and even survival depended on fulfilment of that target. Reluctant collective farmers were kept on their toes through the medium of compulsory procurement quotas — whether they had enough left after fulfilment of those quotas to feed themselves was viewed as strictly their problem (Dyker, 1985, ch. 1).

There can be no doubt that the system worked well as a vehicle of rapid growth, particularly industrial growth. Over the first 40 years of its existence it reported rates of growth of National Income consistently above 5 per cent per annum, and industrial rates of growth which often reached double figures. Equally

3

important, the Nazi onslaught of 1941–2 was repulsed. The experience of other countries suggests that the same results might have been achievable on a different institutional basis. Nevertheless it is fair to say that the sheer weight of Stalin's mobilisatory impetus proved highly effective in implementing very rapid structural change in the Soviet economy. Massive transfers of labour out of overpopulated agriculture permitted the development of a labour-intensive industrial infrastructure to complement the highly capital-intensive 'grand projects', while compulsory grain procurement quotas ensured that there would always be enough food (if only just) to feed the new proletariat. Many of the grand projects in turn focused on bringing into play the massive reserves of industrial raw materials present in the Urals and West Siberia regions. Once on stream, these projects ensured plentiful and cheap supplies of ores and energy materials to manufacturing industry. Thus Stalin could count on abundance of labour *and* raw materials. The latter point is particularly important in that it freed the Soviet Union from the kinds of Balance of Payments worries which afflict most developing countries as they set out on industrialisation programmes, with all that that means in terms of the demand for oil, etc. The only thing that Stalin *did* have to obtain from the outside world was technology, and just because the USSR was in those early days so very far behind, that could on the whole be acquired quite cheaply. Thus in putting maximum pressure on enterprises to produce as much as quickly as possible, the Soviet leadership could feel confident that enterprise managers would not run into unbreakable bottlenecks, whether in terms of labour or materials supply. Bottlenecks certainly did emerge, but they were negotiable ones, and Stalin actually used them to pinpoint the priorities of the industrialisation programme (Wilber, 1969, ch. V). Through the system of Material Balances, which charted supply and demand for each product on a double-entry book-keeping basis, the planners disposed of a crude, but flexible tool of product-flow planning which fitted in ideally with Stalin's 'priority principle' approach. And because of the unconstrained resource situation the Soviet planners were able to force out rapid aggregate growth *without having to worry too much about productivity and cost trends*. This is the essence of the 'extensive growth' pattern.

By the 1960s all of this was changing. As the scope for further transfers of labour from the countryside became increasingly limited, as the female participation rate rose to levels which seriously threatened the rate of natural increase in European parts of the USSR, so the labour supply situation became increasingly strained. Meanwhile hydrocarbon deposits west of the Urals were being depleted, and in 1963–4 commercial exploitation of West Siberian oil and gas began. There is no disputing the richness of hydrocarbon deposits in Siberia, but difficult geographical and climatic conditions ensure that capital costs are very high. By the early 1970s the most accessible of the West Siberian deposits were themselves being depleted, and capital costs rose remorselessly as prospectors were forced farther north and east. Unit capital costs in gas extraction doubled 1970–3 (Dyker, 1983, p. 161), and by 1980 output at the great Samotlor oil field had peaked and gone into decline. There were to be no more Samotlors. Faced, then, with a sharply rising long-run marginal cost curve in energy production, the Soviet authorities found themselves under severe pressure to cut back on energy consumption so as to give the Oil and Gas Ministries some breathing space in relation to the exploitation of more marginal fields. Whether in terms of human or material resources, then, the priority had now to shift onto productivity and cost-effectiveness.

The traditional system of planning was, however, peculiarly ill-suited to this task. The tyranny of monthly or quarterly output targets had given enterprise directors every reason to want to hang onto surplus labour 'just in case', the more so that central planning had proved especially bad at providing industrial establishments with 'fiddly' components. To this day, for instance, Soviet engineering factories find it necessary to make their own nuts and bolts. Soviet lorry drivers would get their bonuses for fulfilling targets for ton/kilometres, estimated on the basis of petrol consumption. So if something went wrong and they were unable to do the ton/kilometres, they might just pour off some petrol down the gutter, to keep up appearances (Turovsky, 1984, pp. 163–4). Oil and gas extraction enterprises in Western Siberia, suffering on the same treadmill of endless production quotas for their 'name' product, have found little incentive to do anything with valuable accessory gas and gas condensate (Dyker, 1983, pp. 169–70). Lack of sensitivity to costs apart, the system of centralised planning showed itself increasingly helpless in the face of the burgeoning complexity of a rapidly growing economy. This manifested itself initially in increasing disarray on the investment front — Khrushchev's first, rather ineffectual, round of planning reforms was, indeed, focused specifically on that issue. By the 1970s the problem of overcentralisation was taking a new twist, as technical progress revolutionised the electronics and communications industry. In the age of the micro-chip the idea of planning through output targets began to seem positively antediluvian. But as the planning system itself became increasingly obsolescent, so it tended to condemn its 'victims' to the same fate. Once again, the tyranny of short-term output targets creates a powerful disincentive for the enterprise manager to do anything which disrupts continuous production, i.e. anything involving fundamental technical change. However committed the central authorities may be to innovation, they simply did not dispose of a vehicle adequate to implement it.

The evolution of Soviet agriculture presented an altogether different picture. The impact of collectivisation was largely negative right from the start — on agriculture itself and indeed on the Soviet economy as a whole. Stalin's theory of 'pumping-over' resources from agriculture to finance the 'primitive socialist accumulation' required by the industrialisation drive found little applicability during the crucial period of the 1930s, because the process of forcible collectivisation itself was so damaging to agriculture as to leave nothing to pump over. Even so, millions of peasants died of starvation in the early 1930s. There was more effective pumping-over during the Second World War, and in the post-war recovery period, but while this may have aided the causes of victory and industrial reconstruction, it deepened profoundly a process of demoralisation of the peasantry which had been begun by collectivisation itself. The demographic impact of extensive industrialisation (43.4 million people migrated from country to town 1926–39 — Gregory and Stuart, 1986, p. 113), combined with the appalling loss of life during the war itself, left the rural population skewed towards the middle-aged and the female, and added specific manpower shortages to morale problems. It is not surprising, then, that on Stalin's death agricultural output was not much greater than it had been in the late 1920s.

Khrushchev attacked these problems on two main fronts. On the one hand he raised agricultural procurement prices sharply. This improved incomes and incentives for the peasants and facilitated sharp increases in the flow of investment into agriculture. On the other, he sought to strengthen the state and collective farms through amalgamations and through the transfer to them of the machinery previously held by the Machine Tractor Stations. At the same time he tried to make the internal organisation of the farms more flexible by encouraging development of the 'link' system, under which small, peasant work-teams are allowed a certain degree of operational autonomy. The merits of at least some of these policies was reflected in a 50 per cent increase in aggregate agricultural output between 1953 and 1958. But this was followed by a new period of stagnation, as the policy package started to break up under pressure. Khrushchev felt by the late 1950s that there had been enough price increases already, although transfers of MTS machinery to collective farms — which had to be paid for — placed a big extra burden on farm finances. As a result agricultural investment trends lost their buoyancy, while peasant incomes fell. Meanwhile the link system was running into difficulties, and Khrushchev had taken to repressive policies to stop peasants spending too long on their private plots. At the same time the costly Virgin Lands scheme, a classic example of extensive development tactics in agriculture as marginal lands were brought into cultivation for the first time, had run out of steam. By the time Khrushchev fell from power, then, most of the agricultural problems he had inherited from Stalin were still, in some degree, on the agenda.

Background: the evolution of the political system

Stalin was a *tyrant*. For better or worse he ruled by imposing his personal will through lieutenants responsible only to him. He was quite uninhibited about using terror as a means of keeping the population at large in submission *and* as a way of preventing his lieutenants from developing any political independence. Having originally risen to power by building up support in the Communist Party, he then largely destroyed the apex of the Party in the Great Purges of 1936–8. From that time until his death he chose to rule largely through the medium of the secret police, though the Party continued to play an important role, politically and economically, at the provincial and city level. After Stalin's death a power struggle between his lieutenants developed. It was won by Nikita Khrushchev, who had taken over Stalin's position as head of the Party secretariat (Khrushchev called himself First Secretary rather than General Secretary). Beria, the police chief, was shot, and Malenkov, who took over the premiership in 1953, had by 1957 been forced into retirement. Political adroitness apart, the basis for Khrushchev's success was the fact that he allied himself with a resurgent Party identity. Central Committee Plena and Party Congresses became more frequent, and the Politburo (known as the Presidium during the Khrushchev period) began to take on some of the characteristics of a genuine cabinet, with policy issues playing counterpoint to personality clashes. Thus the Party, and in particular its professional apparatus — the Central Committee secretariat and the national network of regional secretaries — re-emerged with something like its old 'vanguard of the proletariat' image. However the socio-political content of this re-emergence was anything but radical. For the apparatus, and for Khrushchev, Stalin's greatest crime had been to oppress and abuse the Party. Now that Stalin was gone, the Party could look forward to a future freed of the threat of terror, in which political careers could be built on solid foundations. It was only a short step from notions such as these to the reality of consolidation of privilege, including the privilege of passing on your status to your children, of political 'family circles' which sought to ensure survival through mutual back-scratching — in a word to the development of Djilas's new class.

We should certainly not exaggerate the extent of collective leadership under Khrushchev. Especially after his defeat of the so-called Anti-Party Group in 1957, the First Secretary enjoyed a position of political dominance. He even felt strong enough, in 1962, to split the Party into two separate hierarchies, one for agriculture, one for industry, in an attempt to raise the political status of an agricultural sector still shell-shocked from Stalin's rough treatment. In so doing he inevitably disturbed the family circles, and disrupted normal patterns of promotion. Perhaps that was why, less than two years later, the Central Committee of the Communist Party voted him out of office. Both Lenin and Stalin died in office. Khrushchev's dismissal, by the highest organ of the Party, seemed to promise a new phase in Soviet history, a new quasi-constitutionality in the Soviet mode of political succession.

That promise was not, in the event, fulfilled. All Soviet General Secretaries (Brezhnev revived Stalin's title) since Khrushchev have died in office. The spectacle of Brezhnev's last years, when personal physical decline highlighted policy drift, underlined how embarrassing the issue of political succession remains in the Soviet Union. On Andropov's death in 1983, only a year after his succession to Brezhnev, the Central Committee does, indeed, seem to have deemed it best to choose a General Secretary with one foot already in the grave. But this is not to say that the Central Committee had been ineffectual — far from it. The fact is that no

Soviet leader since Khrushchev has dared to attack *apparatchik* power and vested interest: Brezhnev and Chernenko were both model apparatus men, and from the purely political point of view their incumbency may have been precisely what the Central Committee, numerically dominated by *apparatchiki*, wanted. The picture is, of course, complicated by factionalism and intergenerational tension within the apparatus, as we shall see later on. What does clearly emerge from the post-Khrushchev pattern is the notion that *policy-making* may have suffered at the hands of *politics*. Let us put flesh on this idea by studying the fate of Kosygin's 1965 industrial planning reform, the major legislative initiative of the Brezhnev era.

In replacing the traditional gross output success-indicator with aggregate sales, Kosygin sought in 1965 to push enterprises in the direction of producing for the customer, not just for the plan. The introduction, for the first time, of profit as a key success-indicator was calculated to back up the sales indicator and bring in a genuine incentive to cost economy, so as to stop the kind of misallocations and abuses that were discussed earlier. For the first time enterprises would have to pay a charge on their fixed capital stock, and there is no doubt that in the event a good deal of dishoarding of 'just in case' accumulations of equipment did follow. But it quickly became evident that the new indicators could only work properly if some play of market forces were allowed in the system — without that sales was in practice little different from gross output, while profiteering was too easy and difficult to control. Distinguished economists like Nemchinov had argued the need to introduce some such 'wholesale trade in the means of production' as early as 1960 (Nove, 1968, p. 262), and limited forms of wholesale trading were, indeed, introduced in the late 1960s. Meanwhile the link system came back into favour in agriculture, while farms were allowed a new degree of independence to set up subsidiary industrial operations.

But by the beginning of 1968 the *apparatchiki* were on their guard, as they viewed developments in Czechoslovakia with increasing suspicion. It had already become clear from the Czech economic reforms of 1967 that wholesale trade in the means of production could have far-reaching implications for the traditional role of the apparatus man in the economic sphere. It is precisely the local Party secretary who has in the past played the key role of trouble-shooter, trying to sort out supply foul-ups through political cajolery and *blat* (influence → corruption), trying to keep economic developments in his fief in line with Party priorities. By early 1968 the Czechoslovak *apparatchiki* were beginning to realise that by permitting the introduction of a form of market socialism they had done themselves out of a job (Urbanek, 1968). With the breaking of the Prague Spring in 1968, the lifting of censorship and the retreat of the Czechoslovak Communist Party from its traditional 'leading role', the threatening picture was complete. In the context of economic and political reform the apparatus stood to lose its two main roles as they had developed since the death of Stalin — economic problem-solving and political control. That was too much, and the Soviet tanks duly rolled into Prague in August 1968. Interestingly enough, the Hungarians were allowed to push through their *economically* very radical New Economic Mechanism in the same year. Kadar's firm grip on the whole development, which ensured minimal political repercussions and minimal publicity outside Hungary, seems to have been enough to reassure the Russians. The Czechoslovak disease, by contrast, was viewed as both more virulent and more infectious. But by killing the Prague Spring the Soviet tanks also killed the reform movement in the USSR itself.

By the early 1970s the hesitant steps of Kosygin's reform in the direction of decentralisation were beginning to show some rather perverse effects. In particular, they were destabilising the problematic investment sector. As we shall argue later on, the reason for this was quite certainly the *insufficient* degree of development of wholesale trade in the means of production. The Party men chose to interpret it as evidence that decentralisation of a Soviet-type economy does not work, that market concepts have no place in Soviet socialism. The political convenience of this interpretation hardly needs stressing. About the same time a wave of repression against the decentralising link movement in agriculture was unleashed, and at least one proponent of the system ended up in jail (Dyker, 1985, pp. 89–90).

Developments in the world situation around this time facilitated reaction. With the quadrupling of the prices of oil and gold at the end of 1973 Brezhnev found himself with much-enhanced hard-currency purchasing power. He seems to have thought that the increased imports of Western technology which this made possible could serve as a substitute for serious economic reform (Kaser, 1975, pp. 204–5). Meanwhile the 1973 Soviet grain harvest was the best yet by a long way. This is the economic background to 'mature Brezhnevism', and the theme of thankful immobilism is strongly echoed in the political sphere. During the Brezhnev period security of tenure in the political establishment reached unprecedented heights, and more than 90 per cent of the 1976 Central Committtee still alive in 1981 were re-elected in that year (Donaldson, 1985, p. 9). To quote a distinguished American political scientist, 'If Khrushchev brought the Soviet elite the gift of security of life, Brezhnev assured it security of office' (Bialer, 1980, p. 91). The inter-generational problems which this inevitably entailed will form an important part of the subsequent discussion.

Background: the international dimension

Stalin's successors inherited a kind of empire in Eastern Europe. It was an empire built up in the immediate post-war period essentially as a buffer against a United States that was immeasurably the stronger of the two principal allies, in economic terms and in terms of conventional and nuclear defence capability. It was an unstable empire. It quickly lost Yugoslavia and Albania completely, and subsequently to a degree lost Romania. It retained control over Hungary, Czechoslovakia and East Germany only through the use of military force. But control over the 'iron triangle' of Poland, East Germany and Czechoslovakia has remained a cornerstone of Soviet military doctrine. On the economic side Stalin ruthlessly exploited Eastern Europe in the cause of reconstructing the war-devastated Motherland. Even Yugoslavia came in for the treatment, and that was one of the factors lying behind Soviet-Yugoslav tensions. By the mid-1950s, however, this phase was definitely over, and Khrushchev saw Soviet advantage within Comecon in the development of a genuine division of labour. That, again, was something the Romanians, bent on the building of socialism in one country, did not like, and was one of the reasons why Bucharest started to assert greater independence.

With the fourfold increase in oil prices in 1973 a new phase in Soviet-East European relations begins. The opportunity cost to the Soviet Union of supplying oil to Eastern Europe had now risen dramatically. A system was introduced in January 1975 whereby intra-Comecon international trade prices were calculated on the basis of a five-year moving average of world prices, adjusted annually. This ensured an improvement in the terms of trade for the Soviet Union, as energy prices were pulled up towards the world level, but it also meant that as long as the trend in world energy prices continued upwards intra-Comecon delivery prices could never quite catch up. After the world price of oil peaked in 1982 and started to fall, the Soviet Union found itself in principle the gainer from these Comecon price rules. But the trading relationship in question normally involves the exchange of 'hard' Soviet goods, which could equally well be sold in the West, for 'soft' East European goods, i.e. manufactures which do not meet world market standards of technology or quality. There are exceptions to this rule — the Soviets must be very thankful for exotic foodstuffs from Hungary and Bulgaria, and certainly get the benefit of some technology transfer via machinery imports from the GDR and Czechoslovakia. Overall, however, the economic benefit to the Soviet Union of the East European connection has been called increasingly into question, and the collapse of the Polish economy in 1979–80 only served to highlight the issue. There is no reason to believe, on the other hand, that this has had any serious effect on Soviet strategic thinking.

The main landmarks of the history of East-West relations since the War have been widely discussed and analysed. It did not prove possible to resolve any of the major differences between NATO and the Warsaw Pact, even under Khrushchev's reinterpreted rubric of 'peaceful coexistence'. But East-West trade grew dramatically, fuelled by the Oil Crisis, the inadequacies of Soviet agriculture, and the need felt by all the Comecon countries for Western technology. Soviet imports from the West and total Comecon imports from the West both increased more than tenfold between 1960 and 1975. Through the 1970s primary materials came to bulk larger and larger in total Soviet exports (by value). The mass of Soviet imports of grain came from North America, except in times of embargo, while the trade in machinery and technology transfer has been mainly with Western Europe. East-West trade is still very small beer in comparison with total intra-Western trade, but the strategic significance of all its major components — energy materials, machinery and foodstuffs — has given it a political significance out of proportion to its relative size.

US defence expenditure fell sharply after the end of the Vietnam war, and by 1976 was down to 5.4 per cent of National Income (*SIPRI Yearbook 1979*, pp. 36–7). Meanwhile rapid Soviet economic growth in the period up to the mid-1970s had enabled the USSR to close the gap in total GNP between the two superpowers, while the principle of centralisation was used to maintain a very high level of military priority. As a result the Warsaw Pact was able to achieve parity, perhaps rather more than parity, in the military balance. By 1983–4 the Soviet Union had more than twice the number of men under arms as the USA, more than four times the number of tanks, and substantially larger numbers of combat aircraft and intercontinental and submarine-launched ballistic missiles. The USA still retained a 30 per cent superiority in number of strategic warheads, but had nothing to place in the balance of the Soviet Union's significant strategic defence system development, consisting mainly of SAM missiles (Jones, 1985, pp. 17–18). We should be very careful about interpreting these figures in terms of *effectiveness* — a large part of the Warsaw Pact tank park, for instance, is obsolescent (Jones, 1984, p. 29; 1986, p. 33). But few on the Western side have doubted that Soviet offensive capability has for many years now been sufficient to ensure that any kind of coexistence would be on the basis of MAD — mutually assured destruction. By placing severe limitations on the deployment of ABMs (anti-ballistic missiles, i.e. anti-missile missiles) the SALT-1 treaty of 1972 may be said to have institutionalised MAD.

The signing of the SALT treaty, coupled with the growth in East-West economic intercourse and a new, perhaps poorly founded, Western optimism about the possibility of making progress on human rights in Eastern Europe, were all elements in the development, during the 1970s, of an improved atmosphere in inter-bloc relations. This improved atmosphere found expression in the term détente. The high point of détente was the signing of the Helsinki Agreement in 1975. But Helsinki was also the beginning of the end for détente, as it quickly became evident that Western and Soviet interpretations of the clauses on human rights differed widely. With the Western world starting to move into recession in 1980, and with the fall in oil prices from 1982, any hopes for substantial increases in Comecon exports to the West were dashed. At the same time the combination of sharp increases in interest rates and substantial cumulations of debt from the mid-1970s was beginning to create debt service problems for the smaller East European countries. In 1980 Poland was forced to seek a rescheduling of her debts to the West. It should be stressed that the Soviet Union itself was untouched by these financial difficulties — in its reserve position and international credit rating it remains formidably strong. Nevertheless the Soviets do seem to have felt that in the context of the world economic situation prudence should be the watchword. Soviet imports of machinery

David A. Dyker

from the West fell sharply in the late 1970s (Economist Intelligence Unit, 1985, p. 17).

Three further developments finally destroyed what was left of détente. In 1979 the Soviet Union sent troops into Afghanistan in support of the tottering Marxist regime. They quickly found themselves with a full-scale war on their hands as *mujahadin* resistance to occupation hardened. There had been considerable Soviet military involvement in Third World countries with substantial 'Marxist' movements throughout the 1970s, particularly in Africa, but this was the first time that regular Soviet forces had intervened in a country officially classified as neutral. The US response was to declare a partial embargo on grain exports to the USSR — at a time when Soviet agriculture was going through one of its most difficult phases since collectivisation. The embargo did not stop the Russians obtaining the grain they needed in 1980 — they were still able to get some of it from the USA, and they got the rest from the Canadians, Argentinians and Australians. But the price paid was some 10–20 per cent higher than it had been in 1979. Secondly, America elected in 1980 a President committed to taking a tougher line with the Soviets, and with left-wing regimes in Latin America. Finally in 1981 General Jaruzelski seized control in Poland — with Soviet backing — and proceeded to declare martial law and repress the Solidarity movement. The US response under President Reagan was an attempt to restrict the flow of high-technology equipment to the Soviet Union. That flow does, of course, largely involve West European countries, and America has not found it easy to establish a united Western front on this matter. But US policies certainly made East-West trade that much more difficult. Over the period 1981–5 the value of East-West trade fell sharply in absolute terms, and marginally as a proportion of total world trade (United Nations, 1985, Table 5.4.2).

The pressures for reform

It was not long before it became clear that Brezhnev's wager on technology transfer had not paid off. By the late 1970s the Soviet growth rate was down to 3 per cent — to under 2 per cent if we accept CIA recalculations in GNP terms. While Brezhnev had seen technology transfer as a *substitute* for planning reform, the experience of the 1970s suggested that it should rather be seen as a *complement* to planning reform. The sluggishness of central

14

planning in relation to domestic innovation proved equally damaging to imported innovation, and even turnkey projects produced no dramatic improvement in perennially excessive lead-times (Dyker, 1985, pp. 68–9). Meanwhile the continued escalation of hydrocarbon extraction costs in Siberia was depriving the USSR of the large-scale rental incomes which increasing world oil prices had initially brought.

It came as no surprise, then, when a new decree on the industrial planning system was published in 1979. But Brezhnev's 'mini-reform' was a disappointment, and on balance it moved the system towards greater rather than less centralisation. It had no perceptible effect on industrial performance. Nevertheless industrial production was still growing steadily, if more slowly than before. The same could not be said of agriculture, where output in 1982 was just about the same as it had been in 1973. Brezhnev's last major legislative initiative was the promulgation, in the middle of 1982, of a Food Programme for the period up to 1990, coupled with a decree on the agricultural planning system. These measures aimed to fashion a more integrated planning approach for the whole food complex, to leave more scope for autonomous decision-taking to farms, to create a new impetus in favour of the link system under the rubric of the 'collective contract', and to foster development of the private agricultural sector in co-operation with the socialist sector. Aggregate agricultural performance did, indeed, improve through 1982 and 1983, but the succeeding two years were again marked by stagnation. By the third quarter of 1984 Western food exports to the Soviet Union, coming mainly from the USA, were once again on the increase (United Nations, 1985, section 5.4 (ii)).

Specific sectoral weaknesses apart, the main significance of the slow-down in Soviet growth rates in the late 1970s and 1980s lies in the fact that the USSR thereby stopped catching up with the industrial West, at a point where the gap between the two in terms of GNP and GNP per capita was still very large. At the present time Soviet GNP is probably under 60 per cent of US. But while the Soviet economy is overwhelmingly predominant within the Warsaw Pact area, the USA accounts for just about half the total GNP of the Atlantic Pact countries. This helps to explain why the Soviet military posture has put such a strain on the Soviet economy. The CIA estimates that the Soviet Union has been spending 12–14 per cent of its National Income on defence since 1970 (Joint Economic Committee, US Congress, 1983). These figures are certainly not beyond dispute. The DIA (US Defense Intelligence Agency) reckons that the proportion rose through the 1970s to some 14–16 per cent by 1981. The Japanese economist, Kniti Mochidzuki, has used an Input-Output approach to estimate that the Soviet defence ratio may have declined from 10–11 per cent in the early 1970s to a little above 8 per cent by 1980 (Mochidzuki, 1983). Even if we take the lowest of these figures, however, the Soviet Union still turns out to be spending a larger proportion of its National Income on defence than any other industrial country, and a substantially larger proportion than its own Warsaw Pact allies (Joint Economic Committee, US Congress, 1985, pp. 477–9). Thus the defence burden puts the Soviet economy under severe pressure, and this pressure has been the greater in that the return on investment, the other main nonconsumption element in National Income, has fallen sharply over the last decade or so. The Soviet leadership from Brezhnev through to Chernenko may well have found themselves wishing from time to time that they could switch defence expenditure into investment, in order to shore up falling growth rates. In fact, the ratio of investment to National Income has fallen slightly in recent years.

To these macro-economic pressures we must add the pressures emanating from recent advances in computer and communications technology. It is these advances which have given the Americans hope that they can turn the SDI (Strategic Defense Initiative — 'Star Wars') dream into an operational defence strategy, and it is in precisely these areas that the technological weaknesses of the Soviet economy are most glaringly apparent. Returning to an earlier theme, if the micro-chip is the basis of SDI, and if central planning cannot handle the micro-chip then we should at least keep an open mind on the possibility of a change in the traditionally conservative military attitude towards planning reform.

The overall proportion of Soviet GNP being spent on consumption has probably not changed very much since 1965. Growth rates of consumption have fallen more or less *pari passu* with those of National Income, but the Soviet consumer is still living in a world of steady, if slower, improvement. What has caused increasing embarrassment in recent years is the gap between consumption trends and personal income trends. While money incomes grew at an average annual 4.6 per cent 1976–83, total turnover of retail trade and services grew at a rate of just 3.7 per cent

(United Nations, 1985, Tables 4.5.3 and 4.5.7). Over the same period savings deposits grew at an average rate of 9.4 per cent (United Nations, 1985, Table 4.5.9). A substantial part of this rise in savings deposits must reflect the inability of customers to find anything they want to spend their money on. The hypothesis of a growing repressed-inflationary gap is further substantiated by reports of lengthening queues, and some evidence that the second economy in the supply of consumption goods and services has been increasing in size (O'Hearn, 1980). These phenomena do not amount to a crisis. But there is a good deal of pressure on the Soviet government to improve the performance of the system in relation to consumption *in purely quantitative terms,* never mind qualitative. Thus reform beckons on two counts — it promises a more consumer-oriented planning system, and it promises higher aggregate rates of growth of consumption.

The economic pressures, then, are susceptible to approximate quantification. The question of *political* pressures is a much more speculative one. But we are on fairly solid ground when we pinpoint inter-generational tension as a key factor here. By slowing the rate of turnover of cadres right down Brezhnev did, in fact, make it virtually certain that his demise would open up the floodgates of youthful ambition. Sure enough, we find that during the brief Andropov interregnum the rate of personnel turnover had already quickened considerably (Donaldson, 1985, pp. 10–11). What was the new generation like? Donaldson argues that:

> The formative experiences of the new generation are rooted in de-Stalinization and the untidy reformism of the Khrushchev years. Better educated and materially more secure than their predecessors, the newer leaders tend to come from urban rather than rural backgrounds and were recruited into the party at an early age rather than co-opted in the middle of their careers. They would likely be more confident in the power and accomplishment of the Soviet state, less comfortable with idle sloganeering, and yet more embarrassed by recent periods of inertia and drift. They probably share . . . an 'itch for improvement', and they are likely to be somewhat impatient in their desire to proceed with change. And yet, while they have an obvious edge over their predecessors in education and sophistication, as victims of Brezhnev's 'cadres' policy they suffer from a kind of narrowness of experience, having been denied

opportunities to move across specializations or between geographical regions. (Donaldson, 1985, pp. 12–13)

There can, then, be no doubt as to the generational pressure for *change*. Whether that pressure amounts to a sustained impetus towards systematic *reform* is something on which we shall have to suspend judgement for the time being.

Gorbachev's rise to power

Mikhail Sergeevich Gorbachev was born on 2 March 1931 in the village of Privol'noe in Stavropol' province. He seems to have combined farm work with school in his teenage years, but went to Moscow State University to study law in 1950. He was an outstanding student. On graduating in 1955 he went straight into professional Party work, serving as deputy head of the *agitprop* (propaganda and agitation) department of the Stavropol' provincial Komsomol (Young Communist League) in 1955–6. In 1956 he was promoted to the position of first secretary of the Stavropol' city committee of the Komsomol. In 1958 he went on to the second secretaryship of the Stavropol' provincial Komsomol committee, and subsequently to the corresponding first secretaryship. Then in 1962 Gorbachev was nominated Party organiser for the Stavropol' territorial production administration. Khrushchev had created the TPAs to oversee both collective and state farms in particular regions as part of his agricultural reform which also witnessed the splitting of the Party into agricultural and industrial sections. Thus Gorbachev had direct personal experience of the move which made Khrushchev so unpopular with the cadres, and of an early attempt to pursue the 'agricultural complex' theme. In 1963 he was transferred back to the Stavropol' provincial Party organisation, and then in 1966 became first secretary of the Stavropol' city Party committee. Meanwhile, in 1967, he graduated as an agricultural economist after following a part-time course at the Stavropol' Agricultural Institute. In 1970 he was appointed to the first secretaryship of the provincial Party Committee, and in 1971 became a member of the Central Committee of the CPSU.

In 1978 the future General Secretary succeeded Fedor Kulakov as Central Committee secretary responsible for agriculture. The following year he attained candidate membership of the Politburo, and in 1980 became a full member of that body. After Andropov's succession to the General Secretaryship Gorbachev added the industrial portfolio within the Party secretariat to his agricultural remit, and when the industrial planning experiment came into operation on 1 January 1984 it was he who was in charge. He was also made responsible for lower-level cadres policy. On Chernenko taking over as Party leader Gorbachev added the international affairs and ideology portfolios to his already wide-ranging Central Committee secretariat responsibilities. We have it on Gromyko's authority that Gorbachev frequently chaired Politburo sessions during Chernenko's period in office. On the death of Konstantin Chernenko in March 1985 Mikhail Gorbachev became General Secretary of the Communist Party of the Soviet Union (Brown, 1985).

There is, then, no disputing Gorbachev's qualifications for the job. He has been a full-time Party apparatus functionary since graduation. He can appeal to his own political generation through the level of his educational qualifications, and through his expertise and experience in both industrial and agricultural spheres. He is clearly seen as someone who can be trusted with the Soviet image abroad. His record is, indeed, almost *impeccable*. Thus however much of a new broom he is, or may aspire to be, he is very much an establishment man. Whether that helps or hinders the cause of reform is one of the questions we shall be addressing in what follows.

References

Bialer, S. (1980) *Stalin's successors: leadership, stability, and change in the Soviet Union*, Cambridge University Press, Cambridge

Brown, A. (1985), 'Gorbachëv: new man in the Kremlin', *Problems of Communism*, 34(3)

Bullock, A. and Stallybrass, O. (eds) (1977) *The Fontana dictionary of modern thought*, Collins, London

Donaldson, R.H. (1985) 'Political leadership and succession: the passing of the Brezhnev generation' in J.L. Nogee (ed.), *Soviet politics. Russia after Brezhnev*, Praeger, New York.

Dyker, D.A. (1983) *The process of investment in the Soviet Union*, Cambridge University Press, Cambridge

——— (1985) *The future of the Soviet economic planning system*, Croom Helm, London

Economist Intelligence Unit (1985) *Quarterly economic review of USSR* (4)

Gregory, P. and Stuart, R. (1986) *Soviet economic structure and performance*,

3rd ed., Harper and Row, New York

Heller, A. (1985) 'No more Mr nice guy', *New Socialist*, December

Joint Economic Committee, US Congress (1983) 'Soviet defense trends', September

—— (1985) *East European economies: slow growth in the 1980s*, vol. 1, *Economic performance and policy*, US GPO, Washington DC

Jones, D.R. (1984) 'Survey. The Soviet military year in review: 1982–1983' in D.R. Jones (ed.), *Soviet armed forces review annual 7*, Academic International Press, Gulf Breeze

—— (1985) 'The Soviet military year in review: 1983–1984' in D.R. Jones (ed.), *Soviet armed forces review annual 8*, Academic International Press, Gulf Breeze

—— (1986) 'The Soviet military year in review: 1984–1985' in D.R. Jones (ed.), *Soviet armed forces review annual 9*, Academic International Press, Gulf Breeze

Kaser, M. (1975) 'The economy: a general assessment' in A. Brown and M. Kaser (eds), *The Soviet Union since the fall of Khrushchev*, Macmillan, London

Mochidzuki, K. (1983) 'Voennye raskhody SSSR na osnove rascheta natsional'nogo dokhoda', *Japanese Slavic and East European Studies*, 4

Nove, A. (1968) *The Soviet economy*, 3rd edn., George Allen and Unwin, London

O'Hearn, D. (1980) 'The consumer second economy: size and effects', *Soviet Studies*, 32 (2)

SIPRI yearbook 1979 (1979), Almqvist and Wiksell, London

Turovsky, F. (1984) 'Society without a present' in L. Schapiro and J. Godson (eds), *The Soviet worker*, 2nd edn., Macmillan, London

United Nations (1985) *Economic survey of Europe in 1984–1985*, New York

Urbanek, L. (1968) 'Some difficulties in implementing the economic reforms in Czechoslovakia', *Soviet Studies*, 19 (4)

Wilber, C.K. (1969) *The Soviet model and underdeveloped countries*, University of North Carolina Press, Chapel Hill, NC

2

The Consolidation of Gorbachev's Political Power — a Springboard for Reform?

Iain Elliot

The XXVII Party Congress did little to answer the question which had most concerned observers of the Soviet scene since the accession of Mikhail Gorbachev: would the new man initiate radical reform of the system, or merely introduce a change of style? In the months which followed, Gorbachev seemed to confirm in some remarkable way both the hopes of the over-optimistic and the fears of the hardened sceptic. Much, of course, would depend on the time scale permitted Gorbachev to prove himself.

By the time Gorbachev had held office longer than either of his immediate predecessors, Andropov and Chernenko, there were enough indications of his intentions and capabilities for at least a sound preliminary estimate of his potential as a leader. Several experienced analysts had already committed their conclusions to print. One émigré scientist and biographer, Zhores Medvedev, proclaimed the beginning of 'a distinctively new era in Soviet history', but sensibly modified this statement by saying: 'There is a new leader and a change in political generation . . . (But Gorbachev was) neither a liberal nor a bold reformist'; he preferred administrative modifications and economic adjustments to structural reform (Medvedev, 1986, pp. 243 and 245). Another prominent émigré, Alexander Zinoviev, agrees with Medvedev (most unusually) that one should not count on the liberalisation of Soviet society simply because Gorbachev and his wife were more cultured and more acquainted with Western society than their predecessors (Zinoviev, 1985, pp. 2–3).

Several Western scholars have taken a similar stance. Elliot Goodman, for instance, accepts that Gorbachev could attack mismanagement of the Soviet economy with some success, but questions what would happen after a few marginal gains: 'Then one runs up against the basic structure and political principles of the Soviet regime. Would the new leadership risk basic structural transformations that would alter the nature of the regime itself?' (Goodman, 1986, p. 181).

Jerry Hough, on the other hand, notes Gorbachev's 'attractive personal qualities' and remarks on various indications of his new approach: 'It is precisely with such an accumulation of subtleties that the Soviet Union initiates major changes of policy . . .' He then hedges his bets, acknowledging that these 'subtleties' might come to nothing (Hough, 1985, p. 54). Archie Brown argues that 'Gorbachev has the political will to make significant innovations in both Soviet domestic and foreign policy' and maintains that it would be a mistake to assume *a priori* that he lacks the political means to make changes (Brown, 1986, p. 1064). The West German journalist and biographer Christian Schmidt-Häuer concludes his study on an optimistic note: 'Is Gorbachev good not only for Russia, but also for the rest of the world? The answer is a conditional yes — especially if the West helps him. He is ambitious for power — not power for its own sake, but power to improve his own society' (Schmidt-Häuer, 1986, p. 169).

To assess Mikhail Gorbachev's potential as a reformer requires some further discussion of what exactly we imply by 'radical reform'. Neither his energy, nor his determination to jolt the USSR out of the rut into which it had settled under Brezhnev, are in doubt. The speed and thoroughness of his personnel changes were fully recorded within a year of his taking office. But he needs to go much further to earn the title of Reformer. Radical reform, as defined in Chapter 1, has a clear enough meaning which goes beyond ending minor abuses and improving the operation of the existing system; for students of Russian history, the concept of reform is normally more closely associated with the liberation of the serfs under Alexander II than with the governmental reorganisation of Peter the Great.

Eighty years ago reforming Russia meant moving from tsarist autocracy to democracy based on respect for individual freedoms and parliamentary pluralism; it did not seem an impossible prospect. Having travelled widely and discussed political developments with many prominent Russian politicians, Bernard Pares wrote in 1907: 'With or without convulsions, the Reform Movement is certain to sooner or later have its legitimate results' (Pares, 1907, p. 568). Can Mikhail Gorbachev be judged in these terms, or is he merely a Communist Party *apparatchik* determined to improve the efficiency of the Soviet system?

It is relevant to raise these questions, rather than limit our examination just to movements within the Party structure, because such issues are being discussed in the USSR itself, possibly even in the top Party leadership. A document published in *The Guardian* (22 July 1986) attracted world-wide attention because the newspaper's Moscow correspondent, Martin Walker, claimed that it was the manifesto of a group calling themselves the 'Movement for Socialist Renewal', which includes 'party and government officials of senior rank, stretching up to the Central Committee'. He stated: 'This is the authentic voice of the Soviet elite, thinking aloud and debating with itself.' He believes that Gorbachev himself has read large parts of the manifesto and endorses many of the reforms it proposes, but is unable to carry out the extensive reforms he wishes because he is restrained by conservative elements in the leadership.

Among the proposals put forward in the manifesto are:

(1) an independent press on Western lines, capable of exposing corruption and abuses of power at the highest level, like the Watergate scandal in the United States or the Rainbow Warrior affair in France;
(2) freedom of speech and an end of persecution for political and religious beliefs;
(3) replacing one-party rule with a range of socialist parties providing the electorate with a choice of programmes;
(4) more independence for local industrial management, encouraging initiative and responsiveness to consumer demands;
(5) greater freedom for private enterprise in the service and consumer supplies sector;
(6) a move away from the system of collective and state farms towards a regime allowing individual farmers the right to rent land and machinery from the state in return for a proportion of their produce;
(7) expanding private plots to increase the supply of foodstuffs to the towns;
(8) developing private trade, allowing individual producers to sell directly to consumers in the market place.

From both internal and external evidence it seems most unlikely that the document, which was datelined Leningrad, November 1985, actually originated among top Party officials. Indeed it bears some distinguishing marks of the dissident intellectual circles which have produced various similar documents in the past. (See for example, the 'Programme of the Russian Social Democrat Party', a clandestine document which led to arrests and heavy sentences in 1985; also Elliot, 1983, pp. 55–8.) Yet its sweeping indictment of the existing Soviet system is substantiated by a wide range of sources from eyewitness accounts to the official Soviet media, and its proposals provide a checklist against which to assess Gorbachev's progress to date, and indeed his intentions for the future.

Since we are concerned here with the prospects for political reform, we must go on to examine Gorbachev's record regarding basic freedoms: of the press, of speech, of movement, and the right to form opposition parties. What has he achieved, and what evidence is there for his intentions? First, however, it is worth asking how free he is to make reforms should he wish to do so. Are there still opponents in the leadership, or has he succeeded in creating his own team? What is there in Gorbachev's background, and in the career patterns of those promoted under him, which might lead one to expect a radically new political outlook?'

The road to the top

The accession of Gorbachev on 11 March 1985, only a few days after he celebrated his fifty-fourth birthday, was hailed in the Western media as if the event somehow matched in its exciting expectation of change the election in 1960 of John F. Kennedy, at 43 the youngest US President ever. In fact Lenin and Stalin were in their forties when they took power, Khrushchev and Brezhnev in their fifties; Andropov and Chernenko were exceptionally old to become General Secretary, rather than Gorbachev being remarkably young. Moreover, he was not exactly a 'new leader' as the press eulogies termed him, nor did his emergence as Party boss immediately bring a fresh administration as would the election of a new US President. As we saw in the last chapter, Gorbachev joined the secretariat as early as 1978; he entered the Politburo as a candidate member the following year, becoming a full member in 1980. He is the product of a system which does not encourage radical innovations or original free thinkers; yet that system allowed a man from a peasant family, who began his career at 15 as an assistant operator of a combine harvester, to reach the top.

Managerial efficiency and loyalty to the current Party line are the qualities most likely to have taken Mikhail Sergeevich Gorbachev to the Kremlin from the little village of Privol'noe. At school, and in his teens, his public loyalty had to be to Stalin. He did not get where he is now by protesting against the Stalinist sycophancy in his school textbooks, nor by opposing the post-war repressions which not even remote villages escaped. In fact he was loyal enough to the Stalin regime not only to be a Party member at the early age of 21, but to impress the local Komsomol organisers to such an extent that they recommended him to study for a law degree at Moscow University, from which he graduated in 1955.

Soviet jurisprudence, especially in those years, was not quite the same thing as it is in the Western democracies. True, the Speaker of the US House of Representatives, Thomas 'Tip' O'Neill, was impressed by Gorbachev after talking to him for more than three hours in the course of a Congressional visit to the Kremlin on 10 April: 'He appeared to be the type of man who would make an excellent trial lawyer, an outstanding attorney in New York, had he lived there.' But O'Neill was not actually referring to Gorbachev's grasp of legal niceties: 'He's a master of words and a master in the art of politics and diplomacy. He's hard, he's tough' (*International Herald Tribune*, 11 April 1985).

Lev Yudovich, a Soviet lawyer now living in West Germany, was a postgraduate at Moscow University when Gorbachev arrived to study law under such spirtual mentors as 'the semi-educated conformist hack A. Denisov, whose lectures were little more than a succession of quotes from Stalin's speeches' (Yudovich, 1984, pp. 2–3). At a time when Zhdanov was imposing even tighter Party control over higher education, when the anti-Semitic campaign against 'cosmopolitanism' was at its height, when Stalin was planning a new purge, Mikhail Gorbachev launched into his Party career. He became a Komsomol organiser, disliked by his fellow students, says Yudovich, because of 'his demonstrative political orthodoxy and the hard line he took during discussions of people's personal affairs'.

Another acquaintance of these days was Zdeněk Mlynář, later a prominent theoretician in the Czechoslovak Communist Party under Dubček, and now living in Vienna: 'We were more than just fellow students, we were also good friends' (*L'Unita*, 9 April 1985; *International Herald Tribune*, 22 April 1985). Mlynář says that the young Gorbachev was opposed to Stalin's liquidation of 'enemies of the people'. But Mylnář himself expresses surprise that Gorbachev voiced such heretical views, especially to a foreigner. Indeed, as a Komsomol official friendly with a foreigner, albeit a communist from a fraternal socialist country, Gorbachev would certainly have been expected to write reports on Mlynář. Were such comments a form of *provokatsiya*, rather than a genuine indication of liberal views?

They met again in Stavropol' in 1967, when Gorbachev expressed much more orthodox views, criticising Khrushchev (deposed three years before) for 'impetuous subjectivist interference in the economy and the system'. Whatever he said to foreign students at university, Gorbachev presumably devoted at least as much effort to cultivating Party officials as he did to his studies, since after he graduated he remained a Komsomol official. He may have come to the attention of Ivan Kapitonov, at that time first secretary of the Moscow Party committee, then of the Moscow provincial Party committee. In 1965 Kapitonov was given secretariat responsibility for Party cadres — a very useful contact for an ambitious man.

In 1955 Gorbachev returned to Stavropol', not to practise law, but to work for the provincial Komsomol committee. Within a decade he had climbed through the local Party ranks to become in 1970 the top Party official of Stavropol' province, a post which brought him full membership of the Central Committee in 1971. He gained valuable experience in the administration of agriculture in Stavropol', a major grain-producing area, and this policy experience fed directly into the building of his political career.

For four years Fedor Kulakov had been Party leader of Stavropol' province; he was transferred in 1964 to Moscow to take general charge of agriculture within the secretariat, after supporting the Brezhnev coup which ousted Khrushchev. Kulakov remained in the secretariat with responsibility for agriculture until his sudden death in July 1978. This was Gorbachev's great opportunity; in November 1978 he moved to the secretariat in Moscow to take over Kulakov's portfolio, at 47 one of the top two dozen Party leaders in the USSR. By then Gorbachev had the support of such valuable patrons as the KGB chief Yurii Andropov, who frequently relaxed at the resort of Mineralnye Vody in Stavropol' province where he was born and spent his childhood. Probably through Andropov, he became a protégé also of the veteran ideologist Mikhail Suslov, another former Stavropol' first secretary. (Although that was during the war, before schoolboy

Gorbachev was actively involved in politics, Stavropol' remained Suslov's territorial base.)

Being in charge of agriculture has not been regarded as the best preparation for supreme power in the USSR. Yet this had the advantage of making Gorbachev appear less of a rival for potential successors to the ailing Brezhnev. When Andrei Kirilenko faded from the scene, Konstantin Chernenko remained as Brezhnev's apparent choice. But Andropov skilfully outmanoeuvred them, entering the secretariat in May 1982 and emerging as General Secretary the following November; as we have seen, he rewarded Gorbachev for his support by making him responsible for economic affairs and personnel. This entailed supervising on Andropov's behalf the removal of some of the most corrupt and inefficient of Brezhnev's appointees in the Central Committee and government ministries.

In the USSR, however, corruption and inefficiency are not necessarily sufficient grounds in themselves for dismissing high officials; there is usually a political reason, with the other accusations serving as a convenient excuse. For instance, Army-General Nikolai Shchelokov, Minister of Internal Affairs, was dismissed for corruption within weeks of Andropov taking office. He was a close ally of the Brezhnev-Chernenko faction, and as head of the MVD police was long a rival of Andropov, for 15 years KGB chief. It was widely rumoured that he would be sentenced to death and shot, but as Andropov's drive slackened and he was succeeded by Chernenko, Shchelokov seemed likely to survive. However, Chernenko too lost influence through illness, and in November 1984 Shchelokov was stripped of his rank and honours; he died in December, rumoured to have committed suicide. Vitalii Fedorchuk, a ruthless career KGB general selected by Andropov to succeed him as KGB chief in May 1982, took over as Minister of Internal Affairs in December 1982 and proceeded to 'eliminate shortcomings in the performance of the MVD' (*Pravda*, 26 January 1983). (Fedorchuk was himself replaced on 25 January 1986 by Aleksandr Vlasov, formerly the first secretary of the Rostov provincial Party committee, where he had gathered useful experience in the fight against corruption.) Similar political rivalries can be discerned in other high-level dismissals.

Mikhail Gorbachev himself had to contend with rivals while playing a central role in the new Andropov team supervising the economy. Vladimir Dolgikh, secretariat secretary responsible for heavy industry, was closely associated with Chernenko; both had backgrounds in the Krasnoyarsk Party apparatus. In June 1983 Grigorii Romanov, the 60-year-old first secretary of the Leningrad provincial committee, moved to Moscow as secretary for the defence industries. Now he, like Gorbachev and Chernenko, was a member of both Politburo and secretariat.

The three men who were to become full members of the Politburo under Gorbachev at the April 1985 plenum, first entered the ruling bodies when Andropov was General Secretary and Gorbachev was responsible for economic and personnel matters. Nikolai Ivanovich Ryzhkov, born on 28 September 1929, had proved himself managing heavy engineering in the Urals; in 1975 he became First Deputy Minister of Heavy and Transport Engineering, and four years later was appointed First Deputy Chairman of the State Planning Committee (Gosplan). Egor Kuzmich Ligachev, born on 29 November 1920, made his career in the Party apparatus of Novosibirsk, then served from 1961 to 1965 in the RSFSR propaganda department before becoming first secretary of the Tomsk provincial committee. Ryzhkov entered the Central Committee secretariat in November 1982, Ligachev in December 1983.

At the same December plenum Viktor Mikhailovich Chebrikov, who had replaced Fedorchuk as KGB chief in December 1982, was promoted to candidate membership of the Politburo. Chebrikov, born on 27 April 1923, pursued a successful Party career in Dnepropetrovsk (the former Brezhnev fief from which so many of the Brezhnev mafia came), before moving to Moscow in 1967 as Party watchdog in charge of KGB cadres administration. Andropov made skilful use of his KGB power base to ensure his own advancement, and Gorbachev rewarded the KGB for its support by returning a Politburo vote to that organisation, so crucial to the maintenance of the system. It was also in December 1983 that Vitalii Vorotnikov, the RSFSR premier, and Mikhail Solomentsev, head of the Party control committee, were promoted from candidate to full membership of the Politburo.

On 9 February 1984 Andropov died; it was not until 13 February that Konstantin Chernenko was declared the new General Secretary, after much debate in the Politburo. Two days later the press published an unusual closing speech by Gorbachev, in which he avoided praising Chernenko, but appealed to the 'spirit of unity that has characterised this Central Committee Plenum'. To avoid any public confirmation of the factional dispute at the top, Gorbachev was prepared to bide his time as heir apparent, confident that the ailing Chernenko would not leave him waiting long. The Kremlin old guard had won a brief reprieve, but in less than a year their chosen representative was too ill to appear in public.

While *Pravda* was publishing bogus interviews with the invisible President, or his letter to a Canadian schoolgirl and other such ploys, its editor, Viktor Afanas'ev, was revealing to the foreign media that Chernenko was indeed ill and that his 'second secretary' was Gorbachev. (Afanas'ev was to become even more prominent under Gorbachev, having his own TV programme answering readers' letters about the new policy of 'Acceleration'.) During his December 1984 visit to Britain, the heir apparent exuded an air of confidence. He even played truant, missing the visit to the grave of Karl Marx, and on another occasion surprised his hosts by popping into No. 10 Downing Street while Mrs Thatcher was away in Peking. Mr Allan Gormly, the managing director of the British engineering company John Brown, which had benefited greatly from Soviet orders and hoped for further profitable deals, put into words a widespread impression when he described Gorbachev as 'good humoured and personable' (*The Times,* 12 March 1984).

President Chernenko died at 19.20 on 10 March 1985 and his successor to the General Secretaryship was announced within 24 hours — a smoother succession than ever before. On 12 March the Soviet press, which had pretended for months that Chernenko was still active, devoted page one to Gorbachev and relegated the deceased president to page two.

Forming a new team

Change at the top depends on a slow process of compromise and consensus. A new General Secretary cannot change the administration at a stroke, nor can he immediately initiate dramatic changes in domestic and foreign policies, should he wish to do so. Even after Gorbachev had used his first opportunity to make significant leadership changes at the April 1985 Plenum, only six of the 23 men in the Politburo and secretariat had not held positions in one of the two top bodies under Brezhnev; death from old age was the main — admittedly compelling — reason for replacement. Of the full Politburo members, however, half had received promotion under either Andropov or Gorbachev on the basis of their proven record of administrative ability.

Chernenko had made no major personnel changes during his brief tenure, but in his first weeks as General Secretary, Gorbachev presided over an extensive replacement of ministers and local Party secretaries reminiscent of the early days of Andropov's rule. This suggests that preparations for creating a new Central Committee power base were well under way even before the date for the XXVII Congress (25 February 1986) was announced at the April Plenum. Signs that Gorbachev was about to launch radical reforms were less in evidence. True, an editorial in *Pravda* called for Party organisations to tackle certain 'key problems':

> They embrace essentially all aspects of our life: intensification of the economy; cardinal acceleration of scientific and technical progress; achievement of the highest world level in labour productivity and the perfecting of management and planning. It is necessary likewise to raise the quality of production, intensify the struggle against mismanagement and wastefulness, and bring all reserves for increasing food production more fully into play. (*Pravda*, 20 April 1985)

Yet such appeals were not new, nor was the repeated demand to strengthen discipline. Indeed, *Pravda* went on to point out that 'attention to this very acute issue has lessened recently'. Were the bureaucrats already beginning to settle into their bad old ways? Certainly there were still men in the Politburo who relied on trusted comrades in the 1981 Central Committee for their support, and had no great desire for a thorough house-cleaning.

Gorbachev began his reorganisation of the Soviet leadership at the Central Committee Plenum of 23 April 1985 — not by retiring the remaining septuagenarians, but by promoting to full voting membership of the Politburo two members of the secretariat, Egor Ligachev, aged 64, and Nikolai Ryzhkov, aged 55. Neither had served their apprenticeship as candidate members; the KGB chief Viktor Chebrikov, also promoted, had been a candidate since 1983. Marshal Sergei Sokolov, who had succeeded the late Dmitrii Ustinov as Defence Minister in December, became a candidate member, while Viktor Nikonov, aged 54, was appointed to the secretariat with responsibility for agriculture. This graduate of the

Azov-Black Sea Agricultural Institute had risen to the post of RSFSR Minister of Agriculture in 1983.

Then at the plenum on 1 July, Grigorii Romanov, although only 62, 'retired on health grounds', which appeared to confirm rumours that Gorbachev's main rival for the succession had attempted to block him at the last moment by proposing the dull septuagenarian Viktor Grishin as General Secretary, and had therefore been ousted. Eduard Shevardnadze, 57, moved up from candidate to full membership of the Politburo, and at the next day's meeting of the Supreme Soviet it was announced that he had replaced Gromyko as Foreign Minister, although his experience was limited to a few trips abroad and years of fighting corruption in his native Georgia as a police general and later as Party leader (Elliot, 1985, pp. 2–11).

Gorbachev rewarded Andrei Gromyko for his support by proposing him as President, thus retaining his expertise, while bringing foreign policy decisions more directly under the General Secretary's control. In April 1984 Gorbachev had proposed the aged Chernenko as President, saying that 'proceeding from the supreme interests of the state and Soviet society, the General Secretary should concurrently hold the post of Chairman of the Presidium of the USSR Supreme Soviet' (*Pravda*, 12 April 1984). Yet now the General Secretary was prepared to forgo that honour — perhaps from modesty, but more likely from political expediency. Like his predecessors, he could always become President when he deemed the time right. In the light of his age, it seemed probable that Gromyko would not hold the post for long.

The appointment of Lev Zaikov and Boris El'tsin expanded the number of Central Committee secretaries to 11, but with the ousting of Romanov, only Gorbachev and his colleagues Ligachev and Ryzhkov remained full members of both Politburo and secretariat. The new General Secretary was firmly in charge, but his team was composed of men brought into the top leadership of Politburo and secretariat under his predecessors.

The April plenum left Nikolai Tikhonov to celebrate his eightieth birthday on 14 May still holding the office of premier (Chairman of the Council of Ministers). Geider Alievich Aliev, who reached the age of 62 four days earlier, remained in the post of First Deputy Premier, to which he had been appointed under Andropov in November 1982, simultaneously gaining full membership of the Politburo. He came from Azerbaidzhan, where he had served as head of the KGB and later as first secretary of the republic's Party organisation. Viktor Vasil'evich Grishin, aged 70, who stood loyally by Chernenko through his last days, was still head of the Moscow Party committee, as he had been since 1967. But within a year Gorbachev would have greatly changed the face of the top leadership.

In September 1985 the aged premier Nikolai Tikhonov was replaced by Nikolai Ryzhkov. As with the change in the Presidency, the public had no say in the matter. President Gromyko, as head of state, merely read out a letter of resignation sent by Tikhonov to Gorbachev as head of the Party. Although Gorbachev had no real constitutional right to determine the head of the supposedly elected Council of Ministers, when he proposed his close colleague for the top government post, the Supreme Soviet Presidium 'unanimously supported this suggestion', according to the official report published in the Soviet press on 28 September. An experienced and pragmatic economic manager, Ryzhkov came to the Premiership with a reputation as an advocate of pruning bureacracy and making the existing system more efficient, rather than a proponent of radical changes.

At the Central Committee Plenum on 15 October 1985 Nikolai Talyzin was raised to candidate membership of the Politburo; the day before, it was reported that he had replaced the 74-year-old Nikolai Baibakov as head of the State Planning Committee (Gosplan) after the latter had suffered the indignity of having the draft five-year plan sent back for fundamental revision. Talyzin, aged 56, was another well-qualified technocrat, who had served as Minister of Communications from 1975 to 1980 before becoming a Deputy Premier and USSR representative to Comecon.

During Gorbachev's first year the official media gave a catalogue of widespread dismissals and retirals throughout the USSR, as old and corrupt leaders gave way to a new breed of 'efficient, unblemished servants of the public welfare'. But was this really the point of the changes, or was the General Secretary actually ensuring that the new Central Committee formally approved at the XXVII Party Congress would contain a majority of members who owed their position to the new man? In Turkmenia the Party first secretary, Mukhamednazar Gapurov, was dismissed on 21 December 1985, having been held responsible for various economic failings. But soon the attacks went even further, with *Pravda* on 21 January reporting:

Under him cadres were often promoted to leading posts on

grounds of personal loyalty, family ties or birthplace. It was a breeding ground for nepotism, flattery and careerism, which created an atmosphere of laxity and mutual back-scratching and gave rise to servility and irresponsibility. And this led to a variety of abuses.

On 24 December Viktor Grishin, faithful supporter of Brezhnev and Chernenko, lost his post as head of the Moscow Party organisation to Boris El'tsin, who, speaking at a Party conference the following month in the presence of his chastened predecessor, denounced the leadership of the capital for not being sufficiently strict. According to the *Pravda* report of 24 January: 'An atmosphere was created of ostentation, over-emphasis on successes and hushing-up of shortcomings, and this has given rise to a carefree attitude and inertia.'

In this respect, however, Gorbachev is no different from his predecessors, every one of whom has denounced former leaders. Yet the population is still expected to accept that although previous administrations all contained bad eggs, the present nest is perfect. The argument for an opposition party and free media to expose shortcomings in time to correct them, rather than years later, would appear clear. But this is not an option likely to appeal to the head of the CPSU. The promotions announced at the XXVII Congress included no influx of original thinkers from outside the Party apparatus; an examination of the career background of the new Central Committee reveals no significant rises or falls in the representation of functional groups compared with the previous Central Committee.

There are major differences in other respects, however, between the Brezhnev leadership as announced at the close of the XXVI CPSU Congress in March 1981 and that of Gorbachev after the XXVII Congress in March 1986. Brezhnev expressed his complacency not only in his speech, but also in announcing the re-election of all 14 Politburo members (average age almost 70), all eight candidate members (average age 65) and all ten members of the Central Committee secretariat (average age 68). More than 60 of the 319 Central Committee members were then in their seventies.

Iain Elliot

The Soviet Leadership (December 1986)
Full members of the Politburo

GORBACHEV, Mikhail Sergeevich Born 2 March 1931, Russian, became a candidate member of the Politburo in 1979, full member October 1980; secretary since 1978, General Secretary since 11 March 1985; member of Supreme Soviet Presidium since July 1985; Chairman of Defence Council.

ALIEV, Geidar Alievich Born 10 May 1923, Azeri, candidate 1976, member November 1982; First Deputy Chairman of Council of Ministers since November 1982; holds rank of Major-General from service in KGB.

CHEBRIKOV, Viktor Mikhailovich Born 27 April 1923, Russian, candidate 1983, member April 1985; chairman of Committee for State Security (KGB) since December 1982; holds rank of Army General.

GROMYKO, Andrei Andreevich Born 18 July 1909, Russian, member April 1973; Foreign Minister from 1957 to 1985; Chairman of Supreme Soviet Presidium (President) since July 1985.

KUNAEV, Dinmukhamed Akhmedovich Born 12 January 1912, Kazakh, candidate 1966, member April 1971; first secretary Kazakhstan CP 1960–62 and from December 1964 to December 1986; member Supreme Soviet Presidium since 1962.

LIGACHEV, Egor Kuz'mich
Born 29 November 1920, Russian,
member April 1985; secretary
since December 1983; Chairman
of Foreign Affairs Commission,
Council of Union of Supreme
Soviet since July 1985.

RYZHKOV, Nikolai Ivanovich
Born 28 September 1929,
Russian, member April 1985;
secretary since November 1982;
head of Central Committee
Economic Department; member of
Legislative Proposals Commission,
Council of Union of Supreme
Soviet since July 1985.

SHCHERBITSKII, Vladimir
Vasil'evich
Born 17 February 1918, Ukrainian,
candidate 1965, member April
1971; first secretary Ukraine CP
since May 1972; member of
Supreme Soviet Presidium since
1972.

SHEVARDNADZE, Eduard
Amvrosievich
Born 25 January 1928, Georgian,
candidate 1978, member July
1985; Foreign Minister since July
1985; promoted MVD General in
1968.

SOLOMENTSEV, Mikhail
Sergeevich
Born 7 November 1913, Russian,
candidate 1971, member
December 1983; Chairman, Party
Control Committee since June
1983.

VOROTNIKOV, Vitalii Ivanovich
Born 20 January 1926, Russian,
member December 1983; Chairman, RSFSR Council of Ministers
since June 1983.

ZAIKOV, Lev Nikolaevich
Born 3 April 1923, Russian;
member March 1986; secretary
July 1985; member of Supreme
Soviet Presidium since 1984.

Candidate members of the Politburo

DEMICHEV, Petr Nilovich
Born 3 January 1918, Russian,
candidate 1964; secretary from
1961 to 1974; Minister of Culture
from November 1974 to June
1986; First Deputy Chairman of
USSR Supreme Soviet (Vice-
President) from June 1986.

DOLGIKH, Vladimir Ivanovich
Born 5 December 1924, Russian,
candidate May 1982; secretary
since December 1972; head of CC
department of heavy industry and
energy.

EL'TSIN, Boris Nikolaevich
Born 1 February 1931, Russian,
candidate February 1986;
secretary from July 1985 to
February 1986; first secretary of
the Moscow city Party committee
since December 1985.

SLYUN'KOV, Nikolai Nikitovich
Born 1929, Belorussian, candidate
March 1986; first secretary of
Belorussia CP since January 1983.

SOKOLOV, Sergei Leonidovich
Born 1 July 1911, Russian, candidate April 1985; Defence Minister
since December 1984, promoted
Marshal of the Soviet Union in
1978.

SOLOV'EV, Yurii Filippovich
Born 1925, Russian, candidate
March 1986; first secretary of the
Leningrad provincial Party commit-
tee since 1985.

TALYZIN, Nikolai Vladimirovich
Born 1929, Russian, candidate
October 1985; First Deputy Chair-
man USSR Council of Ministers;
Chairman of USSR State Planning
Committee (Gosplan) since
October 1985.

Members of the Central Committee Secretariat

Full Politburo members: Gorbachev, Ligachev, Zaikov; Candidate
Politburo member: Dolgikh; plus:

BIRYUKOVA, Aleksandra Pavlovna
Born 1929, Russian; secretary
March 1986.

DOBRYNIN, Anatolii Fedorovich
Born 1919, Russian; secretary
March 1986.

MEDVEDEV, Vadim Andreevich
Born 1929, Russian; secretary
March 1986; head of CC department for science and educational
institutions.

NIKONOV, Viktor Petrovich
Born 28 February 1929, Russian;
secretary April 1985; deputy head
of Commission for the Agro-
Industrial Complex of Supreme
Soviet Council of Nationalities
since 1983.

RAZUMOVSKII, Georgii Petrovich
Born 1936, Russian; secretary
March 1986, head of CC depart-
ment of organisational Party work.

YAKOVLEV, Aleksandr Nikolaevich
Born 1923, Russian; secretary
March 1986, head of CC
propaganda department.

ZIMYANIN, Mikhail Vasil'evich
Born 21 November 1914, Belo-
russian; secretary March 1976;
Deputy Chairman of Foreign
Affairs Commission of Supreme
Soviet Council of Nationalities
since 1974.

KAPITONOV, Ivan Vasil'evich
Born 23 February 1915, Russian;
Chairman of the Central Auditing
Commission of the CPSU since
March 1986; secretary from
December 1965 to March 1986.

Only four of the 14 full members in the 1981 Politburo were still there in 1986 — Gorbachev, Gromyko, Shcherbitskii and Kunaev — and of them only the General Secretary enjoyed the crucial power role of a post in both Politburo and secretariat. Gorbachev's team includes two others with this central position: Egor Ligachev, the chief ideologist, and Lev Zaikov, who exercises secretariat responsibility for the defence industries, and for industry as a whole since the promotion of Ryzhkov. Brezhnev's Politburo had five with double status. Gorbachev's secretary responsible for agriculture, Viktor Nikonov, has no Politburo post since Gorbachev himself can speak with authority in this area. Again unlike Brezhnev, Gorbachev is young enough not to need an heir apparent. In 1981 Brezhnev had three secretariat secretaries with candidate Politburo membership, while under Gorbachev in 1986 only Vladimir Dolgikh retained that status.

Thus Gorbachev was able to promote trusted and tested appointees to the central corps of the top leadership with posts in both Politburo and secretariat. It was early however to talk of a 'Gorbachev's team', since the majority of the top leadership (15 out of 27) were in either the Politburo or the secretariat under his predecessors, as can be seen from the rostrum of leaders that emerged from the Congress. Let us now examine some of the significant details of that new rostrum.

Marshal Sokolov was not promoted from candidate Politburo membership, keeping military representation in the Politburo below that of the KGB, and confirming that Gorbachev is intent, as have been his predecessors, on keeping the professional military firmly under Party political control. Vice-President Vasilii Kuznetsov, 85, and the veteran head of the international department of the secretariat, Boris Ponomarev, 81, lost their candidate member status, but as a sign that they were retiring honourably retained their seats in the Central Committee. The promotions of the two new candidate members, Nikolai Slyun'kov, first secretary of the Belorussian CP and Yurii Solov'ev, first secretary in Leningrad province, were expected, since candidate membership would normally go with their positions.

The position of Party chief of Uzbekistan, the most populous Central Asian republic, has long carried with it the status of candidate Politburo member. However, the former incumbent, Brezhnev's close colleague Sharaf Rashidov, was posthumously disgraced after his death in 1983, and the new Uzbek leader, Inamzhon Usmankhodzhaev, had not yet put his house in order. On 27 July 1986 *Pravda Vostoka* announced that Narmakhonmadi Khudaiberdyev, Uzbek premier from 1971 to 1984, had been expelled from the CPSU for encouraging a network of corruption and falsifying cotton statistics. A week before, the passing of death sentences on two officials found guilty of similar crimes was reported. Central Asia then, would be without Politburo representation, while Brezhnev's old crony, Dinmukhamed Kunaev, would manage to retain his Politburo seat only until replaced as Kazakh first secretary in December 1986.

The secretariat underwent the most significant changes, as Gorbachev introduced into this key body trusted assistants to supervise the main areas of policy formation. Ivan Kapitnov, 71, was transferred to head the Central Auditing Commission, which watches over Party probity, and Ponomarev, as mentioned above, was honourably retired, having faithfully preserved an element of continuity in Soviet foreign policy with the time — and views — of Stalin. Anatolii Dobrynin, Ambassador to the United States since 1962, was brought in to take general responsibility for foreign affairs, presenting a more acceptable face to the world than Ponomarev, who was too closely identified with encouraging Third World subversive movements and opposition communist parties in the West. Replacing Gromyko and Ponomarev, with their three decades of experience, allowed Gorbachev to impose his own style on foreign policy, as on the domestic scene.

Vadim Medvedev, whose academic background and experience

as head of the Central Committee department for scientific and educational institutions seemed to qualify him to take responsibility within the secretariat for ensuring more rapid technological progress, now appears to be developing another area in which he has published widely; he has taken charge of the department for relations with ruling communist parties.

Aleksandr Yakovlev, head of the propaganda department, is another new secretary with experience of the outside world. An exchange student at Columbia University in 1959, he did not learn to love the United States; his many publications are bitterly hostile to the West. He served as Ambassador to Canada from 1973 to 1983, and evidently impressed Gorbachev during the latter's visit to that country in May 1983, since a month later he was appointed director of the Institute of World Economics and International Relations of the USSR Academy of Sciences. In 1985 he accompanied Gorbachev and Dobrynin to the Geneva summit meeting with President Reagan, whose 'irresponsibility' and 'maniacal anti-Sovietism and hatred for the Soviet people' Yakovlev predicted would lead mankind into disaster (Yakovlev, 1985, p. 399).

Georgii Razumovskii was also a Gorbachev protégé, serving under him as head of the administration of the agro-industrial complex in the Council of Ministers from 1981 to 1983. He then became first secretary of the important agricultural territory of Krasnodar, again working closely with Gorbachev, and in summer 1985 the latter appointed him head of the department for Party organisational work. In November 1985 he became chairman of the Legislative Proposals Commission of the Council of the Union of the Supreme Soviet, a post formerly held by Gorbachev himself, as well as Ligachev and Ryzhkov.

Perhaps Gorbachev's most evident innovation in personnel policy was the appointment of the first woman in the top leadership for over two decades. Aleksandra Biryukova is not only a sop to feminists in East and West; she was appointed to supervise light industry, with the job of ensuring better consumer goods and improving services.

The average age of the Politburo is now down from 70 under Brezhnev to 64, and the new people in the top leadership have a proven record of efficient administration over a wide range of industries and institutions. But all of them, as loyal Party officials, regard 'liberalism' as a pejorative term, and none has shown any evidence of favouring fundamental changes in the Party state structure; like Gorbachev, their efforts have been devoted to making the existing system work better, rather than dramatically reshaping the power structure which has brought them to the top.

After a year in office Gorbachev had replaced more than a third of the Council of Ministers, more than half the departmental heads in the Central Committee apparatus, and two-fifths of the Central Committee members. There were sweeping changes in the leadership of the republics and provinces also. But do these extensive personnel changes signify preparations for reform, or are they simply the normal steps of a new General Secretary to secure his position and remove dead wood in order to make the machinery of government more efficient? Gorbachev has spoken repeatedly of the need to win popular support for his policies, and certainly a remarkable improvement in labour discipline and individual initiative is required to achieve the growth planned to the end of the century. Yet despite talk of extending social justice, Gorbachev rules with the consensus of a privileged elite; ordinary workers are called upon to improve their labour productivity, but they cannot expect a commensurate rise in consumer goods and services. As we shall see in Chapter 3, that is not where investment priorities lie.

Campaigns against drunkenness, corruption and unearned income might be popular in principle, but in practice they adversely affect the already dull lifestyle of most people. Everything from birthday parties to car maintenance and domestic repairs has become more difficult and expensive to organise. Because a single party controls almost every aspect of society, it is easier to limit the self-indulgences of the masses than to reduce the privileges of those in charge; this must increase resentment amongst the population, and make it less likely that ordinary citizens will identify and co-operate with the aims of the regime.

In their thorough examination of Gorbachev's first year in power, two American scholars (Gustafson and Mann, 1986, p. 17) conclude:

> The requirements of a modern society and economy drive today's Soviet leaders toward a truth that is particularly difficult for descendants of Bolshevism: to maintain control one must partially surrender control. This point departs so sharply from Soviet practice that it is hardly surprising that Gorbachev's predecessors shrank from it and that even now, after a decade of near crisis, the Soviet elite and Gorbachev himself find it supremely hard to accept.

Gorbachev has restored the power and authority of the General Secretary and reduced the influence of factions based on particular local Party organisations. Many of the new men have a Siberian connection, for example, but they express diverse views in discussing policy options. It is accepted by the leadership that the years of drift are over and that problems must be tackled without delay, but the traditional reluctance to share power or delegate responsibility continues as a major obstacle to reform.

Gorbachev in action: open government?

The new General Secretary has been much in the public eye. His speeches have been televised live and reprinted in the daily newspapers; how far they are a true reflection of his views is debatable, but they are certainly livelier and much more colourful than anything since Khrushchev. A good example for analysis is his appearance in Khabarovsk during his visit to the Soviet Far East. On 31 July 1986 he made a speech on domestic policy issues which was every bit as interesting as his earlier speech in Vladivostok had been on foreign policy initiatives.

He began with what might seem a somewhat immodest assessment of his brief period of office as General Secretary:

> New ideas and considerations are springing up regarding the realisation of our plans, both in the country as a whole and in its specific regions. But above all I would like to say that everything we have seen and heard over the last few days confirms once again that the Soviet people have welcomed with profound satisfaction — and I would even say their hearts and souls — the measures outlined by the Party, and have responded actively to the resolutions adopted. I have not seen one instance or met with a single fact to make me express a negative judgement on what the Party has done since the April Plenum of the CPSU Central Committee last year and what it is doing in the wake of our Party's XXVII Congress. (*Pravda,* 2 August 1986)

But Gorbachev then went on to emphasise that there was always a danger of slipping back to the self-satisfied stagnation of his predecessors:

43

What has been achieved to date is not enough, not by any means. One ought never to flatter oneself with what has already been accomplished. We should all learn at least that lesson well, the lesson of the previous two decades. And we are right now at a particularly dangerous stage. So far there have been no profound qualitative changes which might consolidate the trend towards accelerated growth.

He spoke of the vital necessity of pressing on with the process of 'restructuring' (*perestroika*), citing Lenin's example when he introduced the New Economic Policy to help the country rebuild after the civil war; Gorbachev paid tribute to Stalin also, albeit indirectly, by referring to the years of the first five-year plans and the post-war recovery. Under his own leadership, said the General Secretary, the USSR is now tackling a challenge every bit as great as in those years:

> Our transformations (*preobrazovaniya*), the reforms (*reformy*) mapped out in the resolutions of the April Plenum of the Party Central Committee and of the XXVII CPSU Congress, are a real revolution (*nastoyashchaya revolyutsiya*) in the entire system of social relations, in the hearts and minds of people, and in the psychology and understanding of the modern period and, above all, of the tasks placed on the agenda by rapid scientific and technical progress.

He insisted that the dogmas which some Soviet scholars put forward as 'eternal truths of socialism' should not be allowed to become an obstacle to progress, and condemned people who see 'restructuring' as a 'shaking of our foundations, almost a renunciation of our principles'. Rather, he argued, it was time to face up to the full complexity of what was being tackled:

> The tremendous scale and volume of work ahead is coming more fully to light, and it is becoming clearer to what extent many concepts relating to the economy, to management, to social issues, to the state system and democracy, to upbringing and education, and to ethical demands, still lag behind today's requirements and tasks and even further behind the tasks of future development. We have to remove layer by layer the problems which have accumulated in all spheres of social life and free ourselves of what is obsolete, opting boldly for creative decisions.

Progress, Gorbachev went on, depended on every individual doing his bit, and not waiting for others; the inertia and self-seeking of recent years had to go: 'All must work harder.' He moved from calling for technological improvements in the USSR as a whole to specific demands that local industries overcome their deficiencies. Managers and planners who merely dig deeper 'into their entrenchments' should watch out: 'I tell you straight, in cases like that there is no need to give the managers a salary, because it is the workers who are doing everything.'

Interestingly, certain sentences in Gorbachev's speech, as seen live on Soviet television on 31 July, were cut out in the version published in the press on 2 August. For example, it was considered advisable not to publicise further Gorbachev's revelation that badly needed cranes from the Komsomol'sk lifting and transport equipment works of the Ministry of Heavy and Transport Machine Building had been banned 'because of systematic violation of technical discipline and low quality'. (In the following passage the phrases omitted in the published version are in italics.)

> In 1975, that is, 10 or more years ago, the Bikin knitted goods factory was put into production. But even ten years later its capacities are utilised by only 40 per cent. *Comrades this is disgraceful.* It is all our money just lying there as dead capital. *Just how much of the National Income is immobilised by things like that?* The planned number of workers is 1,240: in practice only 520 people, 40 per cent of the planned level, are employed at the enterprise. The basic explanation for the poor work of the factory is lack of manpower and specialists. But the question arises: does that mean this issue has only just become clear? It was surely clear at that time also. This means that a plan should have been developed which would have foreseen both the creation of production capacities and the development of certain social requirements. *I mean housing above all, so that they could have built up cadres.* What kind of economics is this? It's not economics. It's economics inside out, an insult to economics.

Significantly, and despite reports that the censorship organisation *Glavlit* had been disbanded (see *The Guardian*, 28 June 1986), someone in Tass ensured that the same cuts were made in the General Secretary's speech as reported in all the newspapers

45

supposedly publishing it in full. The cuts were not made to shorten the speech: the Soviet press happily devotes as many pages as necessary to such policy statements. The real motive is usually more calculated. In the present case, for instance, it may be acceptable to condemn the Bikin knitwear factory as an exception, but less desirable that the population start questioning what this means in terms of the National Income and low living standards — they might, perish the thought, conclude that the political system is at fault!

Yet despite the recurrent brief cuts, the speech was refreshing when compared with the dull droning of Gorbachev's predecessors. He went into detail on the shortcomings of the service and consumer goods sectors, pointing out that unless they improved, there was little hope for rapid economic growth based on improved labour productivity: 'Wages in Komsomol'sk are high, but the question arises: who needs these wages? — if one cannot satisfy one's reasonable requirements on these wages, then the incentive for work is undermined.'

Gorbachev went on to condemn the tradition ('it's already seeped through into our blood, in all of us' was cut) of fulfilling the production plan at whatever cost to the workers. He called for 'the creative activity of the people' to be applied in strengthening discipline and order, but acknowledged that this meant developing democracy and social justice. Claiming that 'the people have now raised their heads' and are joining in the political process, he admitted that this was not without risks for those who raised their heads:

> A proportion of our officials [Tass omitted 'at all levels'] has responded with dismay to the people's heightened and more acute reaction to the processes unfolding in society. Many restless people — committed people, convinced about our system and our ideology and enthusiasts for the cause — were immediately put down as demagogues, and machinery was found to get rid of them after a certain time.

As he discussed the importance of encouraging the population's participation in the political process, Gorbachev came out with comments which again were felt to be too indiscreet to go into print:

> I have said to them: do not hang your heads. You have

raised them — do not lower them. And they said, no we will not. You probably read that. That is the mood of the people, you understand. And if someone starts to break people, to force that initiative into forms that are, you understand, convenient for him, it will be the end of that leader. He does not have the right to enjoy the support of the people and our support, that of the Party committees.

Continuing this theme of public participation, Gorbachev moved to his pet subject of *glasnost'* — 'openness' in the media — criticising local newspapers for not condemning blunders and shortcomings in the way the central papers now were. He spoke directly to the editors present, and to the local Party secretaries who controlled them. But Tass again cut: 'You should not be afraid of your people. That is a very primitive understanding of democracy.' Openness was not to be approached in the tradition of working in fits and starts; it was to become a norm of Soviet life. Self-criticism was an essential requirement, said Gorbachev, but Tass then omitted his explanation: 'We do not have any opposition parties, comrades.' While no opposition *parties* are permitted, it appears likely that the opponents of Gorbachev's 'restructuring' will not easily be suppressed, entrenched as they are in the Party and state bureaucracy.

Another example of this limited 'openness' in the media was a fascinating article which appeared in *Pravda* on 13 February 1986, dealing with the purification (*ochishchenie*) of the Party ranks: 'It is not a purge, but is precisely that, a purification.' The article surveyed a selection of thousands of readers' letters sent to *Pravda* discussing the pre-Congress documents; behind the 'ardent approval' for Gorbachev's policies 'one can discern some worry'. Would there be enough determination to see them through to the end?

Yes, the restructuring of our life is by no means simple. The path approved by the CPSU Central Committee's April (1985) Plenum is thorny and steep, and progress will not be easy. Painstaking daily work by the whole Party and whole people is needed here. Retrogrades and windbags, bureaucrats and bribe-takers stand, and will continue to stand, in the way. While verbally agreeing with the Party's decision, they are in reality afraid of change and therefore try to delay our progress by every means possible.

Certain officials in Uzbekistan were denounced by name. This was part of the general clean-up in that republic following on the posthumous disgrace of Sharaf Rashidov, the former Uzbek CP first secretary and candidate Politburo member. Various other corrupt officials were mentioned, from a police official who went poaching game to the Chairman of the State Committee for Oil Product Supplies. One letter writer said: 'Indignation boiled in my soul, not so much at those rogues, as at those who admitted the riff-raff into the Party, who gave tricksters and thieves their blessing to assume high posts, who gave them patronage and pretended that everything was going normally.'

Of course, the criticism was not permitted to touch the top leadership. One letter ventured the opinion that *between the Central Committee and the working class* there is still a 'slow-moving, inert, flabby Party administrative stratum which is not very keen on radical changes'. A rare allusion in the official media to the widespread privileges enjoyed by the Party elite followed:

> In talking about social justice we cannot close our eyes to the fact that Party, local government, trade union, economic and even Komsomol leaders often objectively deepen social inequality, taking advantage of all kinds of special refreshment rooms (*spetsbufety*), shops (*spetsmagaziny*), hospitals (*spetsbolnitsy*) and so forth . . . Let the chief go with everyone else to an ordinary shop and queue in the common way — perhaps then the queues of which everyone is sick and tired will be eliminated more quickly. The only thing is that the 'specially privileged' are hardly likely to abandon their privileges themselves; a law and a thorough purge of the apparatus are needed here.

Pravda suggested that when a Party official is 'relieved of his duties' the public should be told exactly why: 'You ask in what connection. Did it mean a transfer to other work? A demotion? A promotion? People do not know, so various rumours spread.' Again, however, there was no suggestion that this 'right to know' should go as high as the Politburo, to permit public explanations for the ousting of Romanov or Grishin, for example.

Even so, this article proved to be too daring for Gorbachev's chief ideologist and second-in-command, Egor Ligachev, who made a point of criticising the media and *Pravda* in particular in the course of his Congress speech on 27 February 1986. He recognised that criticism was necessary for social progress, and deplored the fact that certain ministries and local Party officials had interfered with newspapers to prevent the publication of critical articles. On the other hand, he claimed that the media could go too far and have a disruptive effect: 'Criticism should be aimed at eradicating what is obsolete, at strengthening and developing in every way socialist democracy and our social structure.' Ligachev said that no Party organisation or worker should be beyond criticism, and went on to name particular ministries revealed to have been especially corrupt under the Brezhnev regime — and, perhaps more tellingly, to have had close personal links with Brezhnev himself: the Ministry of Internal Affairs (MVD) whose former head, Nikolai Shchelokov, had died in disgrace, and the Ministry of Foreign Trade, whose Deputy Minister, Brezhnev's son Yurii, was removed well before normal retirement age. The local Party organisations mentioned by Ligachev were also significant: Moscow, Leningrad, the Ukraine and Kazakhstan lost their immunity from criticism with the death of Brezhnev; they were the bases of Grishin, Romanov, Shcherbitskii and Kunaev. But Ligachev named also his own Party base, and those of Gorbachev and Ryzhkov (Tomsk, Stavropol' and Sverdlovsk) to emphasise that the present top leadership was not exempt either. It is worth noting, however, that the media nevertheless continued to concentrate attacks on the shortcomings of organisations connected with former leaders, rather than with those now at the top of the tree. And Ligachev's warning to *Pravda* seemed to have been taken to heart, since nothing quite so far-reaching appeared in the months which followed.

When Boris El'tsin, the Moscow Party chief and candidate Politburo member, addressed in a most candid way a meeting of propagandists held in Moscow on 11 April 1986, his comments were reported in a very dull summary published in *Vechernaya Moskva* the following day. It was not until a *samizdat* description of the meeting reached the West that the impact of his remarks could be assessed. He attacked the previous administration of the capital, under Party chief Viktor Grishin and head of the city soviet, Vladimir Promyslov, for inefficiency and abuse of their position. He also discussed very frankly the problems facing Muscovites in their daily life, from shortages in the shops to crime and drug addiction. He called for questions from the floor and received over 300 in written form — some 90 per cent anonymous, suggesting that the officials in the audience did not fully trust

El'tsin in his call for an open debate (El'tsin, 1986, pp. 3–6).

Perhaps the best example of the limits on *glasnost'* was provided by the Chernobyl' disaster, when nothing was said in official media about the accident until two days after the explosion on 26 April, and it was not until much later that any advice was given to the population on taking precautions against exposure to radiation. Gorbachev himself did not speak to the Soviet public about the disaster until 14 May, when he appeared on television, partly to reveal further details of casualties and countermeasures, partly to revile the West for exploiting the accident in its media coverage.

According to the dissident historian Roy Medvedev, interviewed in Moscow by an Italian communist journalist, Gorbachev wanted to reveal more about the accident, but was overruled at a Politburo meeting on 28 April. When he proposed giving 'correct information' he was supported only by the RSFSR premier, Vitalii Vorotnikov, and KGB head, Viktor Chebrikov. 'All the others wanted to limit the news.' Medvedev spoke of internal disputes between a 'coalition of renewal' and another group 'which had considerable influence and which to a certain extent can succeed in making more difficult, or even preventing, the adoption of significant measures' (Jacoviello, 1986). Although Medvedev has retained contacts with some Party officials, it is seldom clear how direct is his source for such reports, or for what purpose the information was passed on. Of course it does Gorbachev's reputation in the West no harm to be seen as more open and forthright than his colleagues.

The media ultimately revealed much more about the accident than most observers would have thought possible, including the names of several high-ranking officials held responsible by investigators. Yet the public, it seems, still had no *right* to know; they were told only what the authorities saw fit to tell them, bearing in mind that much information was reaching the Soviet population from Western broadcasting stations. Some major issues were not discussed, such as whether the accident was caused solely by human error, or whether partly by a fault in the basic technological design which would call into question the siting of so many nuclear power stations close to population centres.

When the Estonian-language daily *Noorte Haal* revealed (in the course of a series running from 12 to 16 August about Estonians conscripted to help with the decontamination) that some military reservists had gone on strike because of the terrible conditions, the series was stopped short. Robert Gale, the American doctor whose aid for the victims and meeting with Mikhail Gorbachev were widely covered in the Soviet media, described later in the West how, when he finally obtained permission to fly over Chernobyl' to see the disaster area for himself, his camera was 'surgically removed' to prevent him recording anything not officially approved for public release (Gale, 1986, p. 25).

We can broaden out our understanding of the limits of the new approach if we look at how it has come through at the level of the republican and local press. On 5 January 1986 the newspaper *Sovetskaya Rossiya* argued that 'our news must be timely, truthful and comprehensive', and published a reader's view that Soviet television should not only show earthquakes and such disasters when they happened abroad, but also those in the USSR:

> It is necessary to have the courage to inform people about unexpected or negative events. They should not learn about them from foreign voices with an anti-Soviet slant. The ideological losses from information that is incomplete or not reported in good time are too great.

On 1 and 5 February the same paper criticised the local press for not exposing corruption among local Party officials, while not, however, questioning Party control in general. The editor of *Sovetskaya Rossiya*, Mikhail Nenashev, was subsequently promoted to the chairmanship of the USSR State Committee for Publishing, Printing and the Book Trade, but the campaign for *glasnost'* continued in his and other newspapers.

But here is a rather different story. The first secretary of Verkhnedonsk district Party committee, A. Mrykhin, objected to criticism brought to light by a correspondent of the province paper *Molot* ('Hammer') and began to persecute him. He so disliked the contents of a particular issue of the district newspaper *Iskra* ('Spark') that he had the whole issue pulped. But Mrykhin was exposed by *Pravda* (on 25 August 1986) as part of its coverage for the Gorbachev line of increasing efficiency through greater openness in the press. This was only one of various similar cases which revealed the extent of Party control over the media. A complete issue of the Pskov provincial newspaper *Za Kommunizm* ('For Communism'), hot off the press, was pulped because the district Party committee objected to an article entitled *Pokazukha* ('Just for show'). This admission that the local press is effectively censored by Party officials appeared prominently in *Pravda* (on 13 June 1986, pp. 1–2).

It is indeed progress of a sort to admit these practices, and to try to ensure that they cease. However, the local and all-union press are still not permitted to criticise the top leadership, and there is no indication that the general practice of Party control over the media is under question. Protecting individual low-level Party bureaucrats from just criticism may now be discouraged, but state censorship is still the rule, and the system itself remains immune from attack in the official media.

Gorbachev himself admitted that there was censorship in the USSR, in the course of an interview for *l'Humanité* reprinted in the Soviet press on 8 February 1986. Although the very fact that he mentioned censorship was in itself new for the Soviet public, it was far from being an honest admission, since the General Secretary said that censorship was 'to prevent the publication of state and military secrets, war propaganda, materials glorifying violence, cruelty, personal insults, and pornography' and did not mention its main function of preserving Party rule. But the Soviet media have since reported earthquakes, floods, train crashes, and even sensational shipwrecks like that of the *Admiral Nakhimov*. There are frank discussions of drug abuse, immorality and hooliganism — not only as inevitable features of life in the capitalist West, but also as growing problems among young people in the USSR (Elliot, 1986).

When the Politburo announced on 15 August 1986 that the grand scheme to divert water from northern rivers and lakes to the lands of southern USSR was to be postponed indefinitely, the media hailed it as the result of extensive public debate. This was probably more true of the simultaneous decision to abandon a project to build a vast monument in Moscow commemorating victory over Nazi Germany; unlike water in the south of the USSR, there is no shortage of massive war memorials, and public opinion could be allowed to sway planners told to economise. But the suspicion remains that whatever way the great water diversion debate was decided by the leadership, the masses in their thousands would be found to voice their approval, while those against the decision would find themselves deprived of a forum. This is substantiated by a comparison of press articles before and after the Politburo announcement.

The arrest of the American journalist Nicholas Daniloff and his threatened trial for espionage demonstrates that the authorities intend to preserve their monopoly over news reporting by continuing to discourage as much as possible unofficial contacts between

Soviet citizens and Western correspondents. While many interpretations of Gorbachev's personal role in the affair can be mooted, it is evident that he has not effected any change in the KGB tradition of contempt for the principle of press freedom. In pursuing greater openness in the media Gorbachev has made the press and broadcasting much more lively and interesting, but progress to date is far from representing a fundamental change in the system.

On the vexed question of human rights, there were again some interesting indications in Gorbachev's first months of how little he was prepared to move. Certainly, had he wished to make major changes, he would have come up against strong opposition within the leadership. In his speech at the XXVII Congress the head of the KGB, Viktor Chebrikov, condemned 'ideological subversion' aimed at diverting the peoples of the USSR from the 'moral and political unity' of Soviet society:

> Certain circles in the West have harped constantly on the theme of imaginary violations of political and personal human rights and liberties in the Soviet Union. They have put forward groundless demands and claims. All of this is calculated to heat up the anti-social aspirations of individual renegades among the Soviet citizenry, and push them onto the path of carrying out hostile direct actions. (*Pravda*, 1 March 1986).

But Gorbachev himself expressed no basic disagreement with this attitude, although he never put it quite so crudely. Interviewed by French TV journalists on the eve of his visit to France, he spoke fairly openly, and actually had the interview shown on Soviet television, then published in the press (1 and 2 October 1985). Asked about Sakharov, Shcharanskii, Jewish emigration and political prisoners, Gorbachev dismissed Western concern as 'absurd' and reminiscent of the propaganda of a Goebbels. He claimed that Soviet citizens enjoyed greater economic and social rights than in the West, and continued:

> As for political rights, I could say that our Supreme Soviet has more worker and peasant deputies than all the parliaments of the developed capitalist countries put together. It would be interesting to stage an experiment, at least for half a year or for a year, and send workers to the parliaments of your countries. We would then see what happens.

53

Yes, indeed. However, on reflection Gorbachev appeared to decide against this interesting experiment, and restrictions on exit visas remained as tight as before. Emigration figures stayed low. In July 1986 only 31 Soviet Jews left with a Israeli visa, compared with over 4,000 a month in the peak year of 1979. In the first half of 1986, emigration of ethnic Germans to West Germany averaged 49 a month compared with almost 500 a month in 1976 (*Vesti iz SSSR*, No. 16, 1986, p. 4). Anatolii Shcharanskii and his family were allowed to leave, and Academician Sakharov's wife, Elena Bonner, received permission to travel to the West for urgent medical treatment, but welcome though these cases were, they appeared to be exceptions granted to capture newspaper headlines rather than indications of a change in policy.

On 19 February 1986 Academician Sakharov sent an appeal to Mikhail Gorbachev asking him to grant an amnesty to prisoners of conscience, naming several of the better known among them. By 3 September he had received no reply, so released a copy of the letter for publication in the West. In December, Anatolii Marchenko, one of the long-term prisoners named by Sakharov, died in prison aged 48. But a few prominent dissidents were released, and after Gorbachev's personal intervention, Andrei Sakharov and his wife returned to Moscow from exile in Gor'kii.

In Poland leading figures in the Solidarity free trade union movement, such as Zbigniew Bujak, Adam Michnik and Bogdan Lis, have been released from prison; although this does not signify a move to liberal democracy, it is in marked contrast to the situation in the neighbouring Soviet republic of Lithuania, where appeals signed by thousands have brought no noticeable improvement in the treatment of political prisoners, religious believers, or those defending Lithuania's national heritage. Such *samizdat* publications as the *Chronicle of the Lithuanian Catholic Church* show how far the official media are from representing the true range of opinion in the USSR. Dissidents from the Baltic states, the Ukraine, and other non-Russian republics, who have advocated some degree of self-determination for their nations, have been handed down additional sentences rather than released from prison camp.

So what scale of political reforms can be expected from Mikhail Gorbachev? Even the most sympathetic observers point to potential for reform rather than achievement. Their evidence for this potential tends to concentrate on two things about the General Secretary: first, his character and personal background; second, the changes he has made in the membership — not the methods — of the leadership.

Soviet accounts of the General Secretary's background are naturally always inclined to stress his positive characteristics. We learn that when he was 18 he was awarded one of the most esteemed Soviet honours: the Order of the Red Banner of Labour (Gorbachev, 1985, p. 10). Unfortunately the account does not say what he did to earn this unusually high honour at such an early age, whether he excelled at operating a combine harvester or 'rendered important services in the sphere of state and public activity, in strengthening socialist legality and law and order', (Ordena i medali SSSR, 1983, p. 51) which, under Stalin, could cover a multitude of sins. The Soviet account talks of his 'brilliance . . . originality of thought and his charm' and describes his wide interests: 'Mikhail Gorbachev is interested in literature and theatre. He studies new works in political economy, philosophy, law, and art with intense concentration' (Gorbachev, 1985, p. 11).

One biographer finds him a 'courageous experimenter' and states that 'his integrity, drive and managerial skills were beyond reproach' (Schmidt-Häuer, 1986, pp. 61, 64). A leading British political scientist says: 'It is worth underlining both the sheer importance of those offices now held by new people and the remarkable extent of the personnel changes in the highest echelons of Soviet political life' (Brown, 1986, p. 1049). While accepting both these conclusions, one need not necessarily assume that this means the Soviet system is about to change dramatically for the better. Brown points out that Gorbachev is 'a true believer in the Soviet system' but is far from complacent about it, and conscious that it must be improved: 'He may yet have a greater opportunity than any individual since the death of Stalin to make an impact on it' (Brown, 1985, p. 23). However, if the prospects for political change depend on the personality of Gorbachev, and his ability to persuade the top leadership to accept new policies, we should not be too sanguine. Compared with the information available about Western politicians, the evidence on the background of Soviet leaders is very flimsy, and with all due deference to Roy Medvedev, reports about debates within the Politburo and secretariat which emerge in the West must be suspect.

Extensive personnel changes could, as we have suggested earlier, have explanations other than the imminence of radical reform. Every Soviet ruler has changed the leadership in order to consolidate his own position. Gorbachev can expect more loyalty and co-operation from those who owe their advancement to him. He undoubtedly wants more efficient administrators than those responsible for the country's economic difficulties. And of course Brezhnev made so few personnel changes that had not Gorbachev removed so many senior officials, they would have died of old age in their Central Committee chairs.

How were these changes made? Did Gorbachev introduce more democratic procedures? On the contrary, his own selection, that of the other senior secretaries, the new Premier and the new President, all took place behind closed doors, without any public discussions or consultations beforehand. Even the stolid ranks of the USSR Supreme Soviet, well practised in rubber-stamping the decisions of the Politburo, registered no little surprise when that apparently permanent fixture in the Foreign Ministry, Andrei Gromyko, became titular head of state.

Anyone who believes that democracy is the least bad of all possible political systems must hope that the peoples of the USSR will some day have more say in choosing their government. This demands rather more choice of candidates than is offered by the 'democratic centralism' of the CPSU. But is it realistic to expect Mikhail Gorbachev to permit political opponents to form their own parties? On his own admission, Communist Party leaders in the provinces, republics and in Moscow itself have proved corrupt and inefficient. Communist officials were publicly named as bearing some responsibility for the Chernobyl' disaster. Yet the Soviet system ensures that sanctions can be imposed on Party officials only by other Party officials. Against this background, can Gorbachev really expect any mass enthusiasm for his policies? We should certainly expect changes from Gorbachev — some streamlining in the management of the economy; better consumer goods and services to reduce discontent; livelier discussion of problems in the media. But fundamental political or social reform — no.

References

Brown, A. (1985) 'Gorbachëv: new man in the Kremlin', *Problems of Communism, 34,* (3)

Brown, A. (1986) 'Change in the Soviet Union', *Foreign Affairs, 64* (5)

Elliot, I. (1983) 'Dissent, opposition and instability' in M. McCauley (ed.), *The Soviet Union after Brezhnev,* Heinemann, London

Elliot, I. (1985) 'And now Gorbachev, the great reformer', *Survey, 29* (1)

Elliot, I. (1986) 'Drugs: Moscow's tardy admission', *The Times,* 12 July, p. 10

El'tsin, B. (1986) 'El'tsin talks off the record' *Soviet Analyst, 15* (16)

Gale, R. (1986) 'The victims of Chernobyl' *Life,* August 1986

Goodman, E. (1985) 'Gorbachov takes charge: prospects for Soviet society', *Survey, 29* (2)

Gorbachev, M.S. (1985) *A time for peace,* Richardson and Stierman, New York

Gustafson, T. and Mann, D. (1986) 'Gorbachev's first year: building power and authority', *Problems of Communism, 35* (3)

Hough, J.F. (1985) 'Gorbachev's strategy', *Foreign Affairs, 64* (1)

Jacoviello, A. (1986) 'Gorbachev was in the minority', *La Repubblica,* 31 May; the interview is discussed by Kevin Devlin in Radio Free Europe Background Report No. 78, 5 June 1986

Medvedev, Zh. (1986) *Gorbachev,* Basil Blackwell, London

Pares, B. (1907) *Russia and reform,* Archibald Constable, London

Schmidt-Häuer, C. (1986) *Gorbachev: the path to power,* I.B. Tauris, London

Yakovlev, A. (1985) *On the edge of an abyss,* Progress, Moscow

Yudovich, L. (1984) 'Gorbachev: first rungs on ladder', *Soviet Analyst, 13* (25)

Zinoviev, A. (1985) 'The Gorbachev phenomenon', *Soviet Analyst, 14* (23)

Note: References to Soviet newspaper articles are given in the text, since their place and date of appearance are relevant to the argument.

3

Industrial Planning — Forwards or Sideways?

David A. Dyker

The Andropov legacy: the industrial planning experiment

As we saw in Chapter 1, the industrial planning experiment announced in 1983 and introduced at the beginning of 1984 provided Gorbachev with a central role in the immediately post-Brezhnev era, and this forms the basis of a substantial degree of industrial policy unity between Andropov and Gorbachev General Secretaryships. To anticipate a little, the industrial planning experiment is not a world-shattering development, and indeed Gorbachev has made it clear that he sees it as merely the first stage in his industrial planning strategy. But by the same token it can provide us with a concrete starting-point for the assessment of Gorbachev's industrial policies.

The main elements in the experiment as originally promulgated were:

(1) As a general principle, the role of enterprises and production associations (groups of enterprises with unified managements) was to increase. That of industrial ministries and their sub-divisions, confusingly called *industrial* associations, was to decrease. Echoing one of the principal themes of Tatyana Zaslavskaya's 'secret' seminar paper (Zaslavskaya, 1983), the decree of July 1983 implicitly pinned much of the blame for planning shortcomings on too much bureaucratic interference from the intermediate administrative level. In moving the centre of gravity of the system towards the level of primary production unit the planners sought to switch its functional emphasis away from commands and instructions, towards prices and norms — norms for materials

utilisation, for bonus-fund formation, etc. That implied greater autonomy for enterprises and production associations, but it also implied more rigorous assessment of plan fulfilment. The ministries and their sub-divisions had always been notorious for chopping and changing plans — sometimes right up to the 31st of December!, this reflecting the arbitrariness of administrative power which was both the strength and the weakness of the old planning system. But through that arbitrariness the ministry could protect weaker enterprises, and make it look as if they were duly fulfilling their plans. Now, producing units would have clearer perspectives on which to base innovation plans, etc., but would at the same time lie under a much more unequivocal commitment to fulfil their obligations.

(2) Key success-indicators were to be sales/deliveries in accordance with contracts for all producing units, and where appropriate 'development of science and technology', quality, growth of labour productivity, and cost reduction or increase in profit. Profit would continue to be the main source of finance for incentive funds. Thus while the experimental system aimed to give the enterprise/production association more autonomy, it was to be an autonomy strictly circumscribed by centrally determined targets or norms.

(3) 'Stable norms' for wage funds, incentive funds, etc. were to be established on a five-year basis. Traditionally, Soviet planners had always relied heavily on the 'ratchet principle'. In their quest for maximum growth performance, and in the face of the massive informational problems set by an overcentralised system, they had tended to plan output targets in terms of past performance plus a standard mark-up. By the same token they had tended to adjust wage and bonus coefficients as a way of maintaining pressure on the best producing units. How effective this was as a way of 'seeking out reserves' is debatable, since it created an obvious incentive for enterprises to maintain a safety margin by following an output expansion path well within maximum production capacity. Quite unequivocal, however, is the effect it had on the incentive to innovate. As we saw, central planning *ipso facto* creates a disincentive to innovation, because in the short term innovation disrupts production. But if the central planners persistently refuse to allow the enterprise the possibility of making up for short-term disruptions through medium-term gains in incentive funds, etc. then the conspiracy against technical change is complete. That is, indeed, one of the main reasons for the strikingly low rate of utilisation of

robots installed in Soviet factories (Ryzhkov, 1986, p. 96). The importance of the stable norms principle is therefore fundamental.

(4) No bonuses would be paid to managerial workers unless plans for sales/deliveries according to contracts were met in full. In this way the drafters of the decree sought to shift the focus of the system away from the aggregate, quantitative, towards the satisfaction of specific, disaggregated demands.

(5) Autonomous production association/enterprise control over 'decentralised investment' was to be re-established. Decentralised investment is a category of investment financed from the production development fund — one of the three enterprise incentive funds — which had been heavily featured in the Kosygin reform of 1965. By the middle 1970s, however, it had fallen victim to the Brezhnev reaction and had effectively disappeared as an independent category. The industrial planning experiment decree also predicated that production units should enjoy greater freedom in financing 'technical re-equipment' (*tekhnicheskoe perevooruzhenie*) or upgrading investments from amortisation allowances and credit.

(6) Production associations and enterprises were to be permitted to use moneys from the association-level Unified Fund for the Development of Science and Technology to finance autonomous R & D work, and to compensate for increased costs in the period of assimilation of new products. Through this measure the Soviet planners aimed to consolidate the impact of the stable norms rule on the innovation process.

(7) Production units would also be allowed more independence in deciding the allocation of the socio-cultural and housing fund, the second of the production association/enterprise-level incentive funds.

(8) Management was to be given greater freedom in the use of the bonus fund, the third of the incentive funds, and in the disposition of wages-fund economies accruing through job rationalisation. Under the rubric of the *Shchekino experiment*, some enterprise managements had been given the right to get rid of redundant workers from 1967 onwards. The reiteration of this principle within the framework of the industrial planning experiment underlined the depth of concern felt by the Soviet authorities about the labour productivity variable.

(9) Budgetary rules were to be changed so that production units could retain a larger proportion of profit on a regular basis. That meant that all three incentive funds — the production development fund, the socio-cultural and housing fund and the bonus fund — would grow in size as well as independence.

We can pick up a number of interrelated difficulties with the philosophy of the industrial planning experiment as originally promulgated. Most fundamentally, it failed to tackle the problem of general overcentralisation. The system of success-indicators was if anything even fussier than the standard system, and it soon became clear that enterprises on the experiment were to benefit from little in the way of relaxation of central control over prices and specification of contracts (Dyker, 1985, p. 81). In this key respect, then, Andropov's industrial planning experiment seemed to share the weakness of every Soviet planning reform proposal since the death of Stalin.

The lack of any strong impetus towards overall decentralisation in turn sets question marks against most of the other features of the 1983 decree. It is all very well to strip the ministries of their power, but in an economy where the central planners are burdened with an impossible work load 'ministerial arbitrariness' may play an indispensable role. In their efforts to grapple with the planning of more than 15,000 commodity groups the officials of Gosplan, the State Planning Commission, and Gossnab, the State Supply Committee, are forced to take short cuts. Even with the help of computers they are unable to guarantee complete consistency between all the elements in the plan. That is one of the main reasons why supply uncertainty is such a perennial problem for the Soviet enterprise, and why ministerial chopping and changing of plans is not as negative a phenomenon as it looks at first sight. To a great extent it does, in fact, simply represent a form of continuous adjustment process, whereby consistency is eventually approximated through a series of 'iterations'. It is certainly not an *efficient* way of doing the job. It requires an army of ministerial administrators, and in the end of the day the standard of co-ordination may still be rather poor. In particular, problems of inter-sectoral, inter-ministerial co-ordination may actually be exacerbated. The alternative, of course, is to introduce a more efficient continuous adjustment process. But that can only mean some form of market mechanism.

We can see the same rigidity of approach coming through when we look more closely at the original experimental success-indicator system. It is undeniable that one of the main weaknesses of the Soviet system in the past has been production for the *plan* rather than for the *customer*. But the draconian rule on bonuses and fulfilment of contracts introduced by the 1983 decree seem to rest on the supposition that low-quality or poorly specified deliveries are always the fault of the delivering enterprise. Certainly the traditional output-based success-indicators have encouraged enterprises to go for quantity rather than quality, but failure to meet contractual obligations is more often than not the result of supply breakdowns upstream. The lack of any powerful impetus within the experiment towards decentralisation made it inevitable that that should continue to be the case, with the emasculation of ministerial powers possibly making things worse rather than better. In that context the very best enterprises working under experimental conditions in 1984 were finding themselves penalised.

This inherent difficulty was exacerbated by more specific planning problems. The original idea was that enterprises would be directly responsible only for dispatching consignments big enough to be containerised. Smaller consignments would be handled by local supply depots (*snabsbyty*). In practice supply depots showed extreme reluctance to accept this role (Tsagaraev, 1984). As a result, enterprises found themselves saddled with the task of dispatching and invoicing hundreds of consignments, ranging from the large to the tiny. 'Why', asked one enterprise director pertinently, 'turn the factory into a corner shop?' (Gnidenko and Divnogortsev, 1984). To make matters worse, consignments were only counted as delivered once payment had been made, again leaving good enterprises at the mercy of tardy payers. 'We have to send "pushers" to all corners of the country . . . (to try to get the money). Sometimes we make deliveries totalling 50 per cent above plan and still barely make our aggregate sales target' (Rudoi, 1984).

One can make the same points in relation to stable norms and the ratchet principle. Every Soviet planning decree since 1965 has proclaimed the former and condemned the latter. Yet nothing changes, and the reason is obvious. As long as planners remain saddled with an impossible workload they will be loath to give up their tried and tested rules of thumb. The constraint that enterprise managers should receive no bonuses whatsoever unless all sales/delivery plans are met can only exacerbate the problem, in that it strengthens the incentive for those managers to conceal the true capacity of their plants. The central planners may be compelled, in turn, to place even greater reliance in their plan formulation on past production trends, i.e. on the ratchet principle.

Where Andropov's industrial planning experiment did seem to offer enterprises genuine new freedom of manoeuvre was in relation to disposition of profits and wages funds. But a close perusal of the history of the Kosygin reform might have warned the drafters of the 1983 decree to expect trouble here. Once again the issue of centralisation is the nub of the matter. If you decentralise the finance for investment in medium-scale upgrading operations and housing, etc., without decentralising the supply system which is supposed to provide the machines, bricks and mortar, you pose the central planners an insoluble bureaucratic problem. Supplies are released on the basis of plan documentation relating to planned levels of production, investment, etc. Since decentralised investments are by definition not planned by the centre, centralised provision cannot be made for the corresponding supplies. The solution found by managers in the late 1960s reform was to go to the second economy for their supplies. That is one of the main reasons for the increase in the intensity of unofficial supply operations around 1970, and by 1971 centralised investment plans were in disarray as supplies were filched away to the decentralised investment sector. That in turn was one of the things which upset the Party stalwarts and fuelled the fires of reaction against planning reform (Dyker, 1985, pp. 60–2). Of course the real source of the difficulty was the failure to establish an effective decentralised supply network to match the decentralisation on the financial side, in a word to make a decisive move towards Nemchinov's 'wholesale trade in the means of production'. It is curious that in drafting the 1983 decree setting up the industrial planning experiment, the Soviet planners seem to have failed to read this lesson of history. Sure enough, early reports from enterprises transferred onto the experimental system on 1 January 1984 complained of serious difficulties in turning production development fund and socio-cultural and housing fund money into concrete investment supplies (Ural'tsev, 1984; Tsagaraev, 1984). Here again, then, the failure to grapple with the fundamental problem of overcentralisation seemed likely to neutralise a promising initiative.

Apart from giving enterprise directors the power to make workers redundant, the main significance of the Shchekino experiment had been in the increased financial flexibility conceded to them. Because Shchekino allowed use of part of the wages-fund economies from redundancies to pay special supplements to the remaining workers, it substantially blurred the distinction between wages fund and bonus fund. The experiment showed good results in terms of productivity throughout the 1970s, but was extended only slowly, probably covering about 10 per cent of the total industrial labour force in 1980. Why so? Brezhnev was certainly nervous that large-scale redundancy might turn into large-scale unemployment. Soviet full employment may, from the economic point of view, simply represent that flip-side of massive underemployment, but it is also a very important piece of political capital for the regime. Particularly in a period of very high unemployment rates in the West, the Kremlin could point to the unusual level of job security in the Soviet Union as a pledge of its socialist credentials, could exploit an unquestionable social asset as a means of diverting attention from low wages and poor consumer supplies.

But there were other problems, more internal to the planning system itself. The Shchekino system had originally been developed in the chemicals industry, and indeed it was quickly generalised throughout that sector. The first difficulty the Soviet authorities encountered as they tried to push the system outside chemicals was that the technology and history of many key sectors, e.g. engineering, simply did not suit Shchekino. In straightforward production-line industries with limited product ranges, like the energy sectors, chemicals and petrochemicals, substantial scope was found for the conflation of jobs — nearly half the redundancies at the Shchekino combine itself from 1967 to 1980 came into this category. But a Leningrad survey showed that the scope for that kind of economising of labour in engineering plants is quite limited (Fil'ev, 1983, p. 61). What keeps labour productivity down in machine-building is the prevalence of large, non-specialised factories, carrying full complements of auxiliary processes and services operating on an undercapitalised, labour-intensive basis. This typically Soviet form of overmanning is *imposed* on enterprises by the basic shortcomings of central planning. It would have been unrealistic to expect enterprise directors in sectors like engineering to rush to rid themselves of their 'safety factor' as long as those basic shortcomings remained unremedied.

Secondly, superior bodies were often less than sympathetic to the experiment. Ministries failed to make appropriate adjustments to wages funds in connection with major investment programmes, leaving some enterprises without the funds to pay Shchekino supplements. Gosplan and the Ministry of Finance changed the rules so that enterprise shares in economies in wage funds not used to pay supplements had to be transferred back to the state budget. Throughout the 1970s workers found themselves deprived of

Shchekino wage supplements as new wage tariffs were drawn up (Fil'ev, 1983, pp. 67–8), once again confirming the resilience of the ratchet principle. Thus the incentive to endorse the system was as dubious for workers as it was for managers, quite apart from the threat of unemployment, and Shchekino remained just an experiment.

But productivity trends did not improve, and when Andropov came to power he made it clear the overmanning was to be priority area for action. His approach was summed up in the *Leningrad experiment*. Similar to Shchekino in its financial dispositions, the Leningrad experiment broke new ground in a number of important ways. First, it was aimed at lower-level white-collar workers — specifically design workers — rather than shopfloor personnel. It thus attacked an important dimension of the overmanning problem in engineering without directly affecting the 'dwarf-workshops' which engineering directors found so indispensable. Secondly, it evinced a much stronger 'moral' tone. At the Elektrosila factory in Leningrad 220 people from the design-constructor department were made redundant over the period July 1983–November 1984 — or rather, strictly speaking, they resigned. Each individual was subjected to a fairly terrifying process of personal 'attestation' which placed the onus on them to show that they were fulfilling a useful role. The unfortunate 220 did not even stay for the attestation, but simply fled. At the Leningrad Metal Factory the principle was introduced that only the best 70 per cent of design workers should receive bonuses — so that nearly one-third of the personnel would always be feeling the noose around their necks (Strugach, 1984). There is an element of technical rationalisation here, as design work becomes increasingly computerised and therefore less labour-intensive. More fundamentally, however, the Leningrad experiment is simply an exercise in clearing out dead wood.

Here, then, as elsewhere, the death of Brezhnev represented a watershed. Andropov was much less worried than his predecessor about the possibility of increased unemployment. He was much readier to admit, or even aver, that many Soviet workers are simply lazy, and that fear of the sack may be the only way to get them to buck up. In practice Andropov's strong views on labour discipline fed directly into his policies on overmanning and labour productivity. As a statement of intent, then, the clauses of the 1983 industrial planning decree relating to workforce rationalisation must be taken seriously. One is left asking the question whether the Soviet authorities could hope to take their industrial managers with them on this matter as long as the latter continued to view overmanning as an essential safeguard in the face of inflexible and unremitting centralisation.

The Andropov legacy:
Soviet socialist self-management

One of the hallmarks of the traditional Soviet philosophy of politics and planning was the principle of 'one-man management' (*edinonachalie*). Deriving from the Leninist principle of democratic centralism and the functional logic of a command economy, the prerogative of *edinonachalie* did not give the Soviet director the power of life and death over his workers. Prior to the introduction of the Shchekino experiment it had been very difficult for any Soviet manager to dismiss a worker, even in cases of flagrant indiscipline. But the planning system was firmly based on a military-hierarchical principle, which meant that when it came to the execution of set tasks the worker had to do what the director told him, just as the director had to do what his ministerial chief told him and so on up to the top. While in the post-Stalin period trade union committees became increasingly active in the area of working conditions, they continued to play an essentially supportive role in relation to plan fulfilment. Khrushchev brought back the 'collective contract' (*kollektivnyi dogover*), originally a product of the NEP period, as a framework within which workers could participate, through mass meetings, in the formulation of trade union demands on working conditions and amenities. 'Permanent production conferences', first introduced in 1958, were slated to develop as a vehicle of shopfloor consultation on technical production matters — very much oriented towards plan fulfilment, but with a nod in the direction of participatory forms. There can be no doubt that these developments, coming as they did at the same time as the first wave of Soviet planning reforms, represented a recognition of the *functional* limitations of the one-man management approach. But they were necessarily limited to the extent that those early planning reforms did nothing to alter the centralised, hierarchical nature of the planning system. On the ideological plane the concept of self-management remained anathema — an alien concept developed by Yugoslav communists as a living critique of what they saw as the degenerate bureaucracy of the Soviet system. The Brezhnev period witnessed little further evolution of these notions, though it did see the birth of the brigade system, of which more in a moment.

Enter Andropov, with a striking new statement on democracy and Soviet socialism. In his key article on 'The teaching of Karl Marx and some questions of socialist construction in the USSR' he argued that:

> the (Soviet) system functions and is perfected through the process of continually finding new forms and methods of developing democracy, extending the economic rights and opportunities of the working man on the production floor, and in all dimensions of socio-political activity . . . This is real socialist self-management of the people, which develops in the course of construction of full communism. (Andropov, 1983, p. 12)

The term he uses for 'self-management' is *samoupravlenie* — exactly the same word as the Serbo-Croat *samoupravlanjanje*. Thus Andropov's ideological innovation seemed to mark a change in the official interpretation of the meaning of authority under Soviet socialism. The *Law on Working Collectives and Increasing their Role in Management* . . ., passed in 1983, embodied the principle that ultimate authority in any collective lies with the mass meeting of all the members of the collective, and brought the term self-management onto the Soviet statute book for the first time.

But Andropov's ideas about self-management were intimately tied up with his ideas about work discipline, and about raising labour productivity. How do you bring these three things together on the shopfloor? Andropov's answer was the system of *brigade autonomy*. Workteams, particularly in construction, had been permitted a degree of operational and financial autonomy from the mid-1970s onwards, but it was only after the death of Brezhnev that the system was widely introduced in its more radical forms in industry. With brigades receiving just an aggregate sales or output target for a period of, say, three months, a wages and bonus fund and the necessary material supplies, they would in principle have substantial freedom to pay themselves more for working harder, especially since under the new regime they had been increasingly conceded the right to make low-calibre brigade members redundant, in the spirit of the Shchekino and Leningrad experiments.

Two serious technical problems immediately arise with these

arrangements. First, the motivational side will only work if the central planners respect the principle of stable norms. As we have already seen, this is one of the most awkward areas of the industrial planning experiment, while the whole history of the Shchekino experiment has shown how strong is the temptation to claw back extra payments by reducing the wages fund after a couple of years. If the principle of stable norms is not observed, then the only rational behaviour for the worker is to play safe, thus ensuring that if wages are to remain low, his work effort will at least be commensurate. Strikingly enough, the Elektrosignal factory in Novosibirsk, which has been operating a radical brigade system for longer than anyone, reports this as one of the major problem areas of the system (Solomenko, 1983).

The other main technical difficulty relates to the supply side. Clearly the system will only work if the brigades can count on the necessary supplies actually coming through. The realities of overcentralised planning, however, make it virtually impossible for ministries and departments to create such conditions on a permanent basis. In a world dominated by supply breakdowns and layoffs, the workers are bound to prefer the certainty of well-paid (sometimes illegal) overtime to the uncertainty of payment-by-results in a high-risk situation. Once again, then, Andropov's ideas about practical self-management served to highlight the problems of the planning system as a whole, rather than indicating any alternative approach to them. Thus the former police chief left his successors a clear diagnosis of the interrelated problems of planning, productivity and labour discipline, rather than any integrated blueprint for their solution.

Gorbachev and the extension of the industrial planning experiment

Originally introduced in just 700 industrial enterprises on 1 January 1984 the planning experiment was extended to another 1,850 enterprises, giving it a coverage of 12 per cent of total industrial output, just one year later. During his brief General Secretaryship Konstantin Chernenko provided little fresh impetus towards economic reform, stressing rather a reinvigoration of the role of the Party in the economy (see Berezin, 1984). But with Gorbachev firmly in charge of economic policy-making, and frequently chairing Politburo sessions in Chernenko's absence through illness (Brown, 1985, p. 8), the experiment continued to provide the framework for economic policy articulation.

In July 1985, shortly after his accession to the General Secretaryship, Gorbachev published his own decree on the industrial planning experiment, covering the generalisation of the experiment to about half of Soviet industry by the beginning of 1986, and to the whole of it by the beginning of 1987. In its title — 'On the extension of the new economic methods and the strengthening of their effect on the acceleration of scientific and technical progress' — the decree summed up the Soviet leader's perception of the technology dimension as the nub of the productivity problem. But its content was low-key, with a definite air of provisionality. Indeed it seemed to set a style very much in keeping with Gorbachev's no-nonsense, down-to-earth political approach — a style based on the notion of 'continuous reform' rather than the grand public pronouncements so beloved of Brezhnev. Let us look at its specific provisions.

(1) On the key *no bonuses unless all contracts met* provision of the original decree the 1985 legislation backtracked. The difficulties mentioned earlier had, it seems, compounded to such an extent as to make the rule unworkable. Gorbachev's decree predicated that managers should receive a maximum of two months' salary for fulfilment of all deliveries according to contracts. Bonuses earned on other counts should *not* be dependent on prior fulfilment of the deliveries according to contracts plan. This reduces the new indicator to just one among many, practically indistinguishable from Kosygin's aggregate sales indicator, and subject to the trade-offs in which Soviet managers are so skilled. One can only speculate on whether this backtracking represented any deepening understanding of the relationship between particular systems of planning indicators and different degrees of centralisation.

(2) Where the decree certainly did appear to show some evolution of approach was in the area of *price incentives for quality and technical dynamism*. Under new experimental regulations industrial products judged to be in the top quality category would now attract a wholesale price supplement of up to 30 per cent. Products in the lower (in the language of the decree 'first'!) quality category would suffer a price drop of 5 per cent in the first year, rising to 15 per cent in the third year. After that they should normally be taken out of production. The new rules ensure that the loss of revenue resulting from such price reductions will affect bonus funds. In the

event of goods being returned to the manufacturer because of low quality or defects, the fines thus incurred or the cost of correcting the defects should likewise come partly out of the bonus fund. Exports of manufactured goods would attract a special price supplement of 20 per cent, and such supplements were, it seems, to be paid into a special hard-currency fund. The most striking thing about this measure is how closely it parallels recent developments in East Germany and Bulgaria.

(3) The other main focal point of the new attempt to build a bridge between planning and technical progress lay in the area of *decentralised investment*. Here Gorbachev's decree amplified and extended the provisions of the 1983 legislation. It was at pains to spell out that all investment financed from the production development fund should properly be considered to come into the decentralised category, i.e. that ministries should not interfere in its allocation. Retooling or upgrading investments financed from the production development fund of estimated value of up to 4 million rubles (1 ruble = $1.42, £0.93 at the official exchange rate on 1 July 1986) in heavy industry, and up to 2.5 million rubles elsewhere, were to be planned independently by enterprises. What this meant effectively is that a whole category of medium-scale investment which had previously been the preserve of the ministries under the rubric of 'below-limit' centralised investment was now to be handed over — experimentally — to enterprises. In this respect the July 1985 decree consolidated and concretised the anti-ministerial theme which had permeated Andropov's decree *and* semi-official critiques of the established system like Zaslavskaya's Novosibirsk Report. Clearly enterprises could not be expected to finance all this investment from retained profits, and the new proposals envisaged large-scale borrowing from the State Bank and the Construction Bank into production development funds. Once again, these provisions are very similar to investment finance arrangements now in operation in the GDR and Bulgaria (Kirov, 1983, p. 124–5). Special priority was to be attached, under the new Soviet decree, to supplies for technical re-equipment and reconstruction investments, and simply replacing equipment under the rubric of technical re-equipment, which implies upgrading of production capacities, was strictly forbidden.

Positive elements there certainly were, then, in the July 1985 decree on the industrial planning experiment. But did they add up to a sustained impetus for qualitative change? Let us look first at the price incentive issue. The aim of making prices more sensitive to the technology and quality dimensions is certainly commendable. But we looked in vain among the clauses of the decree for any movement in the direction of *flexible* prices. It would still be the State Prices Committee which decided on the supplements and reductions, so that the approach could not but further complicate the lives of already hard-pressed Soviet planners. Thus the biggest weakness of the 1983 decree — the absence of any substantial movement towards *general* decentralisation — was if anything merely highlighted by the new provisions of Gorbachev's decree. Again, it is all very well to insist that when goods are sent back to the manufacturer as sub-standard the bonus funds of the latter should suffer. In the absence of freedom of contract the client, with his own quarterly plan to fulfil, remains a 'captive' of the errant manufacturer, unless he happens to be the Ministry of Defence. In that context consignments are sent back by civilian clients only in the most extreme cases. It is significant that Aganbegyan reported in mid-1986 that the quality-incentive provisions of the July 1985 decree had never, in fact, been systematically introduced (Aganbegyan, 1986, p. 21).

The really striking thing about the investment finance arrangements spelt out in the 1985 decree is the way in which they *extended* the principles of Andropov's decree. Despite the manifold reports of difficulties with supply to decentralised investment through 1984, a much larger chunk of investment was now to be exposed to the same supply problems. As if to underline the point, a decree published a couple of months earlier, just after Gorbachev's accession, had made it possible for private citizens to purchase construction materials, including cement, for private building purposes — again without specifying any mechanism whereby the central material-supply network would, or could, make such supplies available (Medvedev, 1986, p. 192).

The proposed transfer of the bulk of medium-scale investment to the enterprise/production association level also raised a whole range of questions relating to the actual allocation of investment. It is one thing to permit the development of autonomous enterprise investment as a basis for small-scale rationalisation, in particular rationalisation of the second economy, the dwarf-workshops, etc. But in extending the same principles to a large proportion of re-tooling and upgrading investments the Soviet authorities seemed to be banking on the existence of stimuli at production-unit level which they had found to be lacking elsewhere in the planning system.

What were they looking for? The campaign in favour of reconstruction and re-equipment that had been running in the country since the 1970s had been signally unsuccessful in its aim of raising the rate of return on investment. The reasons for this were essentially twofold. On the one hand, reconstruction was often used as a cover-up for expansion of existing enterprises, involving complete redevelopment of sites — often inner-city sites — which were cramped and awkward to manage. As a result there has been very little improvement in the strikingly low ratio (less than 40 per cent) of 'active' investment in equipment to total investment within aggregate Soviet fixed capital formation (UN, 1986, Table 3.4.4). On the other hand, the re-equipment rubric was heavily exploited as a basis for maximising the flow of funds from the centre, with replacement equipment frequently representing no improvement in technological level whatsoever (Rumer, 1984, ch. 2). Gorbachev himself cites a case that nicely illustrates both problems.

> The Bryansk machine-building factory, which produces motors for diesel locomotives, is currently being re-equipped. The total work involved is worth about 140 million rubles, and half of that has been spent already. What kind of return has the investment yielded? It turns out that the application of progressive technologies is not envisaged. The work force has already increased by almost 1,000 while the rate of return on capital has fallen. Most important, they plan to produce an obsolescent motor on the new production lines, although an improved model has already been developed and tested. (Gorbachev, 1986a, p. 7)

It is not surprising, then, that the new decree explicitly forbade 'simple replacement'. What is less clear is how this prohibition can be translated into practice. Soviet managers put in requests for equipment they do not need because in a bureaucratic set-up the man who only asks for enough gets nothing. The ministerial administrator bent on survival is constrained to follow the same tactical logic in seeking block-votes from the centre. Moves in the direction of a greater role for the production development fund, and for bank credit, should certainly make Soviet managers count investment costs more carefully. But as long as quantitative plan fulfilment is the overriding imperative they are likely to continue to endeavour to grab as many resources as possible, whatever the cost to the national economy. Thus while we may agree that in the past the ministries have often been the *instrument* of some of the more glaring misallocations in the Soviet economy, we must question any approach which simply assumes that an enterprise manager will be more 'virtuous' than a ministerial bureaucrat. For the one as for the other, it is the general economic environment that is of overriding importance. It may in principle be easier to transform the environment for producing units than for sectoral administrations. But does the 1985 version of the industrial planning experiment actually do this?

The key is, of course, the dimension of 'wholesale trade in the means of production'. As was pointed out explicitly in the Soviet press by a number of Soviet captains of industry in the course of 1985, the only way to solve the supply to decentralised investment problem is to permit enterprises to buy necessary investment supplies on an across-the-counter basis, without the need for allocation certificates (Yashkin, 1985). That would, of course, in turn necessarily involve the decentralisation of a whole range of production decisions, and possibly of whole sub-sectors of the engineering industry. But it would also create much more powerful incentives for the enterprise to go for quality and innovation in its new production lines, since its clients would by the same token be enjoying substantially increased freedom to shop around for supplies. Finally, it would introduce precisely the discipline required to ensure that enterprises would, indeed, follow a more virtuous path in relation to medium-scale investments than had ministerial bureaucrats in the past.

In his first few months as General Secretary Gorbachev was certainly at pains to show that he was seriously interested in this kind of reasoning. At the Central Committee round table on the theme 'Initiative, Organisation and Effectiveness', convened in April 1985, he listened politely as industrial leaders stated plainly that, *inter alia*, the degree of centralisation in the planning system 'is to a certain extent actually having a negative effect on the development of the national economy' ('Initsiativa, . . .', 1985, p. 4). There was confirmation from early 1985 of the continued existence of a kind of 'experiment within an experiment', whereby consumer goods enterprises were being given some freedom to negotiate prices and contracts with suppliers and the retail network by themselves (Bionchuk, 1985). That had been a feature of the early days of the industrial planning experiment, but seemed to have been played down during the Chernenko interregnum. Like previous adventures with the market mechanism it remained strictly limited to specific regions and specific sectors of light industry. But Gorbachev clearly wanted to see this body of experience developed fully within its limits.

The July 1985 decree itself was guarded on the crucial issue of the role of the market. Tucked away in the third last paragraph is a poker-faced statement to the effect that the 'Commission for the General Management of the Economic Experiment' had been detailed to produce by the end of 1985 proposals for the 'development of forms of wholesale trade in the means of production'. This cautious phrase did, indeed, sum up the essence of the July 1985 decree on the industrial planning experiment, and perhaps the policy-making philosophy of the new leader. Planning reform was a pragmatic ongoing process: all options were open to consideration, but in the meantime the central core of the Soviet planning system was evolving but slowly.

The Sumy experiment

But there are wheels within wheels. At the beginning of 1985 another, more specific, experiment was set in motion at the Sumy machine-building scientific-production association, based on 'pre-experimental' experience stretching back over fifteen years (Lynev, 1985). What was different and special about the Sumy experiment? Thus the assistant general director of the association:

> The industrial planning experiment has made a significant contribution to the improvement of the economic mechanism. At the same time, however, a number of problems have arisen, which is normal to the extent that with the solution of 'old' problems new ones arise. The main deficiency of the economic mechanism enshrined in the industrial planning experiment lies in its failure to make a substantial impact on the problem of restructuring the system for financing capital investments and the development of production, and for introducing the achievements of science and technology at the enterprise level. But restructuring financing procedures, broadening autonomy and increasing the level of responsibility of the enterprise in these areas are in fact the determining factors for fundamental improvement in other parts of the economic mechanism. (Moskalenko, 1986, p. 25)

The key feature of the Sumy experiment is, then, that it

develops further that aspect of the industrial planning experiment which had, indeed, been specially featured in Gorbachev's decree of July 1985. But three qualitatively new elements are introduced. First, ministries and industrial associations cannot redistribute funds between enterprises and production associations. This is a principle, by the way, which at least some Soviet planners have been trying to establish since 1965. Secondly, stable norms are fixed for the first time for deductions from profits back to the state budget. The same principle applies to payments from profits to the ministry. Thirdly, the Sumy system predicates that investments relating to retooling, upgrading *and* expansion can be financed only from the production development fund. The latter is financed primarily from profits, but is supplemented by Stroibank credits and the *whole* of amortisation allowances. The principle of stable norms is also applied to deductions from profits into the three incentive funds — the production development fund, the bonus fund and the socio-cultural and housing fund. Additional details ensure that a degree of planning pressure on the enterprise is kept up. While norms for deductions from profits into the state budget are known in advance up to 1990 they do rise steadily throughout the five-year period. There is some scope for switching moneys between bonus and socio-cultural and housing funds, but if productivity fails to grow at least twice as fast as wages, then part of the bonus fund is put into reserve, or indeed switched into the socio-cultural and housing fund (Moskalenko, 1986; Luk'yanenko and Moskalenko, 1985).

Perhaps as important as the principles are the actual numbers involved in the Sumy experiment. As can be seen from Table 3.1, nearly half of the total profit was planned to go for re-equipment and expansion investments and R & D work within the association in 1985, and the same proportion is planned for 1990. More than 70 per cent in all of total profit was planned to stay with the association in 1985. At one level, then, Sumy represents a vindication of Kosygin's principle from 1965 — that profit should be the main success-indicator and the main focus for incentives at the level of the production unit. But again there is a qualitative innovation. Under the 1965 regime the role of profit as success-indicator was obfuscated by an insistence that it should be planned in terms of *rates* — rates of profit on capital, rates of growth of profit (Dyker, 1985, pp. 54–6). Under the Sumy experiment the only thing that matters is the absolute level of profit, which the association is invited to maximise. Over the period 1981–5 Sumy made 121

Table 3.1: Planned allocation of profit in the Sumy association

	1985		1990	
	rubles (mlns.)	per cent	rubles (mlns.)	per cent
Total profit	60.8	100.0	151.0	100.0
Payments to the state budget and the ministry	17.4	29.0	48.8	32.0
Deductions for own needs including:	43.4	71.0	102.2	68.0
for re-equipment and expansion investments and R & D	27.7	45.0	66.7	45.0
for bonuses	9.0	15.0	21.8	14.0
for socio-cultural measures and housing	6.7	11.0	18.7	9.0

Source: Moskalenko, 1986, p. 32.

million rubles of overplan profits (Luk'yanenko and Moskalenko, 1985).

But that, as the readers of *Literaturnaya Gazeta* have been quick to point out, could raise a few problems. 'Give *khozraschet*-based autonomy and command over resources to real enthusiasts, and they will, of course, work efficiently to the advantage of the state. But give the same freedoms to botchers, layabouts and cowboys . . .' (Ronichev, 1985). The key problem is prices. Again, as became clear after 1965, if you create incentives for profit without creating a flexible price system, you run the risk of encouraging profiteering. The Sumy management claims that the deliveries according to contracts indicator solves this problem, but the history of the industrial planning experiment suggests that that indicator is a weak reed, whatever the context. Of course the price issue goes far beyond that of profiteering. If prices are wrong, then not even the consciences of the Sumy experimenters can stop them from producing the wrong things, or in the wrong quantities.

As of the end of 1985 the price system imposed on the Sumy association was simply the system detailed in the July 1985 decree on the industrial planning experiment. Prices vary according to quality, but in a way fixed by the State Committee on Prices (Moskalenko, 1986, p. 33). Around the same time supply arrangements at the association were still a long way from wholesale trade in the means of production, and the association management was suffering exactly the same problems in finding supplies for decentralised investment and housing construction as other enterprises on the industrial planning experiment. Basic production planning remained heavily tutored, with 76 (out of a total of 200!) plan indicators coming down from the ministry, including, for example, detailed figures on how much wood should be sawn up for packing. Perhaps even more telling, the new decentralised investment regime could not stop two-thirds of designers' time being wasted on paper-work and obtaining approvals (Lynev, 1985). Now these details come from critical reports, and there is some evidence of further decentralisation to the Sumy management in these areas in early 1986. But a comprehensive report on the experiment published in April 1986 still singled out overcentralisation and supply problems among the major obstacles to further progress ('Samofinansirovanie . . .', 1986, p. 14). What we *can* do on the basis of existing evidence is to question deputy director Moskalenko's dictum that 'increasing the level of responsibility of the enterprise in these areas (is) the determining factor for fundamental improvement in other parts of the economic mechanism'. Surely it is the other way round. There is no escape from the primacy of the wholesale trade in the means of production issue.

Productivity, self-management and unemployment

Like-minded on matters of industrial administration, Andropov and Gorbachev had been, perhaps, even closer when it came to the 'human factor'. United in their implicit condemnation of the easygoing, corrupt, boozy days of Brezhnev, they looked to the strong and sober as the human basis for improved productivity performance. When Mr Gorbachev expanded on these themes in his opening speech to the XXVII Congress of the CPSU on 25 February 1986 the content was participatory, while the tone was utterly that of the Andropovian martinet:

> We must increase the material interest of the workers in better utilisation of national wealth, and in the growth of national wealth. How are we going to do that? It would be naive to think that you can develop the feeling of being master in your own house by words alone. Attitudes to property are formed above all by the real conditions in which a person finds himself, the chances he has to influence the organisation of production, the distribution and utilisation of the results of labour. Thus the problem comes down to the

77

need for further deepening of socialist self-management in the economy.

We must ensure a big increase in the role of working collectives in the utilisation of social property. It is important to apply unwaveringly the principle that enterprises and associations should answer fully for any losses their work incurs. And the state will not accept any responsibility in relation to these obligations. That is the essence of business accountability (*khozraschet*). You cannot be master of your country unless you are real master in your factory or collective farm, your shop or farm unit. The working collective must be answerable for everything, and must devote itself to growth in the common wealth. That growth, and indeed any losses incurred, must be reflected in the level of income of every member of the collective.

And finally, we must resist any attempt to draw unearned incomes from social property . . . (Gorbachev, 1986a, p. 9).

As if to underline that the duality of discipline and self-management was to be anything but a passing phase, the new Programme of the CPSU, published in its final form in 1986, posited that the distant Nirvana of Full Communism would be characterised by a blossoming of 'communist self-management', taking over from socialist self-management, and, would you believe it, by a 'high level of discipline and self-discipline' ('Programma . . .', 1986, p. 7).

But while the theme may have been taken directly from Andropov, the development of that theme, and of its implications, is again something which has flowered since Gorbachev took over as leader. The General Secretary himself has proposed the creation of new 'councils of working collectives'. Establishment economists have been making punchy statements and asking awkward questions:

How can we call a plan firmly-based and how can we guarantee its implementation unless it is brought down to the level of working collectives and the individual work bench? That is the only way we can effectively apply moral and material incentives to mobilise the reserves of productivity which exist in every collective and with every worker. ('Obsuzhdenie . . .', 1986, p. 57)

78

In other words the only way out of the vicious circle of unstable norms and playing-safe is to introduce a degree of voluntariness into the planning process. More generally, 'economic independence [for enterprises — D.A.D.] must be considered . . . one of the indispensable conditions for the broadening of democratic rights in management' (Torkanovskii, 1986, p. 62). Thus the technical problems with the self-management idea which Andropov's original initiative had thrown up are being faced fair and square, at least in the pages of the academic journals. No doubt they have had as thorough an airing in the deliberations of the Commission for the General Management of the Economic Experiment. As we shall see later, ideas like the 'collective contract' (*kollektivnyi podryad*, a stronger concept than Khrushchev's *kollektivnyi dogovor*) originally developed in agriculture in the early 1980s, when Gorbachev was in charge of that sector. How deeply committed the future General Secretary was to the idea is something we shall have to discuss later. What is indisputable is the depth of his relevant practical experience.

But higher productivity can only come if given tasks are executed by fewer workers. As we saw, Andropov's conception of brigade autonomy was intimately connected with his desire to revive the impetus of the Shchekino experiment. It was only in the run-up to the new five-year plan, however, that Soviet economists started to talk openly about the problems that might be posed by large-scale redundancies. The published guidelines for the five- and 15-year plans make no reference to labour force planning as such, though they do issue a guarantee of full employment. At the same time they contain figures on projected productivity growth which are difficult to interpret except on the assumption of a contracting number of people in work. Professor Vladimir Kostakov, deputy director of the Scientific-Research Economics Institute of the State Planning Commission, has been more forthright in arguing that the implications of current plans could create 13–19 million redundancies by the year 2000. While citing familiar (to a Western reader) arguments about early retirement and expanded leisure, Kostakov appears to doubt whether the economy will be able to redeploy all of those made redundant (Walker, 1986a). In his Congress speech Prime Minister Ryzhkov confirmed that the 15-year plan did, indeed, envisage the disappearance of 20 million manual jobs by the end of the century (Ryzhkov, 1986, p. 24). In an interview given to Western journalists during the Congress Professor Abel Aganbegyan, who is close to Mr Gorbachev, stressed that natural wastage would mean that many of those jobs should disappear painlessly, while around 5 million would require, and would receive, retraining (Walker, 1986b). There is, indeed, a good deal of discussion in the plan documents and the glosses thereon about the need to improve the efficiency of the labour placement system in the Soviet Union. At the same time T.S. Khachaturov, the chief editor of *Voprosy Ekonomiki*, has gone on record with the statement that 'there are a lot of people in this country drawing a salary that we could do with getting rid of as quickly as possible' ('Obsuzhdenie . . .', 1986, p. 116). Now Khachaturov is anything but a radical. Statements like this indicate just how much the views of establishment figures on the possibility of throwing people out of work have changed in just a few years.

What do the new plans tell us?

The end of 1985 witnessed the elaboration and public discussion of the five-year plan for the period 1986–90, and of a new long-term plan for the 15 years up to the end of the century. It has been the practice since the Brezhnev period for the Soviet planners to work out a 15-year perspective, but on this occasion the longer period was, in fact, treated in greater detail than the classic five-year period. The end of 1985 also witnessed publication of a Complex Programme for Consumer Goods Production for the Period up to 2000. The original draft of the plans was sent back to the planners by Mr Gorbachev for reworking, and that seems to have been the cue for the replacement of the veteran Gosplan chief, Nikolai Baibakov, by Nikolai Talyzin. Again, the final draft of the five-year plan approved in June 1986 featured significantly higher targets for key aggregate series than had the first published draft of late 1985. We should be in no doubt, then, that the final drafts of these planning documents bear the impress of the new General Secretary and his policies.

The overall strategy for the rest of the century is clear enough. National Income is planned to grow 4.1 per cent per annum 1986–90, but to 'nearly double' by the year 2000, which implies a rate of growth of approaching 4.7 per cent for the whole 15-year period, and one of over 5 per cent for 1991–2000. It looks, then, as if Gorbachev is giving himself plenty of time to streamline the economy before launching into a new growth drive. The fact is, however, that the target for 1986–90 is considerably higher than the average rate achieved 1981–5, and the Soviet economic system is certainly going to have to raise its game substantially if the growth rate is to approach 4 per cent over the next five years. As far as the later period is concerned, the implied target seems somewhat improbable even on the most favourable policy assumptions, unless there are profound changes in the world economy. Certainly 5 per cent reported Soviet growth means something more like 3.5 per cent once allowance has been made for elements of concealed inflation. But even that would put the USSR up with the most impressive performers of recent decades among the developed industrial countries. Nevertheless a number of Soviet economists have expressed the view that the plans should be viewed as strictly minimal ('Obsuzhdenie . . .', 1986, pp. 65 and 75–6). The key is economic reform, but while A.A. Sergeev of the Academy of Sciences implies that effective reform would liberate a massive new growth potential, he also argues that the experiments the Soviet Union has seen so far are not even enough to guarantee the rates of growth projected in the plan documents.

The guidelines themselves are unexciting on the subject of the planning system. Enterprises and associations are to have more independence, and ministries are to be held more closely to account for plan fulfilment, in the spirit of the industrial planning experiment. There is also a good deal of emphasis on the need for better regional and locational planning, and on the value of combining vertical and horizontal principles and creating inter-sectoral complexes in high-technology areas ('Ob Osnovnykh napravleniyakh . . .', 1986, p. 24). But if we are looking for telling comments on the essential planning problem, we have to look again at the glosses on the plan documents. Not surprisingly, we find Academician Belkin calling for more flexible prices, more prices agreed between client and supplier ('Obsuzhdenie . . .', 1986, p. 88). Professor Popov of MGU suggests that there is no need for the centre to determine every price, as long as it determines price *policy* ('Obsuzhdenie . . .', 1986, p. 70). Professor Glichev of the All-Union Scientific-Research Institute for Standardisation argues for a big extension of the 'mini-experiment' (see pp. 73–4) in the province of consumer durables. Complaining that 'wholesale trade' in these goods still effectively means that the responsibility of the producer for quality ends as soon as the goods leave the warehouse, he suggests that 30–40 per cent of consumer durables should be sold in outlets belonging to the producing organisations ('Obsuzhdenie . . .', 1986, p. 75). This approach has, in fact, been used with some success in Bulgaria (Krushinskii, 1985).

Academician Bronshtein goes further in suggesting that excessively detailed price control has in the past been to a great extent conditioned by egalitarian distributional motives ('Obsuzhdenie . . .', 1986, p. 89). If he is right, then we must suppose that this is one factor militating in favour of centralisation which Gorbachev will be glad to be rid of. In proposing that direct links should cover structure, assortment and dates of delivery, as well as quality and technology, Academician Tikhonov is implicitly arguing in favour of a large measure of free contracting ('Obsuzhdenie . . .', 1986, p. 85). But the most striking remarks to emerge from the *Voprosy Ekonomiki* colloquium on the plans come from the conservative editor of that journal, Academician Khachaturov, himself:

> Little has been said about the need to improve the quality of our plans. The point is — how long are we going to have disproportion and imbalances in our plans? The aim of the exercise is to put together plans without surpluses or deficits, meanwhile guaranteeing the sectoral and product group development priorities embodied in the decisions of the Party and the classics of Marxism-Leninism. ('Obsuzhdenie . . .', 1986, p. 116)

The answer to Khachaturov's question is, of course, that *overcentralisation* has made disproportion and imbalance inevitable, and made it impossible for the central authorities to concentrate effectively on strategic decision-making.

We can get closer to a realistic assessment of the relationship between plans and planning reforms if we look at some of the more specific projections of the plan. Everyone agrees that productivity is the key, and once you get beyond the stage of discipline and anti-alcohol campaigns that means equipment and technology. What do the plan documents envisage for the capital investment sphere? The machine-building industry, now led by a new 'super-ministry' — the bureau for machine building — is picked out for special priority. Output is planned to grow by 7.4 per cent annually 1986–90, as compared to an average of 6 per cent 1981–5, and the annual rate of renewal of active capital stock in machine building is to be raised to 10–12 per cent. High-technology engineering sectors are programmed to increase output 1.3–1.6 times as fast as the average for the whole sector. The innovation and investment cycle is scheduled for a sharp acceleration, with R & D lead-times to be cut by 50–75 per cent (presumably over the 15-year period) and construction lead-times slated to come down by 30–50 per cent (by 1995). The aim is to renew more than one-third of the machinery component in the capital stock by 1990, with as much as 50 per cent of total production investment being devoted to reconstruction and re-equipment/retooling of existing enterprises. The Soviet stock of robots is planned to treble in size over the five-year period (Ryzhkov, 1986, p. 26). Nearly 40 per cent of all robots installed in the Comecon area 1986–90 are due to be integrated into flexible production systems (Pullman, 1985).

There is, certainly, no reason why the Soviet Union should not increase the rate of expansion of its engineering industry as a whole over the next few years. When we look at goals for specific types of equipment, however, the prospects seem less settled. In particular, the goals for the computer and robot sub-sectors appear, on the basis of present trends, to be pie-in-the-sky (Dyker, 1987). This ties in directly with the issue of planning reform to the extent that the traditional system is insensitive to that which is small, beautiful and revolutionary. It ties in indirectly to the extent that planning failures, e.g. in agriculture, inhibit the import of micro-chip technology by forcing the Soviet Union to spend its hard currency on more basic things like grain. When we turn to the question of the assimilation of increased volumes of machine production the likely difficulties appear to be very serious indeed. We have already discussed the systematic obstacles which may get in the way of the rationalisation of retooling investment programmed in the planning experiments. At this stage we must introduce the dimension of the *general inefficiency of the design and construction sectors*, which threatens each and every initiative for improved productivity. Here again, however, we find that systemic factors are never far away.

The planned productivity revolution and the investment cycle

There is certainly plenty of scope for reducing lead-times in the Soviet investment process. Investment gestation periods in the Soviet Union are commonly 2–3 times as long as they are in the

West (Dyker, 1983, p. 36), and the situation in R & D is not much better (Amann, 1986). But one of the major reasons why R & D takes so long is simply that research institutes and design organisations continue to be rewarded for the volume of work performed rather than the results they achieve. Indeed, for design and construction organisations alike there is a direct incentive to prolong the R & D design stage. If a design organisation succeeds in reducing the estimated cost of a particular project by introducing technological novelties, it will damage the incentive-fund-forming capabilities of itself and the construction organisation charged with building the project. It is reported that construction organisations often resist the inclusion of such innovations in the initial versions of designs, preferring to introduce them themselves at a later stage as 'suggestions for rationalisation'. In that way, the official estimated value of the project remains at the original, higher level, which means bigger incentive funds (Sukhachev, 1985, p. 13). This kind of thing keeps everybody in the investment cycle happy but does, of course, greatly prolong the negotiation and approval stage, quite apart from its inflationary effect. It thus exacerbates the problem of pure paper bureaucracy, which as we saw makes a terrible mess of investment schedules even under the enlightened conditions of the Sumy experiment.

Under an experiment introduced in Belorussia and Lithuania in 1982, and extended to rural construction in the RSFSR in 1985, the estimated value of projects is agreed between client and construction organisation at the preliminary design stage. After that it must not be changed (Sukhachev, 1985, p. 13). This is certainly a good idea in terms of cutting negotiating time, but it still leaves the system wide open to padding of estimates, particularly since the client himself may not always perceive his primary interest in cost minimisation. It has been pointed out that even in the new five-year plan there is a good deal of confusion about targets set for economy in utilisation of basic materials in construction. Thus targets are set in relation to construction estimates in 'constant' estimate prices. But they are in practice subject to a rate of inflation of 2–3 per cent per annum, so that in these terms overutilisation can look like economy ('Obsuzhdenie . . .', 1986, pp 77–8). If, of course, all the actors in the drama were ultimately rewarded on the basis of the profitability of the operating project there would be no problem, but that is simply to return to the issue of general planning reform.

Turning to the stage of construction *per se*, we have little difficulty in pinpointing purely organisational weaknesses within the building industry. Overcomplexity has been specified as one of the major of these, and it is now proposed (not for the first time — see Dyker, 1983, pp. 73–5) that the system should be simplified by getting rid of supernumerary links in the chain of subordination and by rationalising the pattern of departmental/territorial specialisation. The three basic 'bricks-and-mortar' ministries — the Ministry of Construction (Minstroi), the Ministry of Industrial Construction (Minpromstroi) and the Ministry of Heavy Industrial Construction (Mintyazhstroi) — have always been characterised by quite a high degree of territorial specialisation based on the sectoral profiles of particular regions, so that Mintyazhstroi, for example, has in practice done most of the construction work in all sectors in the Ukraine, the traditional centre of Soviet heavy industry. This principle is now to be extended to other ministries that do construction work — the Ministry of Transport Construction (Mintransstroi), the Ministry of Construction for the Oil and Gas Industries (Minneftegazstroi) and the Energy Ministry (Minenergo) — and strengthened so that for each region there will be a ministry whose local main administration will have overall responsibility for construction in that particular region (Balakin, 1985, pp. 18–19).

These measures are aimed, among other things, at improving the pattern of supply of building materials on the same territorial basis, and under the overall supervision of the construction ministry concerned. They thus seek to rationalise, rather than eliminate, the tendency to organisational autarky in supply networks which has been such a major factor behind poor productivity performance. In this context it has been suggested that, in line with the principles of the industrial planning experiment, building suppliers should no longer be set gross output or marketable output targets, but should be assessed purely on the basis of deliveries to construction sites (Sukhachev, 1985, pp. 15–16). Territorial rationalisation, it is argued, will also facilitate consolidation at the level of the building site. The average trust, we are told (again not for the first time), is too small, and has indeed been getting smaller. If economies of scale are to be exploited, amalgamations will be required. The new, bigger trusts will, however, have greater operational independence, and it has been proposed that their work be assessed purely on the basis of bringing projects into operation, profits and unit costs, without any aggregate output or sales target (Sukhachev, 1985, p. 14; 'Ob Osnovnykh napravleniyakh . . .', 1986, p. 16). It is not clear whether that principle has been embodied in the new statute of the construction and installation trust that was to be introduced on 1 January 1986.

These measures do to a degree fit in with a pattern. They constitute a characteristically Gorbachevian departmentalist type of territorialism, and there are strong echoes of current moves in industry and agriculture in the proposed creation of territorial 'superministries' and 'super-main administrations' in construction. The idea of combining the construction and building materials sectors also echoes the vertical integration dimension of the USSR State Agro-Industrial Committee, which we will be discussing in the next chapter. They remain, nevertheless, very limited measures. The purely organisational dimension is reminiscent of the kind of bureaucratic musical chairs that Khrushchev used to like to play, and could yield similar returns. Where important changes in the actual planning regime are proposed, they may not be crowned with success. As we have seen, for example, the idea of crediting only deliveries according to contract has run into all sorts of difficulties within the industrial planning experiment. 'Large-scale experiments' in construction planning were mooted in 1984, and concrete proposals for, e.g. limited marketisation of construction supply and some decentralisation in price-formation put forward (Kluev *et al.*, 1984). It is, however, quite unclear what happened to these experiments, or indeed whether they were ever set in motion.

But let us assume for a moment that the impact of the proposals and experiments on the organisational dimension of the construction industry is maximal. The fact remains that that dimension is not the only, perhaps not even the most important, dimension affecting construction lead-times. There are currently more than 300,000 construction projects under way in the Soviet Union (Ryzhkov, 1986, p. 26) and it has been estimated that in 1984 it would have required the abandonment of half the projects then under construction to get lead-times back to the prescribed norm (Bulgakov, 1984, p. 12). The current plan documents envisage a halving of average lead-times, though they do not specify a time schedule for the achievement of that aim. It is, of course, client ministries, not construction organisations, that have historically been mainly to blame for dissipation of resources. This brings us back to the industrial planning experiment and Gorbachev's wager on the enterprise/association as the vehicle for a new rationality in investment decision-taking. And even if we can put aside our doubts about that proposition (see above pp. 70–3), there remains the problem of which half of current investment projects is to be abandoned. At least one Soviet investment specialist is clear that this can only be a political decision, and that it could take five to ten years to complete the painful process (Bulgakov, 1984, p. 12).

To repeat our earlier conclusion, the projected new Soviet take-off into rapid growth is crucially dependent on productivity trends, and therefore on investment effectiveness. We have seen that the success of policies for medium-scale investment activity is unlikely without thoroughgoing rationalisation of the investment supply system. We can now add that a more general reinvigoration of the trend in returns on new investment will only be possible on the basis of fundamental organisational change in the construction industry and painful adjustments to the investment profile of the country as a whole. The impetus towards reform in the investment sphere has been very weak. In the words of Prime Minister Ryzhkov, 'in no sector has work on improving the planning and management system been so behindhand. In no sector has the need for improvement been so pressing' (Ryzhkov, 1986, p. 27). Kosygin's efforts to bring design and construction into line with the principles of his industrial planning reform were a complete failure (Dyker, 1983, chs. 3 and 4). The only general piece of legislation to appear on investment planning *per se* in the period between Brezhnev's death and Gorbachev's accession was a very weak document indeed (Dyker, 1986, pp. 164–7). As Viktor Krasovskii, the doyen of Soviet investment specialists puts it:

> can capital investment as a sector really manage to solve the most complex problems of effective renewal of the fixed capital stock of all the sectors of the economy, with their various technologies, constrasting reproductive structure and differing priorities? Certainly the State Construction Committee is in no state to undertake this task, especially if you take into account the grave deficiences in sectoral construction and design technology. ('Obsuzhdenie . . .', 1986, p. 71)

Gorbachev will have to do much better in this area if his plans are to stand a chance.

David A. Dyker

Gorbachev's agenda for reform

Whichever way we look at it, then, planning reform is the key factor in the prospects for industrial production. At the same time Gorbachev has gone out of his way to avoid grand pronouncements and major new decrees on these matters. The nearest we have to a comprehensive statement of intent on basic systemic issues are the speeches made by Gorbachev and his Prime Minister, Nikolai Ryzhkov, at the XXVII Congress of the CPSU. On the basis of these sources we can produce a checklist of signposts for the future:

(1) The effectiveness of centralised planning is to be increased by permitting Gosplan, etc. to concentrate on strategic planning, freed of the cares of day-to-day operational planning.
(2) The sphere of independent action for enterprises and associations is to be 'decisively increased', with an end to 'petty tutelage' on the part of the ministries. The industrial association is to be phased out. Stable norms should be the keynote of centre-periphery relations.
(3) The price system is to be restructured in the direction of greater flexibility. Greater use is to be made of negotiated prices and prices free to vary up to a certain limit.
(4) The system of material supply must also become more flexible, with development of wholesale trade in the means of production again mentioned, but again only in passing. Enterprises should be allowed to sell off overplan production freely, and workers should be permitted to use offcuts 'to build houses, garages, and summer houses' (Gorbachev, 1986a, p. 9). Consumer goods and services enterprises should be allowed substantial scope to contract freely with the retail network for deliveries in accordance with consumer demand. This would implicitly mean the end of the aggregate sales target for those enterprises.
(5) The whole financial system is to be reformed, starting with the fiscal system. The keynote as far as enterprises is concerned is financial self-sufficiency, with incentive funds and investment funds, production and infrastructural, coming out of the profits. The model here is the Sumy system. In a speech made just after the Congress, Gorbachev announced that the Sumy system is now to be extended throughout the chemical and oil machine-building sector (Gorbachev, 1986b, p. 4).
(6) The territorial dimension of planning is to be strengthened,

but there is at the same time a clear warning of the dangers of localism.

(7) There is no place in the Soviet system for corruption and unearned incomes.

In very general terms this checklist does help to clarify Gorbachev's policy stance. The bit about unearned income is a clear signal, confirming earlier intimations that while the leadership wants stronger incentives, which means more inequality of income, it wishes to keep a firm grip on the degree of that inequality. Whether these two propositions are mutually consistent will remain to be seen. At the same time the second economy should be partly legalised. A decree of June 1986 on 'the struggle against unearned incomes' specified stronger measures against misuse of state property and reiterated the call for improved do-it-yourself supplies to ordinary citizens ('O merakh . . .', 1986). But when we turn to specific statements about the industrial planning system as such there is little that goes beyond the industrial planning experiment and the Sumy experiment. The idea that enterprises should be allowed to sell off overplan production freely looks attractive, but once again it has to be said that we have been through this one before with the Kosygin reform (Dyker, 1985, p. 48). Enterprises will only be prepared to produce systematically for special orders if they can be sure that prying planners will not mark down the potential thus revealed as a good excuse for raising the basic plan. In other words the idea will only work if the ratchet is buried and seen to be buried.

This brings us back to the basic problem of overcentralisation and to our conclusions on that subject apropos the industrial planning experiment. It therefore brings us back to the question of wholesale trade in the means of production. Yet Gorbachev gives us no more than the standard one-liner on the issue in his Congress speech. There is no evidence that the Commission for the General Management of the Economic Experiment did indeed report on wholesale trade by the end of 1985, and indeed the matter does not seem to have been raised at the Congress at all. Gorbachev talks in his speech about the necessity of a 'radical reform' (Gorbachev, 1986a, p. 8). Subsequent glosses on the theme suggest that it could mean a combination of the Sumy system and the 'experiment within an experiment' in consumer goods production (Milyukov, 1986). In a post-Congress assessment of the balance-sheet of the industrial planning experiment itself,

David A. Dyker

Aganbegyan is very dismissive, making the same critical points that we have made (Aganbegyan, 1986, pp. 20–1). Coming from someone who may claim the status of 'chief economic adviser' to Gorbachev, this can probably be taken to signal the close of that particular chapter in Soviet planning history. The experiment within an experiment has, indeed, now been formalised by a specific decree — but only for consumer goods production in light industry ('Ob uluchshenii . . .', 1986). Soviet appraisals of the problem do, then, seem to differ little from our own. But as of the present time the reality of the chapter to follow, the reality of radical reform, still belongs firmly in the future.

Our assessment of the content of the Congress speeches is consistent with the picture that seems to emerge from the plan documents — the picture of a patient Gorbachev, setting up his new economic model piece by piece, guarding his political rear, and looking to the 1990s for a final advance on all fronts. But how mindful is the General Secretary of the fate of Kosygin's planning reform, which was also programmed on a gradualist basis? If the incompatibilities between financial and supply planning sides of the industrial planning experiment and its successors are not resolved fairly quickly, then the whole industrial economy may find itself under threat of destabilisaton, as enterprise directors jockey for scarce supplies — with plenty of money at their disposal — and illicit procurement booms. That will create a situation ripe for political reaction, as it did in the early 1970s.

While Gorbachev should certainly be studying the history of the Kosygin reform, he should perhaps also be casting an eye back to the era of Kosygin's predecessor, Nikita Khrushchev. Khrushchev was a would-be reformer whose ideas seemed always to get lost in a welter of continuous administrative reshuffling, often aimed, we should add, at combining the best of sectoral and territorial planning principles. There is some danger that Gorbachev's industrial planning initiatives could share the same fate. The Commission for the General Management of the Economic Experiment apart, we know that there was, at least until recently, also an 'Inter-Departmental Commission for the Improvement of the Economic Mechanism'. It was this Commission, under the leadership of the then first deputy chairman of Gosplan, L.A. Voronin, which was in charge of the Sumy experiment as of late 1985 ('V dos'e chitatelei', 1985). In early 1986 a new 'Commission for the Improvement of Management, Planning and the Economic Mechanism' was created under the chairmanship of Mr

Talyzin, the new Gosplan boss ('V Komissii . . .', 1986). Meanwhile Mr Voronin has been moved to the chairmanship of the State Supply Committee (Gossnab). Has Mr Talyzin's new commission superseded Mr Voronin's old one, or merely upstaged it? One can only guess at the political compromises which these shifting and overlapping jurisdictions may reflect. But there is a good deal of irony in the spectacle of such a supernumerary management structure being entrusted, among other things, with the task of slimming down ministerial establishments! *Plus ça change . . .?*

References

Aganbegyan, A. (1986) 'Perelom i uskorenie', *EKO* (6)

Amann, R. (1986) 'Technical progress and Soviet economic development: setting the scene' in R. Amann and J.M. Cooper (eds), *Technical progress and Soviet economic development*, Blackwell, Oxford

Andropov, Yu. (1983) 'Uchenie Karla Marksa i nekotorye voprosy sotsialisticheskogo stroitel'stva v SSSR', *Voprosy Ekonomiki* (3)

Balakin, V.A. (1985) 'Sovershenstvovat' organizatsionnye formy upravleniya podryadnym stroitel'stvom', *Ekonomika Stroitel'stva* (9)

Berezin, A. (1984) 'Vospitanie kollektivizma', *Ekonomicheskaya Gazeta* (15), 5

Bionchuk, A. (1985) 'Mnogo prishlos' menyat' . . .', *Ekonomicheskaya Gazeta* (8), 7

Brown, A. (1985) 'Gorbachëv: new man in the Kremlin', *Problems of Communism*, 34 (3)

Bulgakov, S. (1984) 'Metodologicheskaya osnova i problemy sozdaniya edinoi sistemy planirovaniya kapital'nogo stroitel'stva', *Ekonomika Stroitel'stva* (10)

Dyker, D.A. (1983) *The process of investment in the Soviet Union,* Cambridge University Press, Cambridge

—— (1985) *The future of the Soviet economic planning system,* Croom Helm, London

—— (1986) 'Planning reforms from Andropov to Gorbachev' in R. Amann and J.M. Cooper (eds), *Technical progress and Soviet economic development*, Blackwell, Oxford

—— (1987) 'The economy' in D.R. Jones (ed.), *Soviet Armed Forces Review Annual* 10, Academic International Press, Gulf Breeze

Fil'ev, V. (1983) 'Shchekinskii metod i perspektivy ego dal'neishego razvitiya', *Voprosy Ekonomiki* (2)

Gnidenko, A. and Divnogortsev, I. (1984) 'Bol'she prav — vyshe otvetstvennost'', *Ekonomicheskaya Gazeta* (30), 8

Gorbachev, M.S. (1986a) Opening speech of XXVII Congress of the CPSU, *Ekonomicheskaya Gazeta* (10), 3–20

—— (1986b) Speech to the workers of Tol'yatti, *Ekonomicheskaya Gazeta* (16), 1–8

David A. Dyker

'Initsiativa, organizovannost', effektivnost'' (1985) *Ekonomicheskaya Gazeta* (16), 3–5

Kirov, Kh. (1983) 'O novom ekonomicheskom mekhanizme v NRB', *Voprosy Ekonomiki* (5)

Kluev, A. *et al.* (1984) 'Sovershenstvovanie sistemy khozraschetnykh vzaimootnoshenii i provedenie shirokomasshtabnogo eskperimenta v sfere kapital'nogo stroitel'stva', *Ekonomika Stroitel'stva* (7)

Krushinskii, A. (1985) '. . . Plyus otvetstvennost'', *Pravda*, 15 July, p. 4

Luk'yanenko, V. and Moskalenko, V. (1985) 'Na shag vperedi', *Pravda*, 30 December, p. 2

Lynev, R. (1985) 'Na khozraschete', *Izvestiya*, 8 August, p. 3

Medvedev, Z. (1986) *Gorbachev*, Blackwell, Oxford

Milyukov, A. (1986) 'Problemy radikal'noi reformy', *Ekonomicheskaya Gazeta* (20), 6–8

Moskalenko, V. (1986) 'Samofinansirovanie kak metod ratsional'nogo khozyaistvovaniya', *Voprosy Ekonomiki* (1)

'Ob Osnovnykh napravleniyakh ekonomicheskogo i sotsial'nogo razvitiya SSSR na 1986–1990 gody i na period do 2000 goda' (1986) *Ekonomicheskaya Gazeta* (12), special supplement

'Obsuzhdenie proektov novoi redaktsii Programmy KPSS i Osnovnykh napravlenii ekonomicheskogo i sotsial'nogo razvitiya SSSR na 1986–1990 gody i na period do 2000 goda' (1986) *Voprosy Ekonomiki* (1)

'Ob uluchshenii planirovanii, ekonomicheskogo stimulirovaniya i sovershenstvovaniya upravleniya proizvodstvom tovarov narodnogo potrebleniya v legkoi promyshlennosti' (1986) *Ekonomicheskaya Gazeta* (20), 2, 15 and 16

'O merakh po usileniyu bor'by s netrudovymi dokhodami' (1986) *Ekonomicheskaya Gazeta* (23), 4–5

'O shirokom rasprostranenii novykh metodov khozyaistvovaniya i usilenii ikh vozdeistviya na uskorenie nauchno-tekhnicheskogo progressa' (1985) *Ekonomicheskaya Gazeta* (32), special supplement

'Programma Kommunisticheskoi partii Sovetskogo Soyuza. Novaya redaktsiya' (1986) *Ekonomicheskaya Gazeta* (11), special supplement

Pullman, M. (1985) 'Sotrudnichestvo v robotizatsii proizvodstva', *Ekonomicheskaya Gazeta* (39), 20

Ronichev, I. (1985) 'Gol ne v te vorota', *Literaturnaya Gazeta* (45), 11

Rudoi, M. (1984) 'K eksperimentu gotovy', *Ekonomicheskaya Gazeta* (51), 8

Rumer, B. (1984) *Investment and reindustrialisation in the Soviet economy*, Westview Press, Boulder and London

Ryzkhov, N. (1986) speech to the XXVII Congress of the CPSU, *Ekonomicheskaya Gazeta* (11), 23–30

'Samofinansirovanie — put' k razvitiyu initsiativy' (1986), *Ekonomicheskaya Gazeta* (18), 11–14

Solomenko, E. (1983) 'Shipy i rozy', *Pravda*, 6 December, p. 2

Strugach, A. (1984) 'Inzhenery i novaya tekhnika', *Pravda*, 2 December, p. 2

Sukhachev, I.A. (1985) 'Orientirovat' khozyaistvennyi mekhanizm na uskorenie nauchno-tekhnicheskogo progressa', *Ekonomika Stroitel'stva* (11)

Torkanovskii, E. (1986) 'Uchastie trudyashchikhsya v upravlenii —

forma realizatsii sobstvennosti', *Voprosy Ekonomiki* (2)

Tsagaraev, S. (1984) 'Eksperiment i vstrechnyi', *Ekonomicheskaya Gazeta* (28), 8

United Nations (1986) *Economic survey of Europe in 1985–1986,* New York

Ural'tsev, B. (1984) 'Otvetstvennost' vo vsekh zven'yakh', *Ekonomicheskaya Gazeta* (35), 8

'V dos'e chitatelei' (1985) *Literaturnaya Gazeta* (45), 11

'V Komissii po sovershenstvovaniyu upravleniya, planirovaniya i khozyaistvennogo mekhanizma' (1986), *Ekonomicheskaya Gazeta* (8), 10

Walker, C. (1986a) 'The capitalist plague comes to Russia', *The Times,* 24 February, p. 12

——— (1986b) 'Kremlin economic expert presents radical blueprint', *The Times*, 6 March, p. 6

Yashkin, T. (1985) 'Shagi v zavtra', *Pravda*, 20 August, p. 2

Zaslavskaya, T. (1983) *Doklad o Neobkhodimosti Bolee Uglublennogo Izucheniya v SSSR Sotsial'nogo Mekhanizma Razvitiya Ekonomiki,* Radio Liberty, *Materialy Samizdata* (35/83), 26 August, AC No. 5042

4

Agriculture: the Permanent Crisis

David A. Dyker

Our treatment of agriculture must differ fundamentally from that of industry, and this for two major reasons. First, Soviet agriculture is in crisis in a way that Soviet industry is not. While industrial policy makers may argue meaningfully about the relative merits of incrementalism and 'radicalism', their agricultural opposite numbers must often wonder whether there is any future in Soviet agriculture as presently organised at all. Secondly, Mikhail Gorbachev comes from a predominantly agricultural background. He worked on the land as a youth, and went back into the local politics of his native, largely agrarian, province as soon as he graduated from Moscow. To a considerable extent he built his political reputation on the relative agricultural success of Stavropol' *krai* in the 1970s, and it was agriculture which brought him back to Moscow in 1978. As we shall see, Gorbachev was careful, during the Andropov and Chernenko periods, not to identify too closely with specific agricultural policies — wisely, one can only feel, in the light of the uniform lack of success attendant on these policies. But Gorbachev has been thinking about and acting on agricultural problems for 25 years. If we wish, therefore, to assess Soviet prospects for the future, we must look at Gorbachev's Stavropol' policies in the past. First, however, some facts and figures.

Profile of the crisis

The Brezhnev/Kosygin administration was highly successful in agricultural policy over its first ten years. In essence it did this by going back to the most positive features of Khrushchev's early phase in the management of the sector — pour in money, improve remuneration and investment flows, go easy on the subsidiary private sector and allow more independence to the peasant work-team within the collective or state farm. But after the record harvest of 1973 things began to go sour. Partly as a reflection of the illiberal political climate of the time, partly, perhaps, because the 1973 harvest left the rural apparatus men believing that they could do without economic reform, the 'normless' or autonomous link (*beznaryadnoe zveno*) system, which gives peasant work-teams autonomous control over day-to-day production planning and the distribution of wages and bonuses, fell sharply out of favour again. Agricultural investment expenditure came increasingly to be dominated by gigantic land-improvement projects like the 'non-Black Earth Programme' which in many cases yielded a return of precisely zero or less. Thus while agricultural investment was maintained at extremely high levels — more than 20 per cent of total investment throughout the 1970s and early 1980s — output and productivity stagnated. It is certainly true that the weather was not kind to Soviet agriculture in the late 1970s and early 1980s. Yet one has to say that if drainage and irrigation money had been better spent, and if the peasantry had been powerfully motivated towards a more 'caring' approach to husbandry, the impact of sub-optimal climatic conditions might have been much less damaging. Peasant morale suffered through the 1970s with a return to the traditional practice of having large work-teams (brigades) with few elements of operational autonomy. It suffered at least as much because improved wages turned out in practice to be a rather illiquid asset. Industrial production shortfalls and distributional failures meant that the rural retail network continued to offer little that the peasants wanted to buy, except vodka (Dyker, 1985, ch. 4).

But the problems of Soviet agriculture in the Brezhnev period did not stop at the level of aggregate trends. Anxious to improve the traditionally carbohydrate-dominated Soviet diet, the planners had, in the early 1970s, gone for and achieved a high rate of growth in the livestock sector. Trends in grain output failed to match, and the result was a permanent gap between feed needs and fodder supply which could only be fulfilled through imports. Over the period 1976–80 the Soviet Union imported an annual average of 9.79 million tons of coarse grain, representing 11 per cent of domestic production (UN, 1982, p. 207), and about one half of total Soviet grain imports. The livestock/meat production

Table 4.1: Rates of growth of Soviet agricultural output and productivity 1966–85

	Output	Output per agricultural worker
1966–70 average	4.0	6.7
1971	1.1	1.8
1972	− 4.6	− 4.2
1973	16.1	15.6
1974	− 2.7	− 3.1
1975	− 6.3	− 5.4
1976	6.5	6.5
1977	4.0	4.4
1978	2.7	3.1
1979	− 3.1	− 2.4
1980	− 2.5	− 2.0
1981	− 1.0	− 0.6
1982	4.0	3.6
1983	5.0	4.8
1984	− 0.1	− 0.3
1985	0.0	

Source: Official Soviet and UN statistics.

problem, then, represented a major tie-up between domestic problems and foreign trade profile.

From Stavropol' to the Central Committee: Gorbachev as agricultural administrator

Kraikom and *obkom* secretaries in predominantly agricultural areas traditionally take the lead on agricultural policy matters, and Gorbachev was no exception. His tenure as first secretary in Stavropol' province 1971–8 was marked by organisational innovation and quantitative success, culminating in quite remarkable grain harvest returns in 1977 and 1978. Was this the fruit of steadfast decentralisation, indeed of clandestine decollectivisation? There were certainly elements of that approach in Gorbachev's agricultural policies for his native province. In the early 1970s he developed the autonomous link system, then still in favour with the Moscow leadership, and by the middle of the decade the system was in general use in all sectors of Stavropol' agriculture (Medvedev, 1986, p. 83; Schmidt-Häuer, 1986, p. 61). More strikingly, he permitted migrant Korean *shabashniki* (moonlighters, 'lump' workers) from Central Asia to lease land from collective and state farms for market garden operations on a private basis. This was strictly illegal, but Gorbachev tolerated it because it helped to satisfy the demand for fresh produce which the 1970s tourist boom in Stavropol' was creating.

By 1977, however, things were changing, and Stavropol' was to become the testing ground for a new approach to grain harvesting, dubbed the 'Ipatovo method' after the district of Gorbachev's province in which it was first tried out. The Ipatovo method was based on large-scale harvesting-transport complexes, containing at least 15 combine harvesters and lorries, plus ancillary teams. The work of the complexes was co-ordinated at district level (Medvedev, 1986, p. 83). The method bore more than a passing resemblance to the old Stalinist machine-tractor station (MTS) system, which had been abolished by Khrushchev in 1958.

Why this policy turnabout? One interpretation is that Gorbachev was merely following political fashion. As we saw, the more radical forms of the link system fell increasingly under a cloud through the early-middle 1970s. There must be some truth in this argument, yet we should not try to make it bear too much weight. The link system was already running into trouble long before 1977, and there is no evidence that Gorbachev's Stavropol' links of the mid-1970s were especially adventurous by the somewhat reactionary standards of the time. The Korean *shabashniki* represent a different thing altogether, but they were unaffected by the Ipatovo experiment. Alternatively, the dramatic introduction of the Ipatovo method can be explained as a response to a specific agricultural problem, coloured, certainly, by a traditionally centralist attitude. It was Fedor Kulakov, then Central Committee secretary responsible for agriculture, who conceived the idea of large, mobile harvesting units. He was aiming to attack one of the perennial 'quality' problems of Soviet agriculture — the inability to harvest grain fast enough to prevent a large proportion of it being wasted. The idea was elaborated in a research institute located in Rostov province. Kulakov decided to try it out in Stavropol' *krai* for a combination of political and technical reasons. Gorbachev was a friend, and could ensure the political and propaganda impetus which Kulakov viewed as essential for the success of the undertaking. Because Stavropol' is so far south, its staple crop is winter wheat, which ripens more uniformly than the spring wheat which accounts for the bulk of the area sown to wheat in the Soviet Union. In addition, the terrain is flat, ideally suited for big combines (Medvedev, 1986, pp. 82–5). The results in Ipatovo district were impressive indeed, with the official plan for grain procurement being overfulfilled by almost 80 per cent in 1977. Some commentators suggest that much of the glory of the Ipatovo system is properly attributed to the link system which had preceded it (Schmidt-Häuer, 1986, p. 61).

In fact, then, the political and economic interpretations of the Ipatovo development converge. Gorbachev changed tack because his patron in Moscow wanted to use Stavropol' as a trying-ground. In this way he raised his stock with Kulakov and in addition took a good deal of the credit for a successful operation. It was ironic indeed that Gorbachev should be elevated to the Kremlin so dramatically in 1978 by the sudden death of Kulakov, possibly by his own hand.

By 1979 Gorbachev was already making it clear that he had reservations about the Ipatovo system. Quite apart from the problem of what to do about spring wheat, farms were finding it difficult to know how to cope with isolated fields of high-value durum wheat. In addition, the system was inherently problematic in terms of responsibility for, and maintenance of machinery (Medvedev, 1986, pp. 100–1). Most important, it was incompatible with the autonomous link system, which by 1980 was already being brought back as a major plank in plans to reverse the downward trend in output which set in in 1979, and indeed continued through 1981 (Dyker, 1985, p. 91). It was not until 1983 that an 'official' statement was made to the effect that the Ipatovo method was only suitable for limited areas of the Soviet Union (Medvedev, 1986, p. 131). But Gorbachev had almost certainly made up his mind on the point by 1979.

All the evidence from the 1970s suggests, then, that Gorbachev, far from being a committed and unwavering radical on agricultural matters, was rather a pragmatist working within the Bolshevik tradition of agricultural administration. The principle of centralisation was not at issue, and there was no question of the farmers knowing best. But workteam autonomy was a good idea, especially if the workteams could be tied in to specific obligations through the 'collective contract' system. There was, indeed, plenty of scope for the application of 'good ideas' in Soviet agriculture, but each one had to be assessed on its merits, and none should be expected to provide a panacea for Soviet agricultural woes.

The Food Programme of 1982 was, in a political sense, very much Brezhnev's initiative. But it was Gorbachev who did all the homework, and we can see most of the main features of his Stavropol' approach coming through here. There was to be less interference in farm management from above, the collective contract system was strongly endorsed, and the private agricultural sector was given the all-clear — with the aim of promoting a Hungarian-style symbiosis between socialist and private sectors. True to the Brezhnev tradition, procurement prices, including meat prices, were to be improved again. At the same time *district agro-industrial associations* (RAPOs) were to be created to promote the cause of integration between agriculture and related industrial branches. They would wield significant powers in relation to the setting of procurement targets for farms, distributing investment finance and fixing prices for intra-association transactions (Dyker, 1985, pp. 85–6). Thus the themes of limited operational decentralisation and rationalised *dirigisme* were both strongly represented, sometimes, indeed, to the extent of disharmony. For while the general dispositions of the Programme stressed greater autonomy for farm managers, the reality of the RAPO system in practice meant more detailed procurement targets for the farm (Kopteva, 1983). The Programme also provided for the writing-off of 9.7 billion rubles' worth of debts owed by weak *kolkhozy* to the State Bank. In addition, interest payments were lifted and a ten-year moratorium declared on repayment of a further 11 billion rubles' worth. That move was unavoidable. As we saw, many of the investments of the 1970s had proved to be money down the drain. But the money belonged to the collective farms, although the investment decisions had often been taken out of their hands. Now while it was perfectly proper to let bygones be bygones, the massive writing-off of debts did create problems of short-term financial planning. The trouble with credit amnesties is, of course, that they may create the expectation of further credit amnesties. As the discipline theme developed under Andropov, after Brezhnev's death, so attitudes towards the throwing of good money after bad started to harden.

While agricultural performance did look up a little in 1982 and 1983, Brezhnev's Programme did nothing to put it back on a clear growth trend. In any case Gorbachev was entrusted with a much broader economic portfolio by Brezhnev's successors, and he may have found it administratively as well as politically convenient to distance himself somewhat from an ailing sector. In addition, there were almost certainly specific disagreements between Gorbachev and Chernenko on policy matters.

David A. Dyker

Gorbachev and Chernenko

Agricultural radical or no, there can be no doubting Gorbachev's genuine commitment to the collective contract system. Andropov's successor in the General Secretaryship does not appear to have altogether shared his enthusiasm. By the middle of 1984 the most radical form of link system, whereby 'hectarers' (*gektarshchiki*) were given a hectare of land and paid a standard price for as much produce as they could deliver, was coming in for substantial public criticism (Omarov and Gostenkova, 1984). In poultry-farming hectarer-type systems of individual contracting were being abandoned and replaced by more conventional hierarchical systems of links and brigades. Under these arrangements workteams retained a degree of operational autonomy, but rates of remuneration were kept firmly under the control of the farm management. Accountants were attached to links and brigades with the obvious purpose of ensuring that actual payments did not get seriously out of line with established rates (Kutsevich and Raenko, 1984).

Some of the reasons proffered for this change in direction were obviously specious. It was argued that excessive decentralisation made overall management and co-ordination difficult, and created too much paper work. That sounds more like an argument for *further* decentralisation! But there was also concern about the weakening of the 'inspirational' (*vospitatel'nyi*) role of the collective under the more individualistic arrangements. This is clearly a coded reference to the role of the Communist Party, one of the few things on which Chernenko, the old cadres man, had very strong ideas. Perhaps most important of all, the authorities were worried about the possibility of wage developments getting out of hand. The operation of the normless link system in the vineyards of Dagestan was criticised because in one state farm the price paid by the farm to the link for a centner of grapes was 13 rubles, while in a neighbouring farm it was only 8.5 rubles. To make matters worse, costs in the former farm were not even particularly low (Omarov and Gostenkova, 1984). But what about the quality of the grapes, and what about timeliness of delivery to the farm? The *sovkhoz* in question must surely have had a good reason, in terms of fulfilment of its own plans, for offering 13 rubles, and if it did not, then it was the farm management's fault, not the link's.

The problem is, of course, that this is a recipe for the rich to get richer and the poor poorer. There is a tie-up here with

Chernenko's ideological preoccupations — kulaks under the bed and all that. But there are more substantial dimensions to the question which bring us back to some of the fundamental weaknesses of the Soviet planning system. The profitability of Soviet farms does vary enormously, and this has as much to do with the absence of systematic land rent as with variations in levels of efficiency. Because of limited inter-regional labour mobility, because *kolkhozniki* and *sovkhozniki* are in any case not permitted freely to change farms, peasants do not on the whole filter from the poorer to the richer farms. Thus some farms are bound to find it easier to create powerful incentives for their links, and to back up these incentives with appropriate investments, than others. Exactly the same problem exists at the level of the link itself. There can be no doubt that the principle of voluntariness in the formation of links was to a considerable extent observed during the Andropov period. One of the side-effects of that was that the best workers tended to club together, leaving the weaker reeds to manage as best they could. In some cases this created an uncomfortably large differential in performance between best and worst links which was bound to be reflected in income levels (Meshcheryakova and Zub, 1984).

None of the foregoing really amounts to a valid criticism of the link system as such. Rather it argues powerfully for a system of land rent, for greater farm independence in relation to overall manning levels, and for more investment in basic training for all agricultural workers. Thus in practice the issue of work-team autonomy is inseparable from those of farm autonomy, the price system and the agro-industrial complex. The 1982 Programme had failed to face up to this problem, and Chernenko's instinct was to solve it by going backwards. But Andropov's successor as General Secretary was surely correct in perceiving that if you give the collective contract system its head, you will lose direct control over the distribution of income in agriculture, however well designed the organisational environment.

Some areas of agriculture continued to enjoy a special regime. One was market gardening, where the pragmatism Gorbachev had shown in Stavropol' continued to prevail. Another was stockbreeding. Arrangements were reported in 1983 under which farms were paying workteams a standard price per centner or head of cattle for fatstock delivered (Sadykov, 1983). Reports from the middle of 1984 describe similar arrangements for fodder production, with aggregate link/brigade wage fund being planned at farm level, but the details of who gets what decided at the lower level (Meshcheryakova and Zub, 1984; Sidora and Ryzhkov, 1984). A big centrefold article for use in farm educational sessions published in October 1984 featured a straight group payment-by-results system in milk production ('Bol'she produktsii . . .', 1984). The point is, of course, that the livestock sector in general, and fodder supply in particular, are in *continuous* crisis in the Soviet Union. Soviet leaders have always shown themselves prepared to be much more pragmatically radical in agriculture when the chips are really down, irrespective of political preferences. *Aggregate* agricultural performance had not been so bad in 1982–3, and Chernenko may have felt under less pressure at the more general level.

The second area in which there seems to have been some disagreement between Chernenko and Gorbachev is in relation to the big-spending approach to agricultural development. That had been Brezhnev's approach, and it had not worked. But Chernenko was a Brezhnevite, and in announcing yet another grand land improvement campaign at the October 1984 Plenum of the CC CPSU Chernenko averred that 'we will, of course, continue in the future to increase capital investment in agriculture, to saturate it with technology and other material resources' (Chernenko, 1984, p. 3). To be fair, the interim General Secretary did illustrate graphically in his speech the inefficiency with which drainage and irrigation work had been implemented under his predecessor and patron. More than 40 per cent of organisations under the Ministry for Irrigation and Drainage (*Mindvodkhoz*) were not meeting cost targets, some projects were nearly ten years behind on original planned completion dates, complementary projects on farms were being neglected, and two-thirds of projects were suffering from serious divergences from design parameters and technical norms. Projected yields were being achieved on only one-third of irrigated lands.

How did Chernenko aim to ensure that the mistakes of the past were not repeated? He certainly recognised that one of the main reasons why the Soviet authorities failed to spend their way out of trouble in the 1970s was that they spent too much money on grand schemes and not enough on everyday supplies. Chernenko complained that portable water-sprinklers were still not in mass production, simply because the factory instructed to produce them had not got round to it yet. Application of organic and mineral fertiliser to irrigated land was still 25–30 per cent below norm.

Quite apart from direct effects on fertility this means that the land is less able to retain water. He also stressed the importance of developing clearer lines of responsibility in the whole area of land improvement, by compelling irrigation organisations, farms, etc. to enter into clear contractual commitments on *utilisation* of irrigated and drained land. There was no mention of the system, reported in 1983 (Logach, 1983), of mixed links made up of production and irrigation workers, or production and Sel'khozkhimiya (fertiliser and pesticide supply) workers. But the theme of giving the men in the field a more direct material interest in the results of their work in land improvement permeated the Plenum documents.

Still on the theme of organisational reform, Chernenko's speech was followed almost immediately by the announcement of a reorganisation of the Ministry for Irrigation and Drainage (Zhukov, 1984). This measure aimed to rationalise the ministry's structure by concentrating operational control at trust or association level — thus reducing to two or three links the chain of responsibility running down from the ministry and bringing the production unit nearer to the optimal size from the point of view of scale economies. In addition, it set out to attack the problem of excessive lead-times in drainage and irrigation work by cutting down on the number of projects simultaneously under way.

These proposals seemed, however, to raise rather more questions than they answered. Minvodkhoz administrators clearly felt that the system of dual subordination introduced in 1982, whereby land improvement organisations were made answerable to the local RAPO as well as the ministry, had confused an already complicated situation. How would the new, bigger Minvodkhoz organisations fit in with the RAPO system? More fundamentally, the problem of too many projects going on at the same time is, of course, a universal one in the Soviet Union. It will evidently continue to impinge as long as bureaucrats do not have to pay for the projects they initiate, and as long as Minvodkhoz and its subordinate organisations are rewarded for the fulfilment of purely quantitative tasks. But while the speeches, decrees and proposals of October-November 1984 said much about goals, and about organisation and reorganisation, they said virtually nothing about how any of this was to be planned. The October Plenum decree duly criticised organisations for being too taken up with output targets ('Postanovlenie . . .', 1984). That is certainly the root cause of many of Minvodkhoz's shortcomings, and equally the reason why enterprise directors do not want to introduce disruptive new production lines, even for something as simple and functional as a water-sprinkler. It is also the reason why all the organisations involved, apart from the farms, ultimately prefer expensive ideas to cheap ones.

> The clash of interests manifests itself even at the stage of designing drainage and irrigation projects. Thus plan fulfilment for design organisations doing work on land improvement schemes is assessed on the basis of the volume of investment expenditures. Naturally, the dearer the project, the greater the volume of investment. This principle does not give the working collectives of design organisations much of an incentive to keep project costs down . . . (Gerashchenko, 1984)

In the last analysis, then, Chernenko produced little in the way of new ideas as to how the big-spending approach could be married up with value for money. True to his pedigree, he seemed to place a good deal of faith in Party mobilisatory campaigns. By the same token, however, he interfered little with the planning structure that had been set up by Brezhnev's Food Programme in 1982. It was easy, then, for Gorbachev to stand back somewhat from agricultural policy-making during the brief Chernenko interregnum, in the knowledge that nothing very much was really changing.

Gorbachev in command

Perhaps because he was preoccupied with political and industrial matters, perhaps because he continued to find it politically expedient to avoid too close an identification with the sick man of the Soviet economy, Gorbachev took few initiatives on agriculture in his first six months or so as General Secretary. He did take an early opportunity to state his belief that investment in agriculture had reached saturation point (Gorbachev, 1985a, p. 3). But there was to be no rapid reversal of Chernenko's conservative line on the link and the collective contract. The spring of 1985 produced the odd report of genuinely 'normless' link arrangements (Purgin, 1985; Babin and Lausta, 1985), but the majority of reports from the usually more flexible beef and dairy sector depicted arrangements under which farms were keeping a tight rein on wages and bonuses (Bogomolov and Glezer, 1985; Bogomolov, 1985; Kostenko, 1985). And while around 50 per cent of crop farming (including fodder) in the Russian republic was on some kind of collective contract system by the beginning of 1985, the corresponding figure for the beef and dairy sector was less than 20 per cent (Nefedov, 1986, pp. 76–7). It was significant, however, that most of the reports from this transitional period criticise farm managements for being slow, even obstructive, in generalising the collective contract system. At one regional conference, chaired by Politburo member Kunaev, conservative farm chairmen and directors were berated for allowing 'levelling' tendencies (*uravnilovka*) to weaken the force of the collective contract (Balganbaev and Kozlov, 1985). We should certainly be cautious about reading a Gorbachev policy line into every nuance in farm management trends. But as of spring 1985 the Soviet leadership seemed prepared to permit the distribution of income in the countryside to move towards greater inequality in the name of more accurate payment-by-results. Overall, however, they still appeared to want, at this stage, to keep firm control over the degree of that inequality.

The theme of payment-by-results was strikingly echoed at the Central Committee colloquium held in April 1985. As we saw in the last chapter, Gorbachev took this as an occasion to listen rather than talk, but the kinds of things people were saying amounted to an unmistakable sign of the times. One *kolkhoz* brigade leader summed up the essence of the agricultural problem thus:

> We often discuss with out workmates the question of whether we have really earned our standard of living through our labour. There are many cases in our region where people in the *kolkhozy* making the heaviest losses live well, even better than in our highly profitable *kolkhoz*. When people live on credit rather than income the whole attitude to work on the part of the worker changes for the worse. Discipline and organisation deteriorate, and there is no real concern with final results. That's why we need real business accountability . . . ('Initsiativa . . .', 1985, p. 4)

Here, then, was a neat summing up of the whole Andropov/Gorbachev approach to discipline and organisation. The golden rule should be that all emoluments are earned. That is the basis of good work discipline, just as handouts will always encourage slackness and poor management. And when Gorbachev made a major speech in the Virgin Lands town of Tselinograd five months later he took the opportunity to repeat the message. Farms were too dependent on grants and credits, and much too ready to blame everything on the weather. The key to the future lay in better utilisation, rather than extension, of drainage and irrigation systems, and in better training of agricultural workers (Gorbachev, 1985b). Discipline and management issues aside, then, Gorbachev diagnosed a fatal weakness of Soviet strategy for agriculture — a continued and obstinate reliance on extensive development measures where intensive ones would be much more appropriate.

Gorbachev's reform of agricultural administration

In November 1985 the Central Committee and the Council of Ministers announced the creation of a new 'super-ministry' for agriculture, with full executive powers, to be called the USSR State Agro-Industrial Committee — Gosagroprom ('V Tsentral'nom Komitete . . .', 1985, pp. 17–18). In so doing they followed the pattern already set for the machine-building industry. Gosagroprom was to take over the competences of the Ministry for Agriculture, the Ministry for Fruit and Vegetable Production, the Ministry for the Meat and Dairy Industry, the Ministry for the Food Industry, the Ministry for Rural Construction, and Sel'khoztekhnika, the rural industrial supplies organisation. *Gosagropromy* were also to be created at republican and provincial level, forming a hierarchical system which would dovetail in with the existing system of RAPOs at district level.

The main duties of the new committee, as laid out in the November 1985 decree, are as follows:

(1) To reorganise the RAPO system with a view to creating a rationalised territorial pattern of specialisation and concentration.
(2) To assume overall responsibility for the entire agro-industrial complex. This would mean taking on a quality-control role in relation to the work of the Ministry for Food Products and the Ministry for Drainage and Irrigation. It would also involve 'close co-ordination' with the Artificial Fertiliser Ministry and the engineering ministries producing equipment for agriculture. The ministers themselves from all these ministries would sit on Gosagroprom USSR.

(3) To rationalise the administration of agriculture. This would include systematic redundancy, with full salary being paid to those made redundant for a maximum of three months. It would also mean putting Gosgroprom managerial workers on to an industrial-management type bonus system, with top bonuses, amounting to 50 per cent of basic salary, being paid for, *inter alia*, economising on the wages fund.

(4) To take reponsibility for material supply to agriculture, for relevant areas of price formation, and for the 'perfecting of economic methods of carrying on business and *khozraschet* relations'.

(5) To play a major role *vis-à-vis* agriculture-oriented research and development, and in relation to agricultural training. Special mention is made of the need to develop training for middle-level supervisors and field workers.

(6) To develop the collective contract, the general principle of payment-by-results, and to improve financial and credit mechanisms as they affect agriculture. In order to simplify and rationalise the financial dimension all agricultural credits are now to be channelled through the State Bank. (Previously investment credits for state farms had been disbursed by the Construction Bank.)

(7) To develop subsidiary agricultural activity in all its forms — peasants' private plots, allotments, and subsidiary agricultural operations run by industrial enterprises.

(8) To maintain unconditional fulfilment of orders (*zakazy*) from the state for agricultural output in given assortment as the main instrument of agricultural planning.

These points were developed, to some extent modified, in the decree 'on the further improvement of the economic mechanism in the agro-industrial complex of the country' published on 29 March 1986 ('V Tsentral'nom Komitete . . .', 1986), just a few weeks after the close of the XXVII Congress. The 1986 decree spelled out, firstly, the details of a new, more flexible, agricultural price system. Republican and local Gosagroprom bodies would now be able to fix 'incentive' prices for products like canned fruit and vegetables, fruit juice and jams selling in their own shops, with 50 per cent of the profit accruing therefrom going into the socio-cultural and housing fund. Collective and state farms would now also be allowed to sell up to 30 per cent of their *planned* level of procurement of fruit and vegetables and table wine to consumer co-operatives and on the *kolkhoz* market at freely negotiated prices — in the past they have been allowed to do this only with overplan production. At a more general level, republican governments are conceded the right to vary some procurement prices — with the agreement of Gosagroprom and the State Prices Committee. The new RAPO statute, subsequently published, details the powers of the district agro-industrial associations to fix operational and accounting prices for some categories of intra-RAPO transactions ('Tipovoe polozhenie . . .', 1986, p. 10).

There is a also a good deal in the March 1986 decree on how the collective contract is expected to shape up as the five-year plan progresses. Immediately striking is the endorsement of family and individual contracts as forms of collective contract — signalling that the hectarer system, in the past the most radical form of intra-farm decentralisation, is back in favour. Equally striking is the way in which the collective contract theme is tied in with the manpower training theme — in much the same way that we ourselves did, earlier in this chapter:

> Successful implementation of the tasks before us demands a rise in the standard of re-training. Re-training must mean full assimilation of contemporary methods of management and the principles involved in working on the collective contract and *khozraschet*, a profound knowledge of intensive, energy-saving and other progressive technologies, and the ability to use resources economically and rationally.
>
> Much more attention needs to be paid to raising the qualifications of field and shop-floor workers — every worker must have a command of the basics of economics . . . ('V Tsentral'nom Komitete . . .', 1986, p. 5)

Where the decree is a good deal less clear is in the crucial area of remuneration. We are told that workteams should, wherever possible, be paid 'out of gross income' (*ot valovogo dokhoda*). This could mean tying personal incomes directly to workteam income, in the spirit of the more radical link experiments, or it could just mean that wages should not be paid out of bank credit. Gosagroprom was due to produce concrete recommendations on the 'out of gross income' principle by the end of June 1986, but no report of these had come to hand at time of writing. In the paragraph which discusses the family and individual contract we are told that payment in these cases should be on the same basis as with the collective contract proper. Does that mean a radicalisation of the collective contract or an emasculation of the hectarer system? We shall return to this key question later on.

The March 1986 decree reiterated the stress on financial levers and financial correctness. As a general rule farms and enterprises belonging to the agro-industrial complex should, it predicated, move towards self-financing (*samookupaemost'*) in terms of capital needs. At the same time the decree extended Brezhnev's 1982 moratorium on debt repayment plus waiving of interest payments for a number of farms and enterprises. It sought to attack the underlying causes of financial weakness in two ways. There is firstly a proposal for the introduction of a degree of automaticity in the adjustment of agricultural procurement prices to increases in prices of supplies to agriculture. Secondly, the decree takes two bites at the recalcitrant problem of rent. From 1987 there are to be special supplements to procurement prices for deliveries from low-profit and loss-making farms. This simply represents an extension of the traditional principle of zoned procurement prices, which has not, it must be said, been particularly effective. Rather more radical is the proposal to levy an income tax on all farms (it would be called 'payment to state budget' for state farms), the rates of which should vary in accordance with land endowment and quasi-rental elements like capital stock. But the decree promises no speedy elimination of financial problems, and it is conceded that the loss-making farm will continue to exist, and will require special planning provisions.

There is little that is new here on the status and importance of subsidiary agriculture — the positive assessments of recent years are repeated with little detail on how development of the subsidiary sector might be facilitated. What is new is the proposition that private subsidiary agriculture should for the first time be included in the plans of state and collective farms. Is this a signpost to 'creeping nationalisation' of the private agricultural sector? Before attempting an answer to that question we must study the clauses of the 1986 decree covering farm relations with superior planning bodies.

It is, indeed, clearly stated that the number of plan indicators imposed on farms should now be reduced, thus reversing the *de facto* trend since 1982 for RAPOs to set farms more detailed plans. But what about the *nature* of key plan indicators? There is certainly a terminological change — a tendency to talk (as far as farms are concerned) of plans for *sales* (*prodazha*) rather than the more Stalinist-sounding procurement (*zagotovka, zakupka*). On the administrative side, the planning of procurement of non-grain/pulse produce is to be decentralised to the republican and provincial levels.

Most significant, however, is the projected change in the *style* of planning. True to the philosophy of stable norms, procurement levels of grain and pulses, and inter-republican and inter-provincial deliveries of other categories of produce, will be fixed for the five-year period as a whole. But it is the level at which plans are to be set that really catches the eye. The grain procurement target is to be held at the level of the plan for 1986 throughout the period up to 1990. But any farm delivering more than the average level for 1981–5 will receive an incentive price 50 per cent above the standard price, even if they fail to fulfil the plan. If they do fulfil the plan, the incentive price will be double the standard price. Thus the plan as it comes through at farm level is now to represent very much a minimum plan, and farms may still receive a pat on the back even if it is not fulfilled. Indeed, the whole approach was described at the XXVII Congress in terms of a Leninist 'tax in kind' (Alekseev, 1986, p. 10). Of course neither the average harvest for 1981–5 nor the planned level for 1986 would bring the Soviet Union anywhere near the five-year plan target of a grain harvest of 250–5 million tons annually by 1990. Soviet agricultural planners do, then, seem to be envisaging a transition to a form of 'slack' planning, in line with the principles of the Bulgarian New Economic Mechanism. Under this dispensation the purpose of targets would be to build in a safeguard against extreme fluctuations in output levels, leaving it to the structure of procurement prices to ensure fulfilment of the five-year production target. That would represent a big step in the direction of parametric planning. On this point at least, then, the March 1986 decree seems to have moved on a good deal from the positions of the November 1985 Gosagroprom decree.

What the foregoing is likely to mean at the level of RAPO-farm relations is not clear. The new RAPO statute tells us that that body will continue to fix sales targets and organise procurements from farms, in pursuit of 'unconditional fulfilment of the orders of the state', though it talks a good deal about contractual relations in this connection. Is the idea that deliveries above the minimum levels should be subject to voluntary pre-contracting between RAPO and farm? This would put the notion of 'planning' the private sector into a rather different perspective. Far from representing an extension of the traditional command principle, it would simply mean an extension of the principle of the collective contract. Just as the individual contract is to be subsumed into the collective within the socialist sector, under the rubric of the link system, so the private sector can be pulled into a complex of contracting which binds together every actor on the agricultural scene from the RAPO downwards. But decrees alone cannot tell us the whole story about this kind of potential development. We leave a final assessment of its prospects until we can broaden out the empirical and argumentational basis of our analysis.

The question of contractual links between private and socialist sector brings us to another major focal point of the March 1986 decree. Republican governments are now to have the right to sell fodder on the basis of counter-trade. In the past this kind of approach has been used by some farms in their relations with the private sector — peasants in their private capacity have obtained feed for their livestock on the understanding that they would deliver a certain proportion of that livestock to the farm (Dyker, 1985, pp. 96–7). The aim of this particular clause in the 1986 decree is surely to generalise the practice. But the decree has more to say on counter-trade than that. Farms which overfulfil their targets will be offered payment in motor vehicles, tractors and other agricultural supplies in demand. Gosagroprom has been instructed to form a special supply reserve for this purpose. The stress on counter-trade reflects a recognition of the limited convertibility of the ruble in the Soviet countryside, a factor which seriously weakened the force of the increased financial inducements of the Brezhnev era.

Counter-trade in investment goods brings us, finally, to the decree's innovations in the province of investment planning and finance. Here we see an extension of the farm's autonomy in relation to medium-scale investment projects, especially technical re-equipment projects, which parallels the provisions of the industrial planning experiment. Farms and enterprises will now be empowered to approve the so-called 'title list', which outlines the main features of a project, for investment undertakings up to a value of 1 million rubles. They will also be allowed to do their own design work on some categories of re-equipment investments. As with industry, the success of this kind of initiative in agriculture will obviously depend totally on the quality and reliability of investment supplies — even with counter-trade, the relevant pieces of equipment have to be in stock in Gosagroprom's special reserve in the first place, and the distribution network has to be capable of getting them out to the farms which have earned them. We shall return to this point.

Taken together, then, the official materials of November 1985 through July 1986 touch on almost every aspect of Soviet agriculture. But they are less than definitive — perhaps by express design — *vis-à-vis* a number of key issues. On the development of the collective contract, on the role of the private sector, on the relative importance of targets and prices in agricultural planning, and on the vexed question of industrial supplies to agriculture, many questions are left unanswered. But the scholarly and journalistic literature provides revealing glosses on these matters. With the aid of such additional materials we now attempt a more in-depth analysis of the factors which are likely to determine the future of Soviet agriculture.

The collective contract

As we saw, the year of Gorbachev's accession produced few developments of interest in this area. But the decree of November 1985 enjoined Gosagroprom to develop the link system further, and by early 1986 things were beginning to warm up again. There were reports of arrangements in milk production under which workteams were being left to work out their own wage structure (Polyakov, 1986; Vasil'ev, 1986a). At regional conferences farm managements were criticised for failing to respect the independence of autonomous brigades and links ('Organizatsiya raboty . . .', 1986).

Yet by the middle of 1986 there had been little clarification of the overall situation. The dairy sector was still being featured as a forcing ground for more radical variants (Drebot, 1986), and scholarly writers continued to hit out at farms which introduced the collective contract system on paper, but changed little in practice (Zhurikov and Martyshkin, 1986). Nevetheless the same writers stressed the fundamental importance of farms keeping control over the remuneration of workteam members, while other reports listed a bewildering number of plan indicators for brigades on the collective contract. On one sheep farm these include membership, wage fund, capital equipment, output target, cost constraints, growth in labour productivity, 'personal accounts' for direct costs and wages, and change in number of animals (Volkov, 1986). We seemed, at this point, then, to be back at the position as it was under Andropov — with a whole gamut of collective-contract-type arrangements and a general commitment to developing the system, but still no unequivocal lead on exactly what the system was supposed to involve.

How best to interpret this ambivalence? As we saw, there is no reason whatsoever to believe that Gorbachev has any strong personal commitment to the link system as such. To the extent that he believes in greater autonomy for farms he may well feel that the details of workteam arrangements have to be left for farms to work out. Where farms have dragged their feet, however, there has been a tendency, even under Gorbachev, to use Party cadres in a very traditional Bolshevik way — in a way that would surely have delighted Chernenko. In the middle of 1985, for instance, about 3,000 communists were sent out to the farms in Volgograd province to 'organise' collective contract systems (Mordvintsev, 1985). No doubt they did the job efficiently enough by their own lights, but this is a clearly no way to develop *autonomous* peasant workteams. Moving from the organisational to the ideological front, there is every indication that the debate about the legitimacy of the link system within socialist agriculture continues to simmer. Thus one academic writer:

> We must never forget that a contractual link can be a collective with a high level of consciousness, pursuing socially important goals — or simply a group, infected with egoism, pursuing narrow, group interests, far removed from the interests of society. Units like this are dominated by a consumerist attitude. What they are looking for is a privileged position and firmer and firmer guarantees of increased incomes. That is the psychology, not of the collective, but of the *shabashnik* . . . In what sense can the contractual link make the peasant the real master of the land? Unfortunately, the concept of 'master' is frequently largely identified with the right to play the boss (*rasporyazhat'sya*) . . ., and to please yourself whether you do any other jobs for the farm. (Kataev, 1986, pp. 27–8)

These propositions certainly raise a whole range of questions. It is particularly striking that in a follow-up article on the issue of 'unearned incomes', now the subject of new legislation, the author went very easy on the *shabashniki*, arguing that the money they make is largely earned, and that they need simply to be brought into line with the norms of the socialist sector (Shokhin, 1986).

Now could there be any better vehicle than the autonomous link for the regularisation of the position of the *shabashnik?* On the more organisational side, what does 'proper collective spirit' mean for the planning of link operations? Kataev is, in fact, quite clear, even with all his socio-ideological reservations, that link autonomy must mean giving the link the power to allocate jobs and distribute wages. If the farm has to take men away from link work for whatever reason, they should pay them full compensation for loss of link earnings (Kataev, 1986, p. 29). It is, one feels, the implications of propositions like these, rather than ideological reservations as such, which may inhibit the politicians and administrators from pressing on with more radical collective contract arrangements.

We saw that the March 1986 decree on agriculture lays down as a principle that families and individuals working on contract should be remunerated on the same basis as with the collective contract. Our investigation of the current state of the latter, however, suggests that there is no single model for the family/ individual contract to follow. Specific reports of the operation of the family contract in fodder production paint a picture of a system less decentralised than the pure hectarer system, in that there are production targets, but looking very like the more decentralised livestock/dairy arrangements discussed above (Glezer, 1986). The farm prepares the ground, applies fertiliser and sows the crop. The family link does the rest. Very substantial increases in yields are reported. The family contract system is now being introduced successfully in animal husbandry itself, and members of family links are earning two to two-and-a-half times as much as peasants working under conventional arrangements. There does seem to be one weakness in the layout of the family contract system as currently working. Premium prices are being offered for above-plan deliveries. To the extent that plans for family links are not based on stable norms this is likely to encourage capacity concealment.

Family links are clearly best suited to 'tending' jobs, where child and pensioner labour can conveniently be pulled in to help. They are also by definition small groups. On that basis the Soviet authorities may feel that in allowing them considerable operational autonomy they gain a good deal while committing themselves to little in terms of a general reorganisation of Soviet agriculture. It is worth noting, however, that there has been an interesting controversy in the Soviet scholarly literature about the ideal size for the link. Katorgin has argued that from the socio-psychological point of view the link should number 8–10 people — just about the size of a largish three-generation family, in fact. But technical considerations demand bigger units, at least for mechanised units (Katorgin, 1985). Kataev comes back with some interesting data which show that while large workteams show best results per tractor, they show worst results per *standard tractor unit* (Kataev, 1986, p. 27). Thus there may be fewer technical constraints on the generalisation of small, family-sized links than has sometimes been supposed.

The private sector

In the past Soviet leaders have viewed the subsidiary private agricultural sector as a necessary evil, but a temporary one, with no place in the future of Soviet socialist agriculture. Be that as it may, the sector was still producing as much as 26.5 per cent of total Soviet agricultural output in 1979 (Shmelev, 1981, p. 69). And whatever the precise meaning of the new idea of 'planning' the private sector, it certainly does reflect an acceptance of that sector as an important and permanent part of the agricultural scene. As we saw, the model is now one of co-operation between socialist and private sectors, and there have been success stories on this dimension in the fodder/livestock-fattening nexus. But we can cite many points of contact between the two sectors which reflect anything but the spirit of co-operation. On many farms there is no longer any common pasture. That means that privately-owned cows have to be pastured by the roadside, and that in turn means that they have to be tended constantly. At the end of the day the socialist sector suffers because the peasants take time off *kolkhoz/sovkhoz* work to do the tending (Kozlov, 1986).

Examples of this kind of difficulty can be multiplied. Because there is no regular basis for peasants to get their private plots ploughed, farm tractor-drivers have to be induced to provide the service as a personal favour. Thus when the inhabitants of Zakharovka village, Lipetsk province, discussed at their 'citizens' meeting' the closure of the local off-licence in the wake of Mr Gorbachev's anti-alcohol campaign, the question on everyone's lips was: 'How are we going to get the private plot ploughed and the hay brought in without vodka?' (Kozlov, 1986). Again, because 'regular' private carpenters, stonemasons, blacksmiths and glaziers are a dying breed in the Soviet countryside, rural householders have to resort to expensive *shabashniki* for maintenance jobs on their property.

But help, we are told, is on the way. In 1986 the Bryansk *oblispolkom* (local government) instructed all its *kolkhozy* and *sovkhozy* to help with spring work on the private plots of the village. In Zakharovka (where they had all the trouble over the closing of the liquor shop) and neighbouring villages, private plots are now being ploughed on the basis of 'agreement' (*dogovorennost'*) with the farms. This comes very close to the language of the collective contract. Thus there is undoubtedly a new element in official Soviet thinking about the private plot. But the force of inertia is opposed to that new element, and there are dangerous implications in the fact that local governments are having to *tell* farms what to do in this connection. It is time now to take a further look at the whole question of the farm's relations with its superiors.

Quotas and prices

One thing is very clear from post-Congress reports. The RAPOs are still interfering too much. 'There are established forms and schedules of statistical reporting. But no, they are inventing new ones every day. The paper flows from the farms to the RAPO and the district Party committees, and from there to the provincial agricultural committee and the Party *obkom*' (Dudorov and Kozlov, 1986). Again:

> look at these so-called 'incoming papers' for the first quarter. What are they about? They contain demands for data on size of work-force, number of machines, utilisation of fuel, stocks of artificial fertiliser, progress with the training of mechanisers . . . Could we do without them? We certainly could . . . (Vasil'ev, 1986b)

But the RAPOs have a cast-iron excuse. Thus a RAPO chairman:

> The multitude of planning indicators, the various requests, the paper-work — it's not our idea. The RAPO receives just as many instructions from the provincial agro-industrial committee, and we are obliged, in our turn, to pass them on to the collective and state farms. Does that mean that the

provincial agro-industrial committee is to blame? Well, it would be a mistake to say that. As became clear later from a conversation with the first deputy chairman of the (Urals) provincial agro-industrial committee, V. Yuchkovich, that committee also receives quite a number of regulatory documents from above. Thus there are daily at least two hundred 'incoming papers' alone. (Vasil'ev, 1986b)

The agricultural material does, then, confirm a basic point which we stressed when discussing the 'anti-ministerial' dimension of the industrial planning experiment. Centralised, hierarchical systems have a logic of their own, and it is very difficult to break the chain of that logic unless you are prepared to modify the principles of centralisation and hierarchy. That is why, horror of horrors, many RAPOs are still trying to impose *sowing* plans, as opposed to just procurement plans, on their farms (Vasil'ev, 1986b; Batov, 1986; Dudorov and Kozlov, 1986). And that is why some Soviet economists argue that the logic of the new legislation points in the direction of transition to a wholly parametric system:

In essence it is a matter of transition to wholesale trade in the means of production and genuine implementation of the principles of full *khozraschet* along the whole chain of production, so that the material rewards of each collective are determined by the qualitative parameters of its output (and in turn by the demand for it), by its cost functions and by its record on fulfilment of contractual obligations. (Bronshtein, 1986, p. 81)

Again:

In the future we could get to a situation where collective and state farms could themselves work out volumes of sales of key agricultural products to the state over the five-year period on the basis of norms. They could simultaneously calculate their requirements for the main categories of industrial supply. This approach would substantially raise the level of balance of sales plans with plans for supplies of inputs. (Alfer'ev, 1986)

But, of course, the norms have to be right, and the most important category of norm is price. An example from Estonia nicely illustrates just how insidious the price problem can be:

> Natural and economic conditions in the Estonian republic are most suitable for the development of the beef and dairy industry and the cultivation of potatoes. But with the present structure of procurement prices, production of these relatively capital- and labour-intensive lines is not profitable enough — you can make much higher profits per unit costs, and with a lot less trouble, if you stick to pork and egg production, using fodder brought in from other regions. The only way to maintain output levels of less profitable categories of produce is through administrative measures, setting targets for sales of all product lines, profitable and unprofitable, to the state. *That is why sowing plans and plans for head of livestock are still being imposed in some parts of the country, despite a number of government pronouncements condemning the practice* (emphasis added). (Bronshtein, 1986, p. 81)

The problem is compounded by the continued absence of a comprehensive system of land rent. In that context it is in practice virtually impossible for the planning authorities to isolate organisational inefficiency as a cause of loss-making. But systematic loss-making, mollified by handouts disguised as credits, has been another of the reasons for the persistence of 'administrative methods' in agriculture, as the authorities have sought ways to cut their own losses (Nefedov, 1986, p. 71). In turn, the more detailed are the instructions from above, the less freedom is left to the farm in the area of investment decision-taking, the *more* difficult it becomes to blame the farm for misallocations of resources. Thus defects in the basic agricultural price system set up a vicious circle of loss-making → administrative interference → distortion of price signals → failure to identify inefficiencies → loss-making. It is clear from the March 1986 decree that the Soviet authorities are aware of the existence of this vicious circle. Measures are being taken to refine the system of land valuation, and in one ingenious experiment being tried out in Estonia the RAPO itself is financed exclusively on the basis of differential rent payments from its farms (Bronshtein, 1986, p. 85). But once again, and not for the last time, we have to pose the question: are experiments enough to break out of a vicious circle which envelops the whole system?

Industrial supplies to agriculture

We have not finished with the problem of prices yet. The March 1986 decree recognises the need to adjust procurement prices to agricultural input prices, thus giving us, perhaps, the first Soviet instance of institutionalisation of cost-push inflation. But no procurement-price adjustment mechanism could cope with the likes of the KSK-100 root-crop combine, which has a productivity lead of 1.5–2 times over its predecessors, but costs 8–10 times as much! Even with prices on their side, agricultural supply organisations have sometimes been guilty of trying to do even better. Thus in 1984 the Rossiya *kolkhoz*, in Gorbachev's Stavropol' province, successfully sued for the return of over ¼ million rubles on account of overcharging (Nefedov, 1986, pp. 72 and 74). These are, indeed, but instances of the general failure of the RAPO system, as originally instituted, to improve the industrial supply to agriculture situation to any significant extent (see Dyker, 1985, pp. 100–2). The creation of the Gosagroprom system represented, among other things, a renewed attempt to come to grips with the problem.

So-called agro-industrial supply depots (*agropromsnaby*) are now being created at provincial and district level. These have the status of legal persons, though they are probably not on *khozraschet* as such, and are charged with overseeing the whole gamut of industrial supply operations in the countryside. Bonuses, etc. for their staff are supposed to depend strictly on *agricultural* results. But the style of supply organisations' work is changing only slowly:

> They come along with arguments based on the assumption, if not of the total ignorance of the customer in these matters, then certainly of his inadequate level of expertise. Most of our suppliers try to pass off the delivery plan of the old Goskomsel'khoztekhnika RSFSR [subdivision of Sel'khoztekhnika, the equipment supply organisation abolished by the Gosagroprom reform — D.A.D.] as the document determining delivery dates. Well, they say, our plan is broken down by quarters, and we will do loads of spare parts also on a quarterly basis (when we feel like it). The amazing thing is that the State Arbitration Commission in some provinces has gone along with these arguments. (Izrailev, 1986, p. 10)

Attitudinal problems are compounded by organisational complications. In some cases the organisations formerly under Sel'khoztekhnika have now been put directly under the provincial agro-industrial committee, on the perfectly reasonable grounds that their work takes them beyond the boundaries of any particular district. But that does mean that they remain outside the RAPO system, leaving open the question of just how 'locked-in' to the local incentive structure they can be (Dudorov and Kozlov, 1986). Electrical maintenance work on farms now seems to be carried out by a specialist association, Sel'khozenergo, again presumably outside the RAPO structure:

> Before its creation we had our own electricians. Under that arrangement it cost us annually 12,000 rubles to pay their wages and maintain our electrical circuits. But now we're paying three times as much just for maintenance. Sel'khozenergo is always trying to fiddle the volume of work they do under various excuses, because volume of work is the main success-indicator for their electricians. (Vasil'ev, 1986b)

Most important of all, supply organs can only be as good as the supplies they themselves receive. Though the minister for agricultural machine building now sits on Gosagroprom, supplies from his ministry remain a major bottleneck. Spare parts are still in continuous deficit, and there are specific shortages of pumps, coolers, vats and tankers for milk production. The KAZ-608 cattle transporter has a working life of just three months (Dudorov and Divnogortsev, 1986). The pattern of tractor production still does not correspond to the pattern of needs for *specific* types of tractor (Suslov, 1986). Nor are these difficulties confined to the level of major mechanised operations on the state and collective farms. Going back to the private subsidiary sector in Bryansk province, we note that availability of potato planners has been as much of a problem as ploughing.

Industrial supply problems have always been particularly severe for agriculture. The new dispositions may promise some marginal improvement in this regard. But that does not guarantee any narrowing of the gap between requirements and provisions, for the new agricultural investment regulations cannot but put much more strain on the supply to agriculture network. With farms now to be left in independent control of medium-sized investment projects, the variety of demand for supplies of equipment can only increase. In addition, however, these demands will be, from the centre's point of view, 'unplanned' in the sense that their micro-economic implications will not be foreseeable in advance. Thus the direction of change in agriculture presents exactly the same problems in the investment sphere as the provisions of the industrial planning reform. And just as with industry, we have in fact been through this one before, again, in the late 1960s and early 1970s, under Kosygin's planning reform. The agricultural legislation of the late 1960s gave farms much increased rights to set up autonomous subsidiary industrial enterprises. They did this with some success, but were predictably unable to procure much in the way of equipment and raw materials from the state supply network. So they turned to the *shabashniki* and the *tolkachi*. This resulted in such a wave of illegal operations in the countryside that Brezhnev effectively emasculated the development in the early-middle 1970s, much as he did with decentralised investment in industry (Dyker, 1985, pp. 60–3). If history is not to repeat itself, the principle of wholesale trade in the means of production will surely have to be extended at least as far as industrial inputs into agriculture.

What price Soviet agricultural renewal?

The crisis in Soviet agriculture runs much deeper than the problems of Soviet industry because at root it is a socio-political crisis. The peasantry, alienated and demoralised by Stalin's treatment, continuously depleted of its young cohorts by the pull of industrialisation and urbanisation, have responded disappointingly to the improved material incentives of the last 20 years — partly, of course, because there has been so little in the Soviet countryside to buy with your rubles. More fundamentally, however, it has proved difficult to break the vicious circle of demoralisation and distrust. After decades of pushing the peasants around, Bolsheviks find it difficult to swallow the idea that the former should be allowed, even encouraged, to take *initiatives*.

Thus the nexus of planning relations between the centre and the farm, and between the farm and the workteam, have been crucial. The first condition of an effective agricultural reform is obviously the abolition of procurement targets, production targets, sowing targets, etc. These are the symbols of the tradition of uninformed *apparatchik* bullying, of an attempt to apply the principles of taut planning in totally unsuitable conditions. Let us underline and illustrate the point by reference to one of the most serious long-term problems of Soviet agriculture — that of soil erosion. The Central Black Earth, Volga-Vyatka and West Siberian regions — the main agricultural regions of the country — have lost a depth of 10–15 centimetres — about one-third — of their humus layer over the past 30–40 years ('Obsuzhdenie . . .', 1986, p. 88). The link between this problem and the institution of target planning is direct, and contemporary reports indicate that the problem remains unsolved:

> (The RAPO) set the 'Forty Years of Kazakhstan' farm a target for sale of sugar beet which reduced the farm to monoculture.
>
> As a result disease is spreading among the plants, and yields and sugar content are falling. The same thing is happening this year. (Dudorov and Kozlov, 1986)

Again:

> . . . some departments are still trying to set targets for sown area by crop.
>
> In crop production we were confronted by a disturbing phenomenon. Every tenth acre of arable land [in Kiev province — D.A.D.] is eroded or threatened with erosion, and the humus content in soils is falling. The continual non-observance of crop rotations has led to a massive increase in the incidence of disease among grain crops and significant falls in harvest levels. (Batov, 1986)

Why do the RAPOs behave like this, even though the March 1986 decree tells them not to? To find the answer, we have to go back to the figures cited at the beginning of this chapter. Soviet agriculture has been in stagnation for more than a decade, and the Soviet government is still anxious to maintain as high a level of food self-sufficiency as possible. That places extreme pressure on agricultural planners, and the pressure percolates down through the system in the form of peremptory demands for maximum short-term output performance for specific agricultural products. The effects on medium-term production possibilities are disastrous.

Thus in seeking to reform Soviet agriculture Mr Gorbachev faces two essentially political choices. First, should he be prepared to countenance an even higher level of agricultural imports, as a way of giving agriculture a breathing space and an opportunity to break out of the vicious circle of target planning, poorly motivated farmers, and poor husbandry of the soil? Secondly, and if that opportunity is indeed given, should he abandon the traditional Bolshevik approach to the extent of total abandonment of direct planning, and a full transition to parametric planning, as suggested by Academician V.A. Tikhonov on Soviet television (EIU, 1985, p. 14)? The trouble with the 'slack planning' approach of the March 1986 decree is that under Soviet conditions, and in some regions, even last year's achieved level with no mark-up may represent a pretty demanding target, especially if ecological problems are taking their toll. Getting rid of targets altogether would permit adjustment to conservation factors by the people on the ground, and should ultimately permit a much more reasoned approach to the whole land improvement business. It would also, of course, permit a full flowering of the collective contract system at work-team level. But in our interpretation Mr Gorbachev's thinking would have to evolve a good deal from the Stavropol' days in order to arrive at that point. We have to say that at the present time, and with all the vast apparatus of legislation to appear on agriculture since the end of 1985, very little has actually changed. That might be just the thing to push Mr Gorbachev in the direction of a much more radical approach. We have, of course, said that about past Soviet leaders — and been proved wrong.

References

Alekseev, A. (1986) 'Novye metody rukovodstva — v deistvie', *Ekonomicheskaya Gazeta* (22), 10–11

Alfer'ev, V.P. (1986) 'Progressivnye normativy — osnova planirovaniya v APK', *Ekonomicheskaya Gazeta* (23), 14–15

Babin, V. and Lausta, L. (1985) 'Vnedrenie podryada — delo postoyannoe', *Ekonomicheskaya Gazeta* (20), 17

Balganbaev, E. and Kozlov, E. (1985) 'Kollektivnyi podryad na fermakh Kazakhstana', *Ekonomicheskaya Gazeta* (11), 16

Batov, I. (1986) 'Pul's perestroiki', *Ekonomicheskaya Gazeta* (14), 11

Bogomolov, F. (1985) 'Izuchat' i vnedryat'', *Ekonomicheskaya Gazeta* (16), 17

Bogomolov, F. and Glezer, Ya. (1985) 'Otlazhivat' mekhanizm podryada', *Ekonomicheskaya Gazeta* (14), 17

'Bol'she produktsii s men'shimi zatratami' (1984), *Ekonomicheskaya Gazeta* (43), 12–13

Bronshtein, M. (1986) 'K kontseptsii khozyaistvennogo mekhanizma APK', *Voprosy Ekonomiki* (2)

Chernenko, K. (1984) Report of speech to CC CPSU Plenum, *Ekonomicheskaya Gazeta* (44), 3

Drebot, A. (1986) 'Kak my vnedryali podryad', *Ekonomicheskaya Gazeta* (18), 10

Dudorov, N. and Divnogortsev, I. (1986) 'U partnerov RAPO — obshchie interesy', *Ekonomicheskaya Gazeta* (15), 11

Dudorov, N. and Kozlov, E. (1986) 'S gruzom privychnogo', *Ekonomicheskaya Gazeta* (21), 10

Dyker, D.A. (1985) *The future of the Soviet economic planning system*, Croom Helm, London

EIU (1985) *Quarterly economic review of USSR* (4)

Gerashchenko, A. (1984) letter in *Ekonomicheskaya Gazeta* (45), 5

Glezer, Ya. (1986) 'Podryad beret sem'ya', *Ekonomicheskaya Gazeta* (25), 10

Gorbachev, M.S. (1985a) Speech reported in *Ekonomicheskaya Gazeta* (24), 3–5

——— (1985b) Speech in Tselinograd reported in *Pravda*, 11 September, pp. 1–2

'Initsiativa, organizovannost', effektivnost'' (1985) *Ekonomicheskaya Gazeta* (16), 3–5

Izrailev, V. (1986) 'Postavshchiki otmalchivayutsya', *Ekonomicheskaya Gazeta* (21), 10–11

Kataev, A. (1986) 'Podryad v zemledelii: nereshennye voprosy', *Ekonomika Sel'skogo Khozyaistva* (5)

Katorgin, A. (1985) 'Razmer kollektiva na podryade', *Ekonomika Sel'skogo Khozyaistva* (7)

Kopteva, A. (1983) 'Khozyaeva polya', *Ekonomicheskaya Gazeta*, (36), 16

Kostenko, I. (1985) 'Osnova zarabotka — rastsenka za produktsiyu', *Ekonomicheskaya Gazeta* (19), 17

Kozlov, N. (1986) 'Tsena platnoi uslugi', *Ekonomicheskaya Gazeta* (25), 19

Kutsevich, V. and Raenko, V. (1984) 'Po dogovoru s pravleniem kolkhoza', *Ekonomicheskaya Gazeta* (28), 15

Logach, N. (1983) 'Soglasovat' plany i deistviya', *Ekonomicheskaya Gazeta* (24), 12

Medvedev, Z. (1986) *Gorbachev*, Blackwell, Oxford

Meshcheryakova, I. and Zub, I. (1984) 'Zadacha byla nelegkoi', *Ekonomicheskaya Gazeta* (33), 13

Mordvintsev, Yu. (1985) letter published in *Ekonomicheskaya Gazeta* (22), 16

Nefedov, V. (1986) 'Orientatsiya khozyaistvennogo mekhanizma APK na intensifikatsiyu', *Voprosy Ekonomiki* (3)

'Obsuzhdenie proektov novoi redaktsii Programmy KPSS i Osnovnykh napravlenii ekonomicheskogo i sotsial'nogo razvitiya SSSR na 1986–1990 gody i na period do 2000 goda' (1986) *Voprosy Ekonomiki* (1)

Omarov, L. and Gostenkova, E. (1984) 'Nuzhny edinye normativy', *Ekonomicheskaya Gazeta* (30), 15

'Organizatsiya raboty khozraschetnykh podrazdelenii' (1986), *Ekonomicheskaya Gazeta* (9), 15

Polyakov, V. (1986) 'Intensivnaya tekhnologiya i kollektivnyi podryad', *Ekonomicheskaya Gazeta* (1), 17

'Postanovlenie Plenuma TsK KPSS o dolgovremennoi programme melioratsii, povyshenii effektivnosti ispol'zovaniya meliorirovannykh zemel' v tselyakh ustoichivogo narashchivaniya prodovol'stvennogo fonda strany' (1984), *Ekonomicheskaya Gazeta* (44), 9

Purgin, V. (1985) 'Kollektivnyi podryad v khlopkovodstve', *Ekonomicheskaya Gazeta* (18), 15

Sadykov, V. (1983) 'Po-khozyaiski, s vysokoi otdachei', *Ekonomicheskaya Gazeta* (45), 16

Schmidt-Häuer, C. (1986) *Gorbachev. The path to power*, I.B. Tauris, London

Shmelev, I. (1981) 'Obshchestvennoe proizvodstvo i lichnoe podsobnoe khozyaistvo', *Voprosy Ekonomiki* (5)

Shokhin, A. (1986) 'Otkuda berutsya netrudovye dokhody', *Ekonomicheskaya Gazeta* (15), 10

Sidora, A. and Ryzhkov, V. (1984) 'Za konechnuyu produktsiyu', *Ekonomicheskaya Gazeta* (36), 13

Suslov, K.I. (1986) 'Kriterii — konechnyi rezul'tat', *Ekonomicheskaya Gazeta* (19), 10

'Tipovoe Polozhenie o raionnom agropromyshlennom ob"edinenii' (1986), *Ekonomicheskaya Gazeta* (27), 9–10

United Nations (1982) *Economic survey of Europe in 1981*, New York

Vasil'ev, G. (1986a) 'Obedinil podryad partnerov', *Ekonomicheskaya Gazeta* (2), 16

Vasil'ev, G. (1986b) 'Struktura novaya, a metody . . .', *Ekonomicheskaya Gazeta* (19), 14

Volkov, A. (1986) 'Podryad zastavil schitat' zatraty', *Ekonomicheskaya Gazeta* (23), 14–15

'V Tsentral'nom Komitete KPSS i Sovete Ministrov SSSR' (1985) *Ekonomicheskaya Gazeta* (48), 17–18

'V Tsentral'nom Komitete KPSS i Sovete Ministrov SSSR' (1986), *Ekonomicheskaya Gazeta* (15), 2, 4 and 5

Zhukov, V.A. (1984) 'Puti uluchsheniya organizatsii upravleniya vodokhozyaistvennym stroitel'stvom', *Ekonomika Stroitel'stva* (11)

Zhurikov, V. and Martyshkin, G. (1986) 'Podryad ne terpit formalizma', *Ekonomicheskaya Gazeta* (24), 11

5

Gorbachev and the World — the Economic Side

Alan H. Smith

Introduction

The purpose of this chapter is to examine the impact of the foreign trade sector on the prospects for economic reform in the USSR. Four major areas of reform pressure will be examined. First, why does the Soviet Union trade with the outside world and how important is trade to the domestic economy? Secondly, to what extent has foreign trade acted as a substitute for domestic reform by permitting access to foreign technology? Thirdly, will changing trade needs and Balance of Payments pressure act as a catalyst to domestic reform? Fourthly, does the system of foreign trade itself act as a barrier to economic development and will changing trade needs result in pressure to change the foreign trade system, which in turn will lead to pressure for domestic reform? It is assumed that the reader may be less cognisant with the operation of the Soviet trade system than with the operation of the Soviet economic system as a whole, and a fairly detailed account of the origins and operation of the trade system has been provided. Finally, the intentions of the new leadership towards trade matters, and in particular the extent to which Comecon may become more or less inward looking, will be examined.

The determinants of foreign trade

The trade patterns of a country are determined by a complex of factors, the most obvious of which in the Soviet case are the size of the land mass and the domestic resource base of energy and minerals, the industrial and agricultural structure, the absolute level of economic development and the relative level in comparison with both trade partners and competitors, and the nature of the planning and trading system. Finally, and possibly most important in the longer term, there is the supply of human resources, including not just the size of the labour force and its distribution, but also its quality and productivity, which are influenced by both the level of training and the degree of motivation.

The neoclassical economist tends to take all this as given in the short run, and attempts to explain trade patterns in terms of the influence of these factors on comparative costs. This chapter, however, will focus on the influence of the Soviet growth model and the state monopoly of foreign trade on Soviet trade patterns, in an attempt to analyse whether changing trade demands will provide a stimulus to either domestic economic reform and/or reform of the trading system itself. It can be argued that this approach is justified by the nature of the Soviet planning and foreign trade systems, which isolate domestic manufacturers from the influence of short-run changes in world market conditions, thereby helping to stabilise domestic production patterns and increasing the influence of long-term trends on trade structure.

As David Dyker shows in his introductory chapter, the Soviet growth model emphasises the growth of gross output through the central mobilisation of resources. It is commonly known as the 'extensive growth model', a term derived by the Czechoslovak reform school from the Marxian concept of 'extensively expanded reproduction', which relies on a high rate of growth of inputs of capital, labour and raw materials into industry, with a relatively low growth of domestic development of new processes and techniques of production, to achieve a rapid rate of growth of output.

There is some empirical evidence to indicate that extensive growth is best suited to countries at an intermediate level of development, which can benefit most rapidly from the acquisition of foreign technology (taken in the wider sense to include both methods of production and techniques of management and organisation) and the diffusion of these techniques throughout the economy. Such economies will normally possess a basic infrastructure, some form of educated elite and a pool of unskilled or untrained labour capable of learning and adopting the new techniques of production. In the early stages of extensive growth, centralisation of decision-making may be the most appropriate way to economise on the relatively scarce resource of labour versed in management techniques. As the *stock* of the most easily identifiable and readily absorbable international production techniques is used up, the rate of growth of output arising through international technology transfer will tend to decelerate, and the economy will become more dependent on the *flow* of new innovations (generated domestically and/or acquired from abroad) for technical progress. Failure to adjust to this change will result in a deceleration of the growth rate (Gomulka, 1971, *passim*). In the longer term, therefore, the rate of growth of output will depend more on the speed with which new innovations can be identified and successfully diffused throughout the economy. At this stage of development, centralisation of decision-making may act as a brake on rapid economic development, to the extent that it slows down the process of technical diffusion and does not fully utilise the economic and social benefits of an educated labour force. This may also have a considerable effect on the long-term structure of exports, and consequently on the capacity to acquire a constant flow of imports. Economies that are capable of diffusing and adapting non-indigenous technology rapidly may in the long term also compete successfully in selling those items in international markets, and reduce or even eliminate trade deficits in manufactures; those that are slower to adapt will suffer from severe competition in external markets.

The Soviet planning system and state monopoly of foreign trade (which is discussed below) were specifically designed to implement a strategy of extensive growth in the first five-year plan, and this was reflected in the growing proportion of imports of machinery and equipment and engineering inputs, including steel and metal products, in the 1930s. Imports were not the only, or even the major, source of acquisition of foreign technology during this period. A number of other techniques, including scanning technical journals, requesting detailed technical specifications from potential foreign suppliers, buying single items for the purpose of reverse engineering and hiring foreign engineers in order to obtain their technical expertise, were widely employed (Sutton, 1968, *passim*).

The economic success of the strategy is reflected in official Soviet industrial growth statistics, which indicate that industrial output grew by an average of just under 20 per cent per annum 1929–36, followed by a substantial slowdown 1937–40. These trends are confirmed by Western re-estimates, which indicate an industrial growth rate in excess of 10 per cent per annum 1927–37 followed by a slowdown to only 1.9 per cent per annum 1937–40

(Kaplan and Moorsteen, 1960). The slowdown in the late 1930s was caused in part by the impact of the purges on the efficiency of domestic management. Official statistics show that rates of industrial growth in the order of 20 per cent per annum were also attained in the immediate post-war period, as the USSR reconstructed its war-damaged industry with equipment which embodied improvements in world technology developed since the initial industrialisation drive (Gomulka, 1986, ch. 7). On this occasion technology was partly acquired through the process of reparation payments from the defeated Axis powers, and by the dismantling of German and Czechoslovak enterprises for analysis and replication.

The extensive growth model does not, however, result only in demand for imported technology and machinery and equipment. Extensive growth relies on a high rate of growth of inputs to the expanding sectors of the economy, which need not necessarily fit in with the supply of unused (or underused) inputs available to the planners. This can result in the short term in a reduced supply of those items for export, but in the long term the demand for certain items may outstrip available domestic supply, imposing a specific constraint to further growth. In certain cases the supply of domestic inputs may be unamenable to further expansion in the short run, or be subject to rapidly decreasing returns to scale, with the result that domestic supply cannot be expanded as quickly as domestic demand is growing, or that the cost of domestic development exceeds the cost of imports.

The problem is aggravated in the Soviet case by the rigidity of the domestic price system, which prevents price signals from providing central planners with an automatic indication of scarcities in specific sectors of the economy. *De facto*, the Soviet planning system allows few opportunities for enterprises to substitute inputs in deficit supply with alternative sources, and the 'ratchet effect' (see p. 59) provides enterprises with a perverse incentive to overindent for (and overconsume) those items that it anticipates will be scarce, in order to insure against future supply uncertainty. Central planners who are chiefly concerned with the fulfilment of aggregate domestic output goals may therefore pursue output growth targets for specific products until domestic sources of supply are apparently fully utilised, and then resort to imports to alleviate emerging supply bottlenecks.

Empirically the following constraints have proved to be the most critical in the Soviet case:

Alan H. Smith

(a) The labour force constraint:
As we saw in Chapter 1, the growth of the Soviet industrial labour force in the 1930s resulted from the transfer of labour from agriculture to industry and the increased employment of women in that labour force. The industrial capital stock grew faster than the industrial labour force during this period, but as the economy was capital-scarce this enabled an increasing proportion of the industrial labour force to be equipped with improved technology (labour-augmenting capital), facilitating an increase in output per worker combined with the maintenance of full employment. As optimal factor proportions were reached and labour force growth decelerated, labour constraints became critical. The labour constraint first became noticeable in the more industrialised centrally planned economies of Eastern Europe, notably the GDR and Czechoslovakia, and formed the basis of the extensive/intensive growth argument. The labour constraint has now become crucial in the USSR also. Ryzhkov's report to the XXVII Party Congress indicated that the labour force would grow by only 3.2 million people in the 1986–90 plan period, and that this increase would be almost entirely channelled into the 'non-productive' sectors of the economy — health, education and other services. Without increases in labour productivity, he argued, demand for labour would grow by 22 million people over the five-year period (Ryzhkov, 1986).

The labour force constraint has several significant implications for the structure of imports.
(i) The pattern of demand for capital goods has shifted from labour-augmenting capital to labour-saving categories (industrial robots, computers, digitally controlled machine tools, etc.). As we saw in Chapter 3, the Soviet Union has a poor record in the domestic manufacture of these.
(ii) The bottleneck could be alleviated by importing more labour-intensive products. *A priori*, this would appear to imply increasing imports from labour-abundant countries in the Third World, possibly involving joint ventures in manufacturing industry in Third World countries. Increased economic co-operation with China could prove to be of value in this respect.
(iii) Labour constraints might be eased by establishing joint ventures on Soviet territory, either to attract labour-saving technology or even to involve direct labour contributions. This approach has been reflected in Comecon joint ventures to develop Soviet energy sources for bloc consumption involving the

130

employment of East European construction workers on Soviet territory.

(b) Consumption constraints:
(i) Agriculture and foodstuffs
The transfer of labour from agriculture to industry has not been costless, but has contributed to the failure of agricultural output to keep pace with the growth of domestic demand. The problem has been complicated by price rigidity. State retail prices for foodstuffs have remained heavily subsidised, resulting in excess domestic demand, while the relatively slow growth of procurement prices, especially for livestock producers, has provided an insufficient incentive to increase domestic supplies (see Chapter 4). Despite the significant increase in investment in agriculture in the 1970s, these problems have become so serious that the demand for imported foodstuffs in general, and animal feedstocks in particular, has continued to grow over the long term, with short-term fluctuations determined by harvest conditions.
(ii) Industrial consumer goods
Increased participation rates in the economy were initially a major source of both increased family income and increased supply of industrial consumer goods. The subsequent deceleration in labour-force growth and the growth of output per worker has contributed to a deceleration in the growth trend of supply of goods to the state retail sector without a commensurate slowdown in the rate of growth of wage earnings, as enterprises have responded to labour shortage by finding ways of increasing wage payments to attract labour. This has contributed to a growing demand for imported consumer goods to reduce disequilibrium in the consumer market. Demand for imported consumer goods has also been affected by the technical obsolescence and poor quality of many Soviet industrial consumer goods, now that more immediate demands have been satisfied.

Consumption constraints have had significant effects on the structure of Soviet trade. In 1950 the Soviet Union was a net exporter of foodstuffs and industrial consumer goods taken together. By 1984, however, the USSR had become a substantial net importer of both foodstuffs and industrial consumer goods.

(c) Material input constraints:
The USSR is well endowed with mineral deposits, and raw materials and energy have formed the major source of Soviet exports, both to Comecon partners in Eastern Europe and to the

industrial West. The commodity structure of Soviet trade with Eastern Europe reflects the 'radial' pattern whereby USSR exports meet the major energy and raw materials needs of the less favourably endowed East European countries, in exchange for imports of machinery and equipment, foodstuffs and industrial consumer goods. Hard-currency earnings from the export of energy, raw materials and precious metals, which accounted for an estimated 87 per cent of Soviet exports to industrialised capitalist countries in 1984, have been used primarily to meet Soviet import demand for machinery and equipment, specialised steel products (including pipelines for use in energy transportation) and foodstuffs.

The combined impact of domestic and East European demand resulting from the policy of extensive growth, and the demand for exports to maintain hard currency earnings, has exceeded the capacity of energy deposits located closest to centres of industrial production in the European sector of the country. This is the background to the drive to develop deposits in the less accessible terrains of Western Siberia and the Arctic, with consequent increases in the cost of exploration, extraction and transportation to the major areas of consumption. Centralisation of decision-making and the absence of freedom of entry into energy markets by independent producers have contributed to a pattern of initial slowness to develop new energy sources, followed by rapid growth of output involving crash investment programmes once a potential source has been identified. The pattern is reflected in the reliance on coal as the major energy source into the late 1960s, with output initially peaking in the late 1970s (output may exceed these levels in the late 1980s with the development of new coalfields), followed by the rapid development of oil production in the 1970s, with peak output being reached in 1983. That is now being followed in turn by the rapid development of natural gas in the 1980s and the planned expansion of nuclear power in the late 1980s and 1990s.

Developments like these have resulted in Soviet demand for imports of machinery and equipment for the energy sector, as crash investment programmes have strained domestic production capacity. A more critical problem in the longer term will be the extent to which domestic (and East European) demand for energy will constrain extra-bloc export availability. This points to a direct tie-up between the input-economising implications of planning reform proposals and the external trading dimension.

The origins of the state monopoly of foreign trade and the current trade system

The nationalisation of foreign trade on 22 April 1918 was one of the first acts of the Bolshevik government. It involved the establishment of a state monopoly of foreign trade whereby domestic private traders and nationalised enterprises were forbidden to deal in foreign markets, and foreign businesses seeking trade with Russia were obliged to conduct all their negotiations with government officials. The initial decision was principally motivated by Lenin's fear of foreign capital, and by the desire to pursue a policy of socialist economic development in a backward, predominantly agrarian, economy in which foreign trade flows had been concentrated in the hands of a few large capitalist import-export houses (Quigley, 1974, pp. 9–14).

Lenin's fears largely centred on the prospect of the domestic market being flooded by foreign (predominantly German) consumer goods and manufactures, which would prevent domestic industrialisation. Foreign capitalists might exploit cheap labour and engage in the wholesale extraction of Russian mineral and agricultural wealth for private gain, protecting their own interests by preventing the implementation of socialist economic policies.

A strategy of complete autarky was not envisaged. In part it was hoped that trade relations would be re-established with newly emergent socialist nations, following the spread of revolution to other countries. This trade would take place on a planned basis, and would be more akin to internal trade within the socialist community (Bukharin and Preobrazhensky, 1970 edition, p. 326). It was recognised that trade with capitalist nations would have to continue, but posited that this trade should be directed and controlled by the socialist state. It was also recognised that even if the activities of foreign capitalists could be controlled, it would still be necessary to exercise central control to stop individual preferences determining the structure of imports and exports. Although the volume of trade in 1918 was insignificant by pre-war standards, official statistics show that industrial consumer goods comprised nearly 60 per cent of Russian imports in that year. It was feared that as the economy recovered from the chaos of war demand for consumer goods would grow rapidly, while exporters would be tempted by higher prices prevailing on foreign markets. It was therefore considered necessary both to restrict imports to items that were crucial to economic development, and to prevent

133

individual entrepreneurs from exporting essential raw materials and foodstuffs. It was argued that these goals could best be achieved, not by restrictions on internal and external capital movements, import and export duties, etc., but by the construction of a solid barrier around the economy, administered by state officials (Quigley, ch. 1, *passim*).

In practice the chaos engendered by the Civil War, not to mention foreign restrictions on trade with Russia, resulted in the virtual cessation of foreign trade relations between 1918 and 1920. With the establishment of NEP in 1921 the principle of the state monopoly of foreign trade came under attack on the grounds that it was counterproductive. Bukharin alleged that the People's Commissariat for Foreign Trade (as it was known from June 1920 until 1926) was too remote from domestic producers to stimulate a sufficient volume of exports to pay for the required volume of imports. Lenin repeated the argument that to break up the monopoly would result in private traders and peasants exporting grain to foreign markets, which would threaten industrialisation by reducing food supplies available to the towns, and leave foreign currency, and hence import policy, in private hands. Eventually Lenin's arguments triumphed, with the support of Trotsky and Stalin, who had previously argued against the retention of the state monopoly.

Quigley (1974, p. 46) identifies four features of the current foreign trade system inherited from the NEP period, although these were modified during the first five-year plan. First, the institution of operational agencies to conduct foreign trade relations; secondly, the principle of product specialisation, with agencies handling either the import or export (or both) of specific products; thirdly, the operation of the agencies on the principle of *khozraschet* (requiring them to cover their costs from their revenues); and fourthly, the institution of a network of trade delegations in overseas capitals, in the form of either special trading companies or departments of diplomatic missions.

During NEP the trade delegations operating outside the USSR exercised a virtual monopoly over the conduct of trade negotiations with foreign suppliers and customers. Links between trade organisations and domestic producers were forged through the establishment of separate internal trading agencies (gostorgs) by the Commissariat of Foreign Trade. Gostorgs were responsible for domestic export procurement and import distribution operations. The gostorgs purchased products for export (principally grain and lumber) from domestic producers (including peasants and other private producers) and passed them on to trade delegations, which then sold the items in foreign markets. In some cases the gostorgs established their own factories to process agricultural raw materials prior to export. On the import side, state combines passed on requests for imports from their component enterprises to gostorgs, which in turn passed the request on to the appropriate trade delegation. There are some indications that foreign trade specialists have recently been examining the administration of foreign trade under NEP as a guide to streamlining current foreign trade operations (see the conclusion to this chapter).

A final feature of the foreign trade system under NEP was the operation of concessions by mixed companies involving state and foreign capital inside the USSR. The major purpose of the concessions was to attract foreign expertise for the implementation of raw materials (chiefly oil and timber) developments and major construction projects, including railways and power stations. Foreign investors were, however, deterred by the repudiation of tsarist debts, and in 1928 concessions accounted for less than 1 per cent of industrial output (Nove, 1969, p. 89).

Thus although the principles of the current system of trade management — including the state monopoly of foreign trade exercised by a central trade ministry or commissariat specialised on product lines — were established in 1918, they were modified by a series of *ad hoc* adjustments during NEP, including the weakening of the monopoly principle by the granting of trading rights to non-Commissariat organisations, both state-owned enterprises and foreign concessions. These modifications largely reflected the fact that private trade was still permissible, and that state enterprises were operating in a quasi-market environment and were empowered to choose suppliers for their inputs and markets for their products. Under such circumstances, the operations of the Foreign Trade Commissariat were not entirely dissimilar to those of a series of merchant import-export houses, with the principal difference that the profits resulting from foreign trade operations accrued to the state, not private or foreign traders, and that the structure of imports and exports was subject to a greater degree of central control.

Stalin implemented a far more effective version of the state monopoly during the first five-year plan and this was reflected in a far sharper separation of domestic and foreign trade operations. The latter was achieved by reinstituting two separate commissariats for foreign and domestic trade in November 1930 (they had been merged in 1926), and by the termination of foreign trade rights for all but the Commissariat of Foreign Trade (i.e. even state-owned enterprises were prevented from engaging directly in foreign trade). Finally in 1935 foreign trade operations were largely taken out of the hands of overseas trade delegations and transferred to Moscow. This considerably improved the Commissariat's powers of supervision and negotiation with Western manufacturers (Quigley, 1974, ch. 2).

Despite a number of organisational changes and *ad hoc* adjustments, the system remained unaltered in its basic essentials in the 50 years between the concentration of trade affairs in Moscow and the accession to power of Gorbachev. This reflects the final triumph of the teleological strategy pursued by Stalin over the genetic approach favoured by Bukharin. The system was explicitly designed to prevent pressures for market clearing from diverting resources from centrally determined priorities, and to facilitate the import of machinery and equipment and industrial raw materials required by the policy of rapid industrialisation — all this against the background of a Western recession which halved the price of Soviet staple exports of grain, crude oil and timber, and resulted in a severe deterioration in the Soviet Union's terms of trade.

The operation of the current system

The basic principle of the system of foreign trade inherited by Gorbachev is that the Ministry of Foreign Trade and the State Committee for Foreign Economic Relations (GKES) and their subsidiary foreign trade associations, specialised principally on product lines, are the only bodies empowered to conduct trade negotiations with foreign suppliers and customers. According to a recent Soviet publication, 90 per cent of foreign trade in 1985 was conducted by 50 foreign trade associations directly responsible to the Ministry of Foreign Trade, while a further 10 per cent of trade was conducted by nine foreign trade associations responsible to the GKES (Pozdnyakov and Sadikov, 1985, p. 23). The activities of the GKES have not been widely discussed in Soviet journals. Pozdnyakov and Sadikov (1985, p. 42) state that the GKES is almost exclusively concerned with export operations involving large-scale construction projects in socialist and developing countries. One of the largest foreign trade associations responsible to the GKES is Atomenergoexport, which is responsible for all activities related to the construction abroad of atomic power stations under technical co-operation agreements. The basic principle of the state monopoly of foreign trade as made effective by Stalin viz. that neither productive enterprises nor private individuals should be allowed to purchase imports directly from suppliers or sell exports to customers other than through the intermediary of the Ministry of Foreign Trade (or the GKES), remains in force.

The Ministry of Foreign Trade operates in close consultation with other central economic agencies including Gosplan, Gossnab, the Ministry of Finance, the State Bank, the Foreign Trade Bank and the State Committee for Science and Technology. As we saw, the major function of foreign trade, as perceived in Moscow, is to overcome bottlenecks in domestic production and ensure stability of supplies to the domestic economy, rather than to facilitate short-run economic optimisation. The essentially non-Keynesian nature of the Soviet economy is reflected in the fact that exports are largely viewed as a means to obtain necessary imports, rather than as a market for domestic producers and a means of ensuring full employment. Soviet trade patterns are derived from the system of planning by Material Balances, with its inherent limitations, and inevitably reflect the 'imports first' principle. Gosplan identifies critical imbalances between domestic supply and demand, and critical weaknesses of either a technical or economic nature in domestic supply patterns, through the process of constructing initial perspective, five-year and annual plans. Import plans are then drawn up to alleviate the most critical imbalances and perceived weaknesses of domestic production, while planners simultaneously look for products that are in excess supply relative to domestic demand — as a source of exports to pay for imports. As argued in Chapter 1, the preoccupation with domestic balance at the expense of economic optimisation was determined partly by the political and economic circumstances facing the Soviet Union at the time of the first five-year plan, partly by the overcentralisation of the planning system. But it has been facilitated by favourable endowment with natural resources relative to domestic demand, which has simplifed the problems of identifying imports and exports alike.

The Ministry of Foreign Trade exercises a critical role in both the formulation and implementation of foreign trade plans.

Bureaucratic inefficiencies in the operation of the Ministry provide a major explanation of inefficiencies in the trade process itself. The process of plan formulation is conducted by the central apparatus of the Ministry which is chiefly comprised of six main administrations specialised according to trading area (trade with the Americas, trade with the European socialist countries, etc.) and eight main administrations specialised according to commodity/industrial sector groupings for either exports or imports (e.g. raw materials exports, consumer goods imports, etc.). In the case of imports of machinery and equipment alone, separate trade administrations exist to deal with imports from capitalist countries and imports from socialist countries (Gruzinov, 1979, pp. 22–3). The main administrations are responsible for liaising with other central economic agencies. Foreign trade plans are implemented by all-union foreign trade associations (FTAs) subordinated to the chief administrations. These are chiefly specialised in the import and/or export of specific commodities or industrial items (e.g. Mashinoimport; Mashinoexport). The major function of the foreign trade associations is to purchase imports on foreign markets or export items to foreign markets according to the instructions of the appropriate main adminstration.

V.P. Gruzinov, the head of a research project undertaken in 1975 by the Ministry of Foreign Trade to examine its system of management, has provided a detailed (but officially sanctioned) account of the operation of the Ministry. He describes in some detail the cumbersome and bureaucratic procedures involved in Soviet import and export activities (Gruzinov, 1979, pp. 31–3). Gruzinov argues that a typical decision to import an item of machinery and equipment involves 40 different steps, which he narrows down to seven major stages. First, a decision to import a certain item is taken by the Council of Ministers of the USSR. Secondly, an import application is passed on to the appropriate FTA. These two stages require considerable consultation between the Ministry, the FTA and the receiving Soviet enterprise. When the preparatory work is completed, the FTA requests tenders from potential foreign exporters (stage three), receives the bids and passes these onto the Soviet customer (stage four). On obtaining a positive response from the Soviet customer (stage five), the FTA signs the contract with the foreign supplier (stage six). Stage seven covers the delivery and installation of the machinery in question under the supervision of the FTA, which has to ensure that the terms of the contract are fulfilled.

On the export side the process is reversed. The FTA seeks foreign customers for Soviet products, and makes an offer which includes such details as quality specifications, price and terms of payment, timing of deliveries, etc. If a provisional acceptance is received, further negotiations with the foreign customer concerning the above details will ensue before the drafting of a contract. The contract must then be approved by the functional departments of the FTA, and signed by the head management of the FTA before being sent to the overseas customer for signature. The FTA then assumes responsibility for delivering the goods specified in the contract, and makes the appropriate arrangements with the supplying Soviet enterprise.

By acting as an intermediary between domestic enterprises and foreign markets and suppliers, the Ministry of Foreign Trade preserves the principle of separation of domestic trade activities from foreign trade activities. As a corollary of this principle, the internal price system is divorced from both the absolute and relative levels of world market prices, and in theory can be protected from changes in world market prices. The divorce is implemented through the financial inconvertibility of the domestic ruble. The ruble is nominally convertible into gold at a rate of 0.987412 grams per ruble, but this convertibility remains entirely fictional. More critically, the domestic ruble is also inconvertible in the classic financial sense, in that holdings of domestic rubles cannot be converted on demand into other currencies. Similarily foreign currencies cannot be converted into domestic rubles, with the exception of small sums for personal use. It is therefore illegal to import or export Soviet currency, which is not traded on international currency markets and is not therefore subject to fluctuations in value resulting from Balance of Payments or speculative pressures.

As a result, the Ministry of Foreign Trade has to operate with two entirely separate systems of prices and accounts, one conducted in domestic rubles and domestic prices and a second conducted in external prices and external currencies. An external unit of account, the valuta or foreign trade ruble, is used to convert operations conducted in foreign currencies into a common denominator for purposes of accountancy and statistical recording. The valuta ruble is equated to a basket of Western currencies according to an official exchange rate which is adjusted by the State Bank on a fortnightly basis.

The Ministry of Foreign Trade conducts all its business in the domestic economy in domestic rubles, in principle buying exports from domestic enterprises at the prevailing domestic wholesale price, and selling imports to domestic enterprises at the industry wholesale price (including turnover tax where appropriate) for 'identical or comparable' products produced domestically (Treml and Kostinsky, 1982, p. 3).

In trade with the majority of market economies the Ministry of Foreign Trade operates in convertible currencies. The appropriate FTA purchases imports from foreign suppliers according to the conditions and prices prevailing in those markets, and pays for these in the appropriate hard currency. Similarly the Ministry of Foreign Trade sells exports to foreign customers according to the prevailing market conditions and receives payment in the appropriate currency. Exports and imports are then converted into valuta rubles at the relevant exchange rates for purposes of accounting and statistical recording. When trade is conducted in convertible currencies, import and export activities can be separated from one another, and FTAs can seek out the best prevailing market conditions for each category of exports and imports. In practice, it appears that FTAs are principally concerned to maintain expected revenue targets, and as a result tend to increase the volume of exports of a given item in response to short-term falls in market prices.

The process of trade with the majority of socialist countries and some market economies (of whom the most important are Finland and India) is somewhat more complicated, being conducted on the basis of bilateral balancing or clearing, where trade imbalances are normally not cleared by convertible currency payments. Officials from the Ministry of Foreign Trade negotiate trade flows with their opposite numbers, normally according to predetermined price rules, and try to secure balance in the value of exports and imports on an annual basis, or over a longer period. Under these circumstances, the import-purchasing capacity of a given volume of exports can be estimated directly.

Treml and Kostinsky (1982, pp. 19–24) argue that in practice domestic prices are more directly linked to world market prices, and in particular to changes in world market prices, than the model outlined above indicates. This argument appears to hold true for imports more than for exports. In most cases manufactured items produced for export differ substantially from similar items produced for the domestic market, and this factor is reflected in the price paid by the Ministry of Foreign Trade to the domestic enterprise to compensate the producing enterprise for the higher costs involved, and to provide an incentive to domestic enterprises to meet export orders. The most critical problems concern the higher quality specifications which are normally required to meet world standards. FTAs collect data concerning quality standards on Western markets, and these are used as guidelines for awarding the State Certificate of Quality to domestic products. In practice, however, many commodities awarded the State Certificate of Quality do not meet the demands of foreign markets, and items produced for the domestic market cannot be exported without substantial modifications (Gruzinov, 1979, p. 205). FTAs are forced to issue precise instructions to domestic producers from foreign buyers concerning product quality, and to supervise quality control throughout the production process. Gruzinov (p. 206) argues, however, that prices paid to domestic enterprises are settled at 'established domestic wholesale prices' with 'appropriate mark-ups' according to such criteria as intended destination, quality specifications, meeting delivery schedules, etc. Treml and Kostinsky (1982, p. 20) estimate that such export price supplements were between 30 and 40 per cent of the domestic wholesale price in the early 1980s. Following on the attempts of the July 1985 decree to improve export quality, exports which receive the State Certificate of Quality now receive a mark-up approaching 30 per cent of the wholesale price, and an additional 20 per cent mark-up on the domestic wholesale price has been awarded for certain manufactured goods which are exported for hard currency (Bash, Belous and Kretov, 1986, p. 5). Additional bonuses are paid to the workers of the enterprise for meeting export quality and delivery schedules, subject to the approval of the State Inspectorate for the Quality of Export Products (Gruzinov, 1979, p. 206).

It appears from the foregoing analysis that although the prices paid by the Foreign Ministry to enterprises are in practice substantially higher than domestic wholesale prices, the initial basis for price estimation remains the domestic wholesale price rather than the world market price. The adjustments made to domestic wholesale prices largely reflect the far higher enterprise costs involved in meeting the quality standards required in export markets, and prices are not determined by demand conditions on foreign markets. On this basis, therefore, it still appears valid to argue that enterprises are insulated from world market conditions, and in particular from changes in world market conditions affecting their products, and that the current system only attempts to compensate enterprises for the additional costs involved in export activities, rather than providing enterprises with an adequate incentive to produce for the export market. Treml and Kostinsky (1982, pp. 20–1) do, however, demonstrate that the price charged to domestic enterprises for imported commodities may bear only a tenuous relationship to the domestic wholesale price of analogous products or close substitutes. In the case of imported machinery, this frequently results from the fact that close substitutes for the item in question do not exist. Under these circumstances, the FTA can exercise a degree of market power in determining the price to be charged to the importing enterprise. Similarly the price of luxury imported consumer goods ranging from tropical foods to consumer durables may be substantially higher than that of 'comparable' domestic items, if such commodities can in fact be identified, and increases in world market prices tend to be passed on to consumers directly.

Foreign trade and economic reform

It was in the early 1960s that the initial slowdown in the industrial growth rate was recorded, following the exceedingly rapid rates of growth of industrial output recorded in the post-war 'catch up' period. Similar decelerations in growth of industrial output were experienced in Eastern Europe, being most severe in Czechoslovakia and the GDR where the labour force constraint was most serious. This gave rise to the reform debates centring on the need to move from extensive to intensive growth and to provide incentives for enterprises to innovate.

As we saw in Chapter 1, the Soviet economy is systemically biased against decentralised innovation (i.e. the development of new products or processes at enterprise level). Enterprises are principally rewarded in the form of money bonuses for fulfilling or overfulfilling centrally determined output targets. Innovation, in the sense of bringing new products or processes into series production, is likely to impose significant costs on enterprise managers and the workforce in terms of output bonuses foregone in the initial introductory stages of development.

Reformers with a market-oriented approach argue along Schumpeterian lines that the lure of extra profits is the prime motive for innovation, with the costs of innovation relating to the destruction of markets for existing producers who fail to innovate being externalised by the innovator. This results in generalised competitive pressure which forces existing producers to seek to improve their products and processes for fear of being innovated against.

Similarly, once a new product or process is successfully brought into commercial production, competitive pressures force existing producers to imitate the innovation. The result is a rapid diffusion of technology. Similarly market-oriented reformers have stressed the role played by international investment (particularly that undertaken by large multinational corporations capable of financing high levels of expenditure on R & D and who are seeking lower labour costs and additional markets) in the international transfer of technology.

These arguments stimulated proposals in Czechoslovakia and Hungary to abolish both the state monopoly of foreign trade and the isolation of the domestic price system from world market prices, and to open the economy to international competition (see Šik, 1971 and Abonyi, 1981). Šik proposed that enterprises should be brought into direct competition with overseas manufacturers, so as to encourage enterprises to respond quickly to changing world market conditions and require them to produce commodities meeting world market specifications as a basis for generating exports. Clearly this requires that enterprises should be deprived of the sellers' market in the domestic economy, which will accept low quality produce, and therefore discourages enterprises from making the changes necessary to compete on world markets. Šik took this proposition to its logical conclusion, arguing that the maintenance of genuine competitive pressures required the threat of bankruptcy for lagging enterprises, and the creation of frictional unemployment.

All this clearly tends to the conclusion that market-oriented reform of the domestic economy and the foreign trade system needed to be complementary if innovation and the absorption and diffusion of foreign technology were to be stimulated, and enterprises provided with the incentive to become competitive on Western markets. Similar arguments linking market-oriented domestic economic reform with exposure of the economy to international competitive pressures, as a way of stimulating domestic innovation and eliminating poor quality output, were put forward by the designers of the Hungarian New Economic Mechanism.

An alternative, less radical, school of thought favours the more centralised 'science to production cycle' approach to the problem of domestic innovation and the absorption and diffusion of international technology (see Shiryaev, 1983). The notion underlying this approach is that the basis for innovation should first be established by pure scientific research; the ideas coming out of that should then be developed in large-scale production organisations and put into series production, while specialised foreign trade organisations working within or in close relationship to production associations take responsibility for selling the resulting products in foreign markets, and for obtaining the required inputs. Supporters of this approach argue that innovation is not entirely spontaneous but involves high overhead costs in both pure research and development. They propose to reduce research costs through Comecon co-operation in research and development, including the establishment of international research organisations to pool costs, joint investment and specialisation in R & D. Specialisation and co-operation in production entails the establishment of joint production enterprises involving two or more Comecon countries, and ultimately developing direct links between Comecon enterprises. This would speed up production specialisation in the manufacture of components (see Nikonov and Stromov, 1986).

The science-to-production-cycle approach implies far less radical domestic economic reforms, and its general principles have, indeed, underlain the reform measures discussed in the USSR in the 1960s and the Andropov proposals currently being implemented in the USSR. Similar proposals were enacted in Bulgaria from 1965 to 1968, again based on the proposition that domestic economic reform and the attempt to attract foreign technology are interrelated. The Bulgarian reforms involved the creation of large-scale economic associations incorporating R & D organisations, a reduction in the number of compulsory centrally-determined indicators, a greater degree of domestic price flexibility, and the creation of specialised foreign trade enterprises which, it was hoped, would enter into direct contacts with foreign enterprises and stimulate export efficiency. These measures coincided with a doubling of Bulgarian imports of machinery and equipment from the OECD in 1966 (Smith, 1983). They were extended on the introduction of the Bulgarian New Economic Mechanism in the early 1980s.

It appears that Kosygin initially associated the acquisition of Western technology with a modified reform programme similar to that initiated in Bulgaria. As David Dyker points out in Chapter 1, however, events in Czechoslovakia resulted in a backtracking even on centralised economic reforms in the USSR and Eastern Europe in 1968 and 1969. Finally Brezhnev was persuaded by the experience of co-operation with Fiat in the construction of the Tolyatti car plant that co-operation with Western firms in large-scale 'turnkey' ventures could bring significant economic benefits without domestic political dangers. We saw earlier that the dramatic increase in oil prices in 1974 opened the way for a full-scale policy of import-led growth, based on the purchase of Western licences and machinery and equipment — but without permitting equity participation by Western firms in joint enterprises on Soviet territory.

Thinking in terms of the science-to-production-cycle suggests that once a new product or process has been researched and put into production, central instructions should ensure its rapid diffusion throughout the economy. A series of studies conducted at the University of Birmingham over a long period (Amann, Cooper and Davies, 1977; Amann and Cooper, 1982 and 1986) indicate that in practice the Soviet economy has been relatively slow to diffuse new technology throughout the economy, and that there has been no sign of a consistent closing of technical gaps between Soviet industry and advanced industrial economies in the West since the early 1960s.

Part of the explanation for this slowness in diffusing technology lies in the reluctance to retire old plants. As a result, older plants utilising outdated technologies can co-exist in the economy with plants using relatively modern technology. In the initial stages of extensive growth, when the economy is capital-scarce, this policy may be rational. It may, nevertheless, have adverse effects on the trade balance, to the extent that the older plant utilises imported materials and components (obsolescence may, indeed, be reflected in high input costs per unit of output) but is not capable of producing commodities of the quality standard required in international markets. In the longer term, as labour (and other inputs) grow relatively scarce, it becomes more important to retire obsolete equipment and provide all workers with modern equipment with low input costs. The replacement of obsolete equipment has, however, been delayed by the 'full employment constraint', involving an unwillingness to make workers redundant in the wake of changes in demand or working practices. The desire to avoid frictional unemployment has also forced planners to maintain a guaranteed domestic market for obsolescent products. Thus the innovation and diffusion of technology issues relate directly to the controversies surrounding the Shchekino system discussed in Chapter 3.

Enterprise managers in turn have little or no incentive to introduce even identified and known technologies. Piecemeal attempts at improving the operation of the existing system by introducing indicators and bonuses linked to the introduction of new commodities or the proportion of output falling into various quality categories (the highest of which is supposed to meet international quality standards) tends to result in a form of simulated innovation, or quality improvements in which old products are re-styled in order to qualify for bonuses without reference to end-users' needs. Although the planners may in principle want enterprises to display greater initiative, the system of bonuses still rewards obedience to central instructions.

Slowness in diffusing technology has contributed to a failure to expand exports in growing markets. This problem has been most acute in the East European countries, which are more dependent on exports of manufactures for hard currency earnings, and has resulted in severe Balance of Payments problems for those countries which placed greater reliance on the 'import-led' growth strategy. Their example provides a warning of the effect of systemic factors that could threaten Soviet attempts to expand the export of manufactured goods without reforms aimed at accelerating the diffusion of new technology and processes.

Poznanski (1986) demonstrates that East European exports of traditional items such as steel, ships and cars have lost their technological lead over competing exports form newly industrialising countries (particularly in South-east Asia), and that there is evidence that the NICs will soon overhaul East European technological levels in the more sophisticated new technologies (electronics, complex chemicals and aircraft) in which the East European countries have yet to make an impact on Western markets. As a result, the market share of the East European countries in OECD imports of chemicals and manufactured items (SITC categories 5–8) declined from the relatively low figure of 1.2 per cent in 1970 to 1.1 per cent in 1983, while that of the NICs grew from 2.8 per cent to 8.6 per cent over the same period. The declining share of the East European countries must be viewed in the light of a positive attempt during this period to boost the volume of East European exports to the OECD.

The USSR has been protected from the need to improve the quality of manufactured items for export to the West, and to respond quickly to changing world market conditions, by its mineral wealth. The two major increases in world oil prices in 1974 and 1979 enabled Soviet oil exports to OECD countries to grow from 647 million rubles ($780 mn) in 1972 to 13.4 billion rubles ($16.4 bn) in 1984. Over the same period natural gas exports to OECD countries rose from only 19 million rubles to 3.1 billion rubles ($3.8 bn). Energy exports in 1984 accounted for 80 per cent of Soviet exports to the industrialised West, while exports of diamonds and ferrous and non-ferrous metals accounted for a further 9 per cent of exports. In addition sales of non-monetary gold, which are not included in the trade statistics, accounted for approximately $2 billion of hard currency earnings in that year.

This has contributed to a situation in which the USSR has not needed to attach much importance to the export of manufactured and semifabricated goods to the West. These constituted just 10 per cent of exports in 1984, two-thirds of which was accounted for by chemicals and paper and wood products utilising relatively unsophisticated production techniques.

Moscow has been somewhat more successful in selling manufactured items in Third World countries. Total exports to developing countries were specified as 10.9 billion rubles in 1985, but only 5.3 billion rubles could be identified by country of destination. Of this amount, 2.2 billion rubles were accounted for by exports of machinery and equipment and 1.8 billion rubles comprised oil exports. Exports worth 0.7 billion rubles which could be identified by country of destination remained unidentified by sector. Exports of aircraft and shipping accounted for just under half of Soviet exports of machinery and equipment, while a further 13 per cent could not be identified by product. The unidentified commodity residuals in trade that is identified by country of destination correlate with exports of aircraft and shipping, and are concentrated on countries that are known to receive Soviet arms.

On the assumption that all the unidentified trade is in military equipment, and that exports of aircraft and shipping also have military uses or emanate from Soviet plants which serve military needs, approximately 70 per cent of Soviet exports to Third World countries in 1984 consisted of military items and civilian items which could be used militarily. It appears from data on changes in Soviet assets and liabilities with Western banks and Western attempts to estimate the Soviet Balance of Payments (Zoeter, 1982) that the USSR has received relatively little payment in hard currency for these items, and that a significant volume of armaments (similar to the volume of the trade that cannot be identified by country of destination) has been delivered on credit (see Smith, 1986).

This raises some critical questions. In the first place, it may be asked whether we are really dealing here with a form of back-door investment — does (or did) the USSR expect to be repaid for these deliveries in the future by deliveries of products (particularly energy and raw materials, but also labour-intensive products, foodstuffs and tropical goods) that could help to alleviate bottlenecks, and if so will the countries in question be able to meet their repayments?

More fundamentally important for the analysis of the prospects for economic reform, why was the USSR capable of selling these forms of manufactures in Third World countries, when it has remained singularly unsuccessful in selling other manufactures to non-socialist countries, developed and developing alike? Three possibilities may be suggested. First: political practice — the recipient countries could not obtain, or did not wish to obtain, weapons from capitalist sources for predominantly political reasons. Second: terms of delivery — was Soviet willingness to deliver arms on favourable credit terms a decisive factor in the importers' decision? Third: quality — are Soviet quality specifications in arms sales sufficiently good to enable them to become one of the world's major arms traders?

These three angles are clearly not mutually exclusive. But if the third has been a major factor, it indicates that Soviet domestic production of manufactured goods is indeed capable of meeting the quality standards demanded in world markets in sectors which receive high priority. Although it is impossible to give priority to all sectors of the economy, this suggests that attempts to give greater priority to enterprises producing for export could have a significant impact on the volume of exports of manufactured items, even outside the context of a wholesale reform of the economic system. One possibility is the creation of specialised enterprises producing predominantly for export markets which receive priority for inputs from the rest of the economy, combined with incentives to attract the best personnel. Such enterprises could also be granted the right to retain a proportion of hard-currency earnings to finance imports of machinery and equipment and even for the payment of bonuses. As noted in Chapter 3, intimations of this approach are present in the July 1985 decree. There is obviously a hint here that some reduction in the demand for access to priority inputs placed on the economy by the military sector could in the long run result in an increase in the capacity to generate exports of manufactures.

Soviet economic strategy and the role of foreign trade

We saw in Chapters 3 and 4 that the new leadership has shown a far greater willingness at least to discuss the problems besetting the economy. The discussions have clear implications for both the structure of foreign trade and the nature of the foreign trade system. Mr Ryzhkov's speeches to the XXVII Party Congress and the June 1986 meeting of the Supreme Soviet indicated a clear strategy of economic development for the next 15 years involving the introduction of new technology to increase labour productivity and reduce energy and raw material consumption per unit of output. Investment will be concentrated on the modernisation and re-equipping of existing plants at the expense of the grandiose, large-scale 'turnkey' projects favoured in the Brezhnev era.

Ryzhkov also argued that the process of modernisation could be achieved without recourse to additional imports from the West. He was particularly scathing in his speech to the XXVII Party Congress about the tendency on the part of industrial managers to import machinery and equipment that could be produced domestically. Gorbachev and Ryzhkov both indicated that improved economic co-operation with socialist countries would play a major role in the expansion of foreign economic relations.

In fact, the Soviet leadership has since the late 1970s placed greater emphasis, in its attempts to overcome domestic bottlenecks, on improving economic integration within Comecon (along predominantly non-market lines) than on increased trade with capitalist nations. These initiatives have been directed at stimulating or maintaining bloc self-sufficiency in three principal sectors — energy and raw materials, the production of foodstuffs, and science and technology. Soviet policy has involved attempts to improve plan co-ordination and joint planning activity leading to joint Comecon investments, particularly in the energy sector, and to develop an agreed investment strategy and pattern of specialisation in production. Measures are implemented in an analogous fashion to national plan formulation, incorporating initial multilateral framework agreements reached by national Party and government leaderships. These are then given more concrete form by agreements between senior representatives of the national planning agencies, which form the basis of special sections in member countries' national plans. The resulting trade flows are then incorporated into bilateral trade agreements between the participating Comecon countries.

Meanwhile the Soviet Union's terms of trade with Eastern Europe have improved considerably, as the effects of the two world oil price increases have fed into the intra-Comecon price formula (which is based on a sliding average of the preceding five years' world market prices). Although the USSR has provided oil to Eastern Europe on terms far less favourable to itself than it could have obtained from exporting oil to the West, the formula has still represented a substantial economic gain to the USSR. Estimates based on Soviet data indicate that the real volume of Soviet imports from Eastern Europe doubled between 1974 and 1984, while the real volume of Soviet exports to Eastern Europe only increased by 35 per cent over the same period. Furthermore the real volume of Soviet exports to Eastern Europe declined in 1982, when the USSR cut oil supplies, and was still below the 1980 level in 1984, while the real volume of Soviet imports increased by 27 per cent between 1980 and 1984. An approximate estimate of the commodity composition of this trade indicates that the real volume of Soviet imports of machinery and equipment from Eastern Europe increased by 130 per cent between 1974 and 1984, while imports of industrial consumer goods increased by 75 per cent in real terms over the same period. The quality of these imports has, however, been attacked by Soviet politicians.

The agreements reached at the summit meeting of Party leaders convened in Moscow in June 1984 reflected a continuation of this policy. The summit communiqué indicated that the leaders of the East European countries had agreed to restructure their economies and exports, in order to supply the Soviet Union with foodstuffs, industrial consumer goods, construction materials and machinery and equipment meeting world technical standards. More significantly, from the viewpoint of economic reform, the summit communiqué also emphasised that improved plan co-ordination and joint planning activity rather than market measures was to be the main vehicle of economic co-operation in Comecon, although the policy appears to have been slightly modified to meet certain East European objections. The precise wording was that plan co-ordination should be the principal instrument of integration and policy co-ordination. This would serve as the basis for drafting members' national plans but would be limited to areas of prime importance for economic co-operation.

The new leadership appears to have made improvements in bloc scientific collaboration its top priority. The first success in this sector was the Comecon agreement, announced at the June 1984 summit and concluded in December 1985, entitled the 'Comprehensive Programme for Scientific and Technical Progress'. The Programme is designed to facilitate a doubling of bloc labour productivity by the end of the century, and a marked reduction in energy consumption per unit of output. These goals are to be pursued through bloc technological co-operation in five priority sectors: electronics, including telecommunications, fibre optics and computers; the automation and robotisation of production; atomic energy; biotechnology for the foodstuffs sector, and the use of new industrial raw materials.

The methods by which agreements like this will be implemented appear to reflect the continued primacy of the joint planning approach, incorporating the science-to-production-cycle paradigm. Both Gorbachev and Ryzhkov were critical at the XXVII Congress of the current state of organisation and administration in Comecon. Ryzhkov provided a more detailed critique, arguing:

> The centre of the integration process is moving towards the joint assimilation of the latest achievements of science and technology, and the development of large scale co-operation . . . primarily in the production of modern types of machinery and equipment. Central planning organs and other economic agencies must organise their foreign economic activities from this standpoint. Much will depend on improving the work of the CMEA . . . the old forms which developed during the period of extensive growth can no longer guarantee dynamic growth of co-operation. It is necessary to seek new ways of introducing spontaneous interaction between enterprises and branches, developing direct economic links and establishing joint associations, construction bureaus and laboratories. (Ryzhkov, 1986)

Ryzhkov did not indicate how direct links between enterprises would actually operate. A recent article by Nikonov and Stromov (Nikonov and Stromov, 1986) has provided considerable detail on the operational content of direct links which gives an indication of possible lines of reform in the foreign trade system. (These will be developed in the next section.) The process is officially known as 'international intra-branch co-operation in production', and is designed to create a framework for enterprises in the same industrial branches in different Comecon countries to enter into long-term agreements on component specialisation and production co-operation. The underlying concept is the extension of production associations across Comecon boundaries. Central agencies of the collaborating countries have to approve framework agreements, and central planners control the relations of the enterprise with the domestic economy. But managers of joint enterprises have greater powers to direct the flows of inputs between collaborating enterprises without needing detailed central approval. The system began operation on a small scale in the early 1980s, but will be considerably expanded in the 1986–90 plan as part of the Comprehensive Programme for Scientific and Technical Progress. Existing agreements operate on a bilateral basis only, and are covered by national trade agreements signed by the respective Ministries of Foreign Trade. Industrial ministries are thereby empowered to conclude intra-branch trade agreements with their opposite numbers enumerating nomenclature of products, technical and economic specifications, etc. Production associations and enterprises can then enter direct negotiations with their opposite numbers and discuss economic and technical details. Final delivery arrangements are again written into foreign trade contracts signed by the appropriate foreign trade association, which determines the commercial conditions of operation, including questions of price settlements.

These developments indicate that the USSR is not contemplating the introduction of active monetary relations between Soviet enterprises and enterprises in other Comecon countries, but is more concerned to decentralise the detail of intra-Comecon co-operation to industrial ministries and enterprises while retaining central control over financial operations. This limited decentralisation of trade relations with Comecon partners will, however, require a greater harmonisation and rationalisation of the price systems in the member countries, if industrial ministries are to evaluate the prospects of international co-operation and central agencies to be barred from intervening in the details of settlements.

Soviet trade strategy has been complicated by the fall in Soviet oil output reported in the first half of 1985 and the fall in world oil prices in the winter of 1985–6, which will affect both Soviet hard-currency earnings and terms of trade with Eastern Europe as the price changes are fed into the intra-Comecon price formula. Oil production fell from a peak of 617 million tons in 1983 to 595 million tons in 1985. This forced the USSR to cut exports by approximately 25 million tons in 1985, and resulted in a trade deficit of 2.4 billion rubles ($3.0 bn) in trade with the industrialised Western countries in the first six months of the year. This deficit was financed in the short term by running down assets with Western banks (by $1.8 bn in the first six months of 1986) and increased borrowing (by $2.2 bn). In the second half of 1985, following Mr Gorbachev's accession to power, a new pattern emerged, and Soviet imports from the industrial West were cut by 13 per cent. Western businesses exporting to the USSR reported a cutback in Soviet orders for Western machinery and equipment, which was sustained through the first three quarters of 1986.

Although Soviet oil production improved in 1986, and daily output in the summer of 1986 was consistent with an annual output level of 610–15 million tons, the fall in world market prices will prove more difficult to neutralise. At 1984 export levels each $1 fall in the price of a barrel of oil costs the USSR approximately $0.5 billion per annum of hard-currency earnings. On this basis a long-term price for Soviet crude oil of $15 per barrel would cost the USSR approximately $6.5 billion annually in terms of 1984 hard-currency earnings (these estimates exclude the effect of bilateral trade with Finland, and assume an equivalent fall in the price of refined oil products).

There is no reason to suppose that it would be especially difficult for the Soviet Union to adjust to a long-run downward trend in oil production. Soviet and East European oil consumption accounts for approximately 86 per cent of Soviet output, and only a relatively small cut in Comecon consumption would be required to maintain the volume of exports to the West. The USSR has not yet come up against an energy bottleneck in total, but has tended to run into constraints relating to specific fuels. The Soviet energy strategy outlined at the XXVII Party Congress indicates a continuation of the policy of substituting natural gas and nuclear power for oil in the Comecon energy balance, in order to maintain oil for export for hard currency. Comecon co-operation in the energy sector is chiefly directed towards this end, involving further joint investments in developing Soviet natural gas deposits in the Yamburg peninsula for bloc consumption. The Soviet authorities do not currently appear to consider that the economics of these policies will be radically affected by a sustained fall in oil prices, but there are some indications of a rethink of nuclear policy following the Chernobyl' accident.

The scenario of a crude oil price stabilising at around $15 is a much more awkward one for the USSR to respond to. It would be unable to compensate for such a substantial fall in oil prices by a proportionate increase in exports, which would in any case tend to encounter output constraints. In addition, it would force the price down further and could invite a price response from competitors with lower production costs than the USSR. Market satiation may also act as a barrier to increased Soviet deliveries of the other items which make up Soviet exports to the West. The European natural gas market is oversupplied and long-term contracts for natural gas are likely to be affected by the oil price. Sales of gold, diamonds and other precious metals could be increased, but the price of these items will ultimately be sensitive to the volume of Soviet supplies. Finally, a sustained fall in oil prices would have adverse effects on Soviet hard-currency earnings from the sale of armaments to oil-exporting countries.

Lower oil prices would also have an adverse effect on the Soviet Union's terms of trade with Eastern Europe, and make it far more difficult for the USSR to increase the volume of imports of machinery and equipment, foodstuffs and industrial consumer goods from Eastern Europe in the long term. Furthermore the economic benefits of co-operative projects to develop Soviet oil and gas would be substantially reduced to East European participants if the cost of alternative sources of supply were reduced. This could also reduce Soviet power to implement joint planning policies and result in greater pressure for more market-oriented reforms in Comecon.

Assuming that the world market price for crude oil averages $15 a barrel until 1989, the application of the sliding world market price system would result in an annual fall in the Comecon oil price of 10 per cent per annum, equivalent to a deterioration in the Soviet Union's terms of trade with Eastern Europe of 4 per cent per annum. This need not result in an immediate cut in Soviet imports from Eastern Europe, as the USSR has been running substantial surpluses in its trade with Eastern Europe since 1975. On the assumption that the real volume of Soviet exports to and imports from Eastern Europe are maintained at their 1985 levels throughout the 1986–90 plan period, Soviet trade surpluses with Eastern Europe (excluding Poland) would be turned into deficits by 1988, and Soviet accumulated surpluses in trade with Eastern Europe (excluding Poland) effectively eliminated by 1990. There is therefore little prospect of much significant improvement in the Soviet Union's real terms of trade with Eastern Europe over the current five-year-plan period. Any increase in the volume of Soviet imports from Eastern Europe will require an increase in the volume of Soviet exports or measures that could prove unpopular in Eastern Europe.

These arguments suggest that the USSR may experience considerable difficulties in increasing the volume of imports of machinery and equipment from Eastern Europe, and in securing long-term economic co-operation from some East European countries (notably Hungary and Romania, which do not have outstanding deficits in their trade with the USSR). There are also substantial doubts about the capacity of the science-to-production-cycle approach to generate new innovations, and in particular to stimulate the diffusion of new processes. Eastern Europe's chances of acting as a 'bridge' for the transfer of Western technology into Comecon joint ventures will also be constrained by East European inability to market manufactured commodities in the West. Thus the need for both the USSR and Eastern Europe to increase the volume of exports of manufactures to the West, if the bloc is not to lapse into a form of Comecon autarky, should act as a stimulus to economic reform.

Pressures to reform the state monopoly of foreign trade

Gruzinov's account indicates that the process of placing orders for imports and securing export markets is highly cumbersome and slow working, and imposes substantial overhead costs on both Soviet and foreign partners. He also indicates that middle-tier officials in the main administrations are risk-averse, reluctant to innovate and unwilling to delegate tasks to subordinates who have closer links with Soviet and foreign producers; this results in further delays and missed opportunities for trade. Gruzinov attributes this largely to the principle of *edinonachalie*, whereby managers are held responsible for all decisions taken below them and are consequently reluctant to delegate real authority. In a framework in which all the steps to be taken in the planning process are clearly defined, individual managers have no incentive to accelerate the process, or to risk official sanctions by omitting unnecessary paper work in order to secure an economic or competitive advantage from which they gain no reward. As a result, Gruzinov argues, (1979, p. 63) 'An enterprising worker who has done a lot may be criticised more often than a person who has done a little and hence made fewer mistakes.'

Gruzinov's complaints about the inherent conservatism of middle-tier management, who have been promoted as a result of their ability to carry out centralised instructions faithfully, are echoed in Zaslavskaya's critique of the domestic planning system contained in the Novosibirsk Report. They raise the same question as that put by Zaslavskaya — is it sufficient to tinker with the existing system, or does the current level of sophistication of the economy require a more radical decentralisation?

The more immediate pressure for foreign trade planning

reform more radical, perhaps, than hitherto envisaged, comes from the foreign trade developments discussed in the last section. First, there is a need to boost the volume of exports of manufactured goods to compensate for the fall in hard-currency revenues brought about by falling oil prices; secondly, changes in the structure of demand for imported machinery and equipment away from turnkey projects towards the re-equipping of existing enterprises will require closer links between the enterprises themselves and overseas suppliers.

Mr Ryzhkov argued at the XXVII Party Congress that 'changing the raw material bias of exports' and improving the export competitiveness of manufactured goods would be a major priority for foreign trade organisations, but admitted that this process would take longer than a single five-year-plan period. The Soviet authorities appear to have become increasingly aware of the problems of exporting manufactured items to capitalist nations in the first 18 months since Mr Gorbachev came to power, and have organised a number of high-level conferences and seminars devoted to the problem. The principal focus of these discussions has been to improve the operational activities of the Foreign Trade Ministry and foreign trade organisations, and to bring them into closer contact with domestic enterprises.

It has now been generally recognised that the current system of foreign trade administration works too slowly to enable or to encourage enterprises to respond to changing world market conditions. Proposals implemented in 1986 were largely directed towards streamlining the operation of foreign trade organisations, sharpening up the assessment of the potential of foreign markets and improving the quality of domestic production, by providing better information to enterprises concerning quality specifications required on product markets and imposing stricter quality control (Pitrovanov, 1986, pp. 2–3; Stefanovskii, 1986, p. 47).

There have been reports that the USSR is preparing a major change in legislation covering foreign trade activities, and that this will involve a weakening of the monopoly powers of the Ministry of Foreign Trade and the transfer of some of its import and export activities to the industrial ministries themselves, and to some large enterprises and industrial associations (Cockburn, 1986). It appears likely that foreign trade associations will be transferred from the jurisdiction of the Ministry of Foreign Trade to that of the appropriate industrial ministry, and will be expected to maintain closer links with industrial enterprises. This should help facilitate the implementation of international intra-branch co-operation within Comecon. The Ministry of Foreign Trade would retain its monopoly position over the export of energy and raw materials and the import of complete plants and installations. These proposals, which are designed to bring end-users of machinery and equipment into closer contact with suppliers in order to facilitate the modernisation of existing plants and bring manufacturers closer to markets, follow logically from the analysis contained in this chapter.

The principle of centralisation does, of course, have clear benefits in the case of imports of complete installations (turnkey projects) which have considerable external effects on the economy requiring central appraisal. Furthermore the negotiating costs of individual transactions are not related proportionately to the size of the project, and there may be substantial economies of scale to be enjoyed from the central negotiation of large-scale projects. In addition, the importance of large-scale projects to the potential supplier may be so great that the USSR is capable of exercising monopsonistic pressures through retention of the central monopoly. These benefits are substantially reduced in the case of smaller purchases of machinery and equipment for the modernisation of plant, and may be offset by the greater need for the end-user to negotiate technical specifications and discuss potential modifications to the imported equipment directly with the supplier.

Although the proposed measures would involve the most radical reorganisation of the system of management and administration of foreign trade for over 50 years, they do not necessarily imply a radical reform in the economic sense. As noted above, Soviet proposals for Comecon intra-branch industrial co-operation do not imply a marketisation of the economy, or the introduction of active monetary measures. Even after allowing for the fall in world oil prices, the categories of exports that remain centralised — energy, raw materials and armaments — should still make up 66–80 per cent of Soviet hard-currency earnings. Control over hard-currency earnings will therefore remain highly centralised, and the Foreign Trade Bank or the Ministry of Finance will be able to exercise a critical role in the determination of import patterns through the procedures it uses to allocate hard currency to industrial ministries and enterprises. This could even in practice mean more rather than less effective centralisation in investment planning.

Will this limited decentralisation prove sufficient to solve the problems facing the trade sector of the economy, or will further measures prove necessary at a later date? What are the implications for reform of the economy as a whole?

In practice the amount of decision-making that can be decentralised to enterprises depends on the creation of criteria by which decentralised agencies can evaluate import and export decisions. In a supply-constrained economy the marginal value of an export is determined by the value of the import which it facilitates. In theory, a market economy can decentralise this information through price and exchange rate signals. Under the existing Soviet system of inflexible prices and exchange rates, the centre alone possesses sufficient information for the economic evaluation of trade decisions. However the organisational detail involved and the problems of information overload at the centre tend to restrict evaluation of imports and exports to a relatively small number of large-scale projects. Foreign trade planners simply cannot attempt to pursue trade flows to the point where the marginal value to the economy of an additional import is exactly balanced by the marginal cost of the export that finances it. The proposed changes may therefore be described as an adminstrative rationalisation which frees the centre from informational overload, and permits industrial ministries and enterprises to have a greater influence over the detailed implementation of centrally determined decisions. It is unlikely to have a serious effect on trade volumes.

Soviet experience, particularly over the last 20 years, indicates that the use of enterprise incentive schemes linked to this form of limited decentralisation has a tendency to throw up unforeseen practices that are perfectly rational from the enterprise viewpoint, but are the opposite of those intended by the planners. This results once again in a further pressure for recentralisation. David Dyker has shown in Chapter 3 that the current round of reform experiments, which give enterprises greater freedom to choose their output mix and link bonuses to sales and deliveries, are no exception. Some Soviet economists argue that these measures, combined with the more stringent quality demands imposed on enterprises by foreign trade associations, have the counterproductive effect of reducing the incentive for enterprises to produce for export markets. Bash, Belous and Kretov (1986) argue that the detailed specifications required to meet export targets frequently mean that export orders cannot be fulfilled from series production, so that enterprises producing for export frequently fail to meet sales targets in the specified plan period. Additional obstacles to the fulfilment of sales targets arise from the longer time period required for a commodity to be accepted as saleable by foreign trade associations. Enterprises, therefore, prefer to produce for the softer domestic market, a problem initially identified by the Czechoslovak reformers. Anxieties about meeting sales targets could act as a major deterrent to increasing the volume of exports of manufactured goods to compensate for declining oil revenues.

Bash, Belous and Kretov also argue that the current system of paying enterprises a mark-up on domestic wholesale prices for commodities delivered for export is too complicated in practice to provide enterprises with a sufficient incentive to produce for the foreign market. They propose a substantial modification of the separation of the domestic price system from world market prices, arguing that enterprise earnings from exports should be directly linked to actual prices obtained for exported commodities.

They also propose that enterprises should be empowered to retain a larger proportion of foreign currency earnings, not just for modernisation of plant and equipment via the production development fund, but also to provide improved amenities for workers, including holidays, through the socio-cultural and housing fund. The argument is chiefly applied to export earnings arising from trade with other Comecon members. To be successful, it would require that money play a more active role in intra-Comecon trade. It is possible that the reference has simply been included to make the proposal politically acceptable.

The critical problem remains, however, that the principal operating features of the system of foreign trade are directly derived from the operating features of the domestic planning system. Although (as NEP experience indicates) it may be possible in an economy as large as that of the USSR to decentralise domestic planning decisions while keeping the state monopoly of foreign trade intact, it is not possible to decentralise foreign trade decisions without a radical reform of the domestic planning system and the price system in particular.

Conclusion

The pattern of extensive growth was initially based on technical modernisation, on the construction of an industrial base incorporating existing world technology according to centralised instructions. The process was effectively repeated in the immediate post-war period, following the destruction of much of the industrial base built up in the 1930s. The state monopoly of foreign trade was an integral part of this process, permitting scarce hard-currency resources to be concentrated on the acquisition of technology, protecting developing industry and allowing planners to maintain a high level of domestic demand without incurring Balance of Payments bottlenecks.

In the longer term economic growth decelerates and greater reliance must be placed on domestic innovation. Schumpeterian analyses suggest that the centrally planned economy is systematically biased against innovation. This argument is denied by Soviet economists who stress the science-to-production-cycle argument. The Birmingham studies suggest, however, that the critical weakness of the Soviet economy does not lie so much in the quality of scientific research as in the rate of diffusion of new technology. East European experience in exporting argues that slowness to develop new technology and the failure to diffuse technology rapidly through the economy results in an inability to compete in capitalist markets which acts as a further constraint on the capacity to import. The USSR has been largely shielded from the trade aspects of these problems by the sheer size of the country, which reduces its dependence on imports, and by its mineral wealth and from 1974 to 1985 by the operation of the OPEC cartel which has enabled it to maintain a level of export earnings sufficient to meet import needs.

The international situation facing Gorbachev when he came to power has tended to make him distrustful of the benefits of trade with capitalist nations, and his policies have emphasised, if not Soviet autarky, then certainly a greater degree of bloc self-sufficiency, involving heavier emphasis on domestic and Comecon science and technology. But can such a policy be successful without a domestic reform that breaks down the barriers to rapid diffusion of technology which have become the major constraint to growth?

This raises an additional question which finds strong echoes in pre-Soviet Russian history. Is it possible at generational intervals to replicate the process of extensive growth — involving centrally imposed technical modernisation incorporating foreign tech-nology — to eliminate recurrent technical gaps? Taken to its logical conclusion, in pure historical terms, this implies that Gorbachev would have to succeed where Khrushchev before him failed (and Brezhnev never attempted), to be the benign inheritor of a Russian tradition which includes Ivan the Terrible, Peter the Great and Stalin.

There are a number of reasons, partly political and partly economic, for thinking that a policy of 'one-off' modernisation may prove unattractive to the new Soviet leadership.

(i) A deliberate strategy which involves the continuous presence of technical gaps between the USSR and advanced capitalist nations is unlikely to prove politically appealing, and would further diminish the attraction of the Soviet planning model to developing countries.
(ii) It can be argued that the pace of international technological change is now so rapid that the process of modernisation must be permanent.
(iii) As Zaslavskaya argues, the process of technical modernisation in the 1930s relied heavily on the use of terror to force an unwilling agricultural labour force into heavy industry. The policy could be partly justified on Marxist grounds, viz. that the peasantry were not the heirs to a revolution fought to establish the dictatorship of the protelariat. The new leadership is therefore faced with the problem of how to introduce positive incentives (or sanctions) to generate the required degree of inter-industry mobility, and whether such an objective can be achieved without a radical change in the planning system. Thus the issues aired in Chapter 3 impinge directly on the issue of long-term modernisation strategy.

The implications are that a policy of trying to eliminate existing technology gaps through imports, not backed up by sustained improvements in the standard of domestic R & D, will prove insufficient to meet other policy objectives. The critical question for the Soviet leadership is whether improved scientific and technical co-operation within Comecon can help to overcome the problems of technical modernisation without radical system reform. If the answer to that question is no, then the next stage in the argument is obvious.

References

Abonyi, A. (1981) 'Imported technology, Hungarian industrial development and factors impeding the emergence of innovative capacity' in Hare, P.G., Radice, H.K. and Swain, N. (eds) *Hungary: A decade of economic reform,* George Allen and Unwin, London

Amann, R. and Cooper, J.M. (eds) (1982) *Industrial Innovation in the Soviet Union,* Yale University Press, London and New Haven

Amann, R., Cooper, J.M. (eds) (1986) *Technical progress and Soviet economic development,* Basil Blackwell, Oxford

Amann, R., Cooper, J.M. and Davies, R.W. (eds) (1977) *The technological level of Soviet industry,* Yale University Press, New Haven

Bash, Yu, Belous, N. and Kretov, I. (1986) 'Ekonomicheskii eksperiment v promyshlennosti i razvitie eksporta', *Vneshnyaya Torgovlya* (7)

Bukharin, N. and Preobrazhensky, E. (1970) *The ABC of communism,* Penguin, Harmondsworth

Cockburn, P. (1986) 'Moscow carries out foreign trade shake-up', *Financial Times,* 4 September 1986

Gomulka, S. (1971) *Inventive activity, diffusion and the stages of economic growth,* Institute of Economics, Aarhus

Gomulka, S. (1986) *Growth, innovation and reform in Eastern Europe,* Harvester Press, Brighton

Gruzinov, V.P. (1979) *The USSR's management of foreign trade,* Macmillan, London and Basingstoke

Kaplan, N.M. and Moorsteen, R. (1960) 'An index of Soviet industrial output', *American Economic Review 50* (3)

Nikonov, A. and Stromov, A. (1986) 'Pryamie svyazi', *Vneshnyaya Torgovlya* (6)

Nove, A. (1969) *An economic history of the USSR,* Penguin, Harmondsworth

Pitrovanov, Ye. (1986) 'Sodeistvie TPP SSSR', *Vneshnyaya Torgovlya* (6)

Pozdnyakov, V.S. and Sadikov, O.N. (1985) *Pravovoe regulirovanie otnoshenii po vneshnei torgovle SSSR,* Mezhdunarodnye Otnosheniya, Moscow

Poznanski, K. (1986) 'Competition between Eastern Europe and developing countries in the Western market for manufactured goods', in *East European economies: slow growth in the 1980s,* vol. 2, Joint Economic Committee, US Congress, US GPO, Washington DC

Quigley, J. (1974) *The Soviet foreign trade monopoly,* Ohio State University Press, Ohio

Ryzhkov, N.I. (1986) 'Ob Osnovnykh napravleniyakh ekonomicheskogo i sotsial'nogo razvitiya SSSR na 1986–90', *Pravda,* 4 March

Shiryaev, Yu (1983) 'Perfection of CMEA countries' economic cooperation', *World Marxist Review* (4)

Šik, O. (1971) *Czechoslovakia: the bureaucratic economy,* IASP, White Plains, New York

Smith, A.H. (1983) *The planned economies of Eastern Europe,* Croom Helm, London

Smith, A.H. (1986) 'Soviet trade relations with the Third World', in R. Cassen (ed.) *Soviet interests in the Third World,* Sage, London

Stefanovskii, D. (1986) 'Sozdanie sektsii po voprosam kachestva eksportnoi produktsii TPP SSSR', *Vneshnyaya Torgovlya* (7)

Sutton, A.C. (1968) *Western technology and Soviet economic development,* vol. 1, Stanford University Press, Stanford

Treml, V. and Kostinsky, B. (1982) *Domestic value of Soviet foreign trade:*

exports and imports in the 1972 input-output table, US Department of Commerce, Washington DC

Zoeter, J.P. (1982) 'USSR: hard currency trade and payments' in *The Soviet economy in the 1980s,* Joint Economic Committee, US Congress, US GPO, Washington DC

6

Gorbachev and the World — the Political Side

Zdeněk Kavan

In her pessimistic assessment of the prospects of reform in the USSR which we quoted in Chapter 1, Agnes Heller goes on to argue that 'nuclear arms reductions, beneficial as they are internationally, have absolutely no impact on the oppressive nature of the internal Soviet system' (Heller, 1985, p. 26). In contrast, Archie Brown is optimistic about the prospects for domestic reform, but suggests that 'an increase in international tension and an accelerated rate of military expenditure would exacerbate the difficulties of economic reform and diminish the prospects for significantly enhancing Soviet economic performance'. He goes on to conclude that 'it therefore makes sense for Gorbachev to reassess Soviet foreign policy to see what innovation might be required in this area, too, to complement his ambitious domestic programs' (Brown, 1986, p. 1060). It is clear that behind these differing conclusions lie not just differing sets of predispositions and sets of empirical evidence, but also, and crucially, differing conceptions of reform and change, and differing understandings of the relationship between domestic and foreign policies. Before proceeding to the analysis of Soviet foreign policy developments and the assessement of the prospects for evolution in this area, therefore, we must review our central concepts.

Reform and change

As we argued in Chapter 1, reform is a particular type of change, to be distinguished from revolutionary change on the one hand, and ubiquitous change on the other. S.F. Cohen remarks that the meaning of reform(ism) is 'always historical, changing from one period to another'. Most writers on Soviet and East European societies use the term reform, however, to indicate changes of policies and institutions designed to 'improve the existing social order within the broad parameters of the existing social, economic and political foundations', (Cohen, 1984, p. 87). These foundations can be understood to mean relations of production, relations between classes and major social groupings, and basic forms of governance of society. That already throws some light on why 'reform' and 'reformism' have been used to describe changes in domestic policies and institutions, rather than foreign policy changes. The social order that reform is applied to is that of the nation state, not the international order. Such reform may have an international dimension, viz. for the sake of a successful domestic reform certain changes in foreign policy may be needed. But the focus is on the domestic side, the aim is to improve the domestic order, and the changes in international relations to be brought about by new foreign policies are derived from the required domestic reforms. In keeping with this interpretation, it might be better to use the more general concept of 'change' when dealing with foreign policy.

Foreign policy and change

Foreign policy is a purposeful activity undertaken by the designated organs of the state to deal with the state's external environment, and with that environment's most important actors — other states and international organisations. There is a close linkage between domestic and foreign policies, and there are a number of reasons for this. No state, however powerful, can isolate its domestic environment from the international one. This is not just because states are affected by the policies of other states, and because the need to be ready to deal with other states' policies imposes certain priorities in the choice of domestic policies — armaments expenditure, for example. For the international system is not reducible to simple aggregations of the interactions between states and their respective foreign policies. We saw in the last chapter that a relatively integrated international economy now exists, which means that developments in given parts of this global economy have effects on the rest, and that these in turn have important political consequences. The international system, comprising both the international economy and the policies of states and other actors, is thus a crucial foreign policy determinant. Major causes of change as well as obstacles to change in national societies are to be found there.

The other determinants of foreign policy are domestic. The main purpose of foreign policy is to preserve and/or develop the state's internal social, political and economic order. The state is not, however, monolithic. It is based on a particular social structure in which different groups derive different benefits from the existing order. Both domestic and foreign policies are thus affected by the relationship between the most significant groups in this structure. Changes in the relationships, social and political, between societal groups may have significant effects on foreign policy.

After these preliminary remarks, we can now proceed to the analysis of Gorbachev's foreign policies. The main contention of this chapter is that though some changes have taken place, and some others will no doubt follow, there are as yet no signs that a radical reorientation of Soviet foreign policy is likely. This is partly because there has still been no radical economic or political change within the Soviet Union itself, partly because the current international environment in any case places severe constraints on the Soviet Union's freedom significantly to alter its foreign relations.

The Brezhnev legacy

Brezhnev left to his successors a Soviet Union suffering from a host of domestic and foreign problems. The crucial one is the weakness of the economy, particularly its relative technological backwardness. Alan Smith has shown in Chapter 5 how this technological backwardness has impinged on general trading patterns. We can now extend the analysis to follow the consequences of economic weakness for Soviet foreign policy. The inability of the Soviet economy to export capital or technology has limited its capacity to project power, and influence developments, in many Third World areas. It has made the Soviet goverment more reluctant to bale out the East European economies (e.g. Poland) more severely affected by the consequences of the international energy crisis. The enormous military expenditure through which the Soviet Union achieved real parity of military power with the United States for the first time in the 1970s bore less fruit than had been anticipated. Paradoxically, 'while Soviet military power increased in the 1960s and 1970s, its political power declined' (Steele, 1983, p. xii). By the late 1970s détente had been undermined, and the new Cold War was setting in; the international communist movement was in even greater disarray than it had been in 1964, the conflict with China remained unresolved, and the difficulties of maintaining control over Eastern Europe had not diminished. The Soviet Union not only failed to increase significantly its ability to participate in the management and influence the outcome of regional conflicts, but witnessed an actual decline in its influence in some regions, like the Middle East. It is true that Moscow acquired the capacity to intervene militarily in more distant regions, but this capacity was used quite sparingly, and mostly indirectly (Angola, Ethiopia) and with a great deal of caution. The results have in any case not been altogether favourable, and no conclusive results have yet come from these interventions.

Of all the foreign problems that Brezhnev faced, the most galling one must have been the demise of détente, and the dramatic deterioration in Soviet-American relations in the late 1970s. This struck at the heart of Soviet foreign policy. The basic line of that policy under Brezhnev, as under his predecessors, was the notion that international relations are essentially determined by the relations between two contending camps — the Western capitalist one and the Eastern socialist one — each dominated by a superpower. For a variety of reasons, peaceful coexistence between these two camps is possible and desirable. But peaceful coexistence depends crucially on the achievement and maintenance of parity of power between the two blocs, and mutual acceptance of the need for certain rules and other means by which international friction and crises can be managed without escalation into armed conflict. In Soviet eyes this presupposes that both superpowers should share responsibility for managing international relations jointly, accept each other's primacy in areas crucial to them, and, most important, accept each other as equals in terms of global interests and responsibilities. The importance of parity of power and parity of treatment has been emphasised time and time again by the Soviet leadership. It was the refusal of the Reagan administration to accept such a notion of parity, as much as the related Soviet intervention in Afghanistan, that spelled the end of détente.

The advantages of détente to the Soviet Union were obvious. By diminishing the danger of superpower confrontation, it enabled

Moscow to seek expansion of its influence globally with relative freedom from major risks — a position which well suited this essentially conservative regime. The SALT agreements and the prospect of further arms control negotiations and agreements offered the possibility of avoiding, or at least minimising, expensive arms races. In this context it is worth noting that the growth of Soviet strategic nuclear power, particularly in a qualitative sense, has on the whole been a response to American initiatives. As demonstrated in Chapter 1, Soviet defence expenditure remained relatively high, but stable in relation to National Income, throughout the 1970s. Sudden escalations in the arms race are much more difficult for the Soviet economy to cope with, simply because it is centrally planned and 'fully employed'. In conditions of slow economic growth this becomes even more of a problem. The strong and public Soviet campaign against the Strategic Defense Initiative from the moment it was announced by Reagan is in the circumstances not at all surprising.

Gorbachev's new broom in foreign policy

Since acceding to power, Gorbachev has used personnel changes to establish his own policy priorities in the foreign policy sphere as elsewhere. Gromyko's reign as Foreign Minister came to an end when he was kicked upstairs to the prestigious but largely honorific position of Chairman of the Supreme Soviet, with Eduard Shevardnadze taking over his former position; Ponomarev was replaced as head of the international department of the Central Committee by Dobrynin; Rusakov was replaced by Medvedev as secretary of the Central Committee responsible for relations with communist countries (see Brown, 1986, p. 1050–1). Some of these replacements have been known to differ from the Gromyko line stressing the bipolarity of international relations and central place of Soviet-American relations. A. Yakovlev, the new head of the propaganda department of the Central Committee, has been an outspoken critic and opponent of this position, and has been publicly and virulently anti-American, but much more agreeable to Europe and Japan (Hough, 1985, p. 52). As we shall see later, the more multipolar approach to international relations does appear to be favoured by Gorbachev himself.

These personnel changes are significant, but their importance should not be exaggerated. The Soviet foreign policy decision-making process is quite complex, and involves a whole range of institutions. The trend since the early 1970s has been for increased involvement of professional/academic experts from the growing number of research institutes specialising on different aspects of foreign affairs, like the Institutes for the Study of the USA and Canada and Latin America, and the Institute of Oriental Studies. Some individuals from these institutions, like G. Arbatov, have attained Central Committee status, and Yakovlev comes from this background. Again, the fact that the Defence Minister is no longer a full member of the Politburo should not be taken to mean that the defence establishment has lost its influence on foreign policy-making. A great number of foreign policy issues have a military aspect — negotiations with China, arms control talks with the USA, Afghanistan etc. — and this requires that the defence establishment be closely involved.

Continuity and change in Gorbachev's foreign policy approach

There is an essential continuity in Soviet foreign policy which can be traced back to the 1920s. It is based on the proposition that international relations are crucially determined by the struggle between socialism and capitalism. With the triumph of Stalin's concept of 'socialism in one country' in the late 1920s the contradiction between the aims of international revolutionary transformation and the interests of the Soviet state were resolved. From that time right up to the present day the interests of the Soviet state and those of world socialism have been held to be identical. The emergence of the Soviet Union as a world power in political, economic, and military terms has been seen as a vital precondition for the survival of *any* revolutionary socialist movement, whether Soviet-backed in origin or not. The development of alternative poles of influence within the communist world with different conceptions of socialism, like China and Yugoslavia, has not altered this perception on the part of the Soviet regime, though it has, of course, meant that the most serious ideological challenges to the Soviet position have come from within that world. It is from the basic principle thus formulated that successive Soviet leaderships have derived their primary operational principle — that foreign policy should always reflect the priorities of domestic policy, while those domestic policies should in turn provide the material basis for the prosecution of foreign policy. The primary concern with the position of the USSR in the world has equally meant that international relationships with capitalist and socialist regimes alike have tended to be seen through the prism of relations with the most powerful capitalist state — since 1945 the USA. Major pronouncements by Gorbachev on the foreign policy sphere underline the extent to which the new General Secretary still cleaves to these basic principles:

> The acceleration of socio-economic development will enable us to contribute considerably to the consolidation of world socialism, and will raise to higher levels co-operation with fraternal countries. It will considerably expand our capacity for economic ties with the peoples of the developing countries, and with countries of the capitalist world. In other words, implementation of the policy of acceleration will have far-reaching consequences for the destiny of our motherland. (Gorbachev 1986a, p. 79)

If we understand the term 'consolidation of world socialism' to encapsulate Moscow's view of the interests of the Soviet state, we can see in this statement a reaffirmation of all these basic principles. There has, certainly, been some movement away from Gromyko's extreme interpretation of the primacy of relations with the USA:

> Wherever the three imperialist centres manage to coordinate their positions, it is more often than not the effect of American pressure or outright dictation . . . For the first time, governments of some Western European countries, the social democratic and liberal parties, and the public at large have begun to openly discuss whether present US policy coincides with Western Europe's notions about its own security and whether the United States is going too far in its claims to 'leadership' . . . Still, the existing complex [under US leadership — Z.K.] of economic, politico-military and other common interests of the three 'centres of power' can hardly be expected to break up in the prevailing conditions of the present-day world. (Gorbachev 1986a, p. 77).

Thus while Gorbachev recognises that the new economic strength of Japan and Western Europe must have pushed the Western world in the direction of a higher degree of multi-polarity, he still insists that in the last analysis it is relations wtih the Americans that really count. What this means in practice is that the Soviet Union takes separate foreign policy initiatives *vis-à-vis* America's allies, not in the belief that it can thereby break up the Western alliance, but rather in order that it can (1) derive specific benefits, mainly economic, from such bilateral dealings, and (2) influence the USA indirectly, through the medium of America's friends, e.g. in relation to arms control. It is in this light that we should gauge the significance of Gorbachev's visit to Paris in October 1985, for instance.

It was, indeed, on the occasion of that visit that the Soviet General Secretary took the opportunity to state clearly how he understood that favourite Soviet term, peaceful coexistence:

> . . . Civilisation must survive at all costs. But this can be ensured only if we learn to live together, to get along on this small planet by mastering the difficult art of showing consideration for each other's interests. This we call the policy of peaceful coexistence. (Gorbachev 1985a, p. 358)

Thus the concept of national interest is linked directly to that of peaceful coexistence. And through his emphasis on the dangers of nuclear holocaust Gorbachev implicitly confirmed — to a West European audience — that for him relations with the United States remain paramount.

It is certainly true that Soviet relations with other communist countries and with Third World countries have developed a dynamic of their own, e.g. in connection with Czechoslovakia in 1968 and Afghanistan since 1979. But for the Moscow leadership even events like the Prague Spring, or the developments leading up to the military intervention in Afghanistan, have to be analysed and assessed by reference to Soviet-US relations. It is for this reason that we take those as the first area for detailed consideration.

East-West relations

The concept of détente has governed Soviet attitudes to the West since the early 1970s. Détente is a slippery concept, however, which has been used in different ways, notably by Eastern and

Western protagonists. For the Kremlin, détente means a kind of joint management of international affairs by the Great Powers, with no necessary implication that the basic sources of underlying conflict can be wholly removed. This means that whilst nuclear confrontation is to be avoided through the maintenance of strategic parity, security arrangements in vital and sensitive areas (e.g. Europe) and crisis management, the superpowers would continue to compete on a global scale. Thus the Soviet concept of parity goes beyond the purely strategic sphere, to a notion which implies the acceptance of the USSR as an equal partner and indispensable participant in any major international affairs initiative in any part of the world — with the qualification that traditional spheres of influence (the Soviet Union in Eastern Europe and more questionably the USA in Latin America) — should still be respected. This broader concept of parity is, indeed, crucially important if we are to understand the purpose of particular dimensions of the Soviet arms build-up, e.g. in relation to sea-power. We should note that at the core of the Soviet conception of détente lies a tension between the increased co-operation required for the maintenance of global stability and the concomitant increased degree of regional competition and conflict. The main policy areas covered by this Soviet vision of détente have been:

(1) continuous arms control negotiation and agreement;
(2) crisis management under the rubric of ongoing global and regional security arrangements;
(3) co-operation measures covering trade, technology transfer, human rights and cultural matters.

We now look at these three headings in turn.

(1) Arms control

There have been a number of arms control proposals and negotiations since the end of the Second World War, some resulting in eventual agreement and many not. These proposals have ranged from the global — in their nature and in the proposed control, limitation or prohibition — such as the Baruch Plan for international control of atomic energy, the banning of nuclear tests and of particular weapons (biological, chemical, etc.), to those limited to particular areas or regions, such as outer space or the sea-bed, or Europe, Latin America, etc. The reasons for arms control proposals and agreements are varied, and reflect shared as well as conflicting interests, changing strategic approaches and economic and political objectives. The whole process of arms control is crucially affected by technological progress. The superpowers share an interest in minimising the risks of accidental or inadvertent war, as well as in minimising the war-producing impact of an uncontrolled arms race. They may pursue arms control in order to minimise the economic costs of the arms race — though economic pressures in this respect operate differently in the US and the USSR. Both sides may negotiate in the area with a view to achieving military and political advantage — in the former context by attempting to achieve and maintain previously nonexistent parity, or to achieve and maintain superiority; in the latter either to exact political concessions through various linkages or to gain prestige and influence by succeeding in presenting itself as the peace-loving nation and the opponents as the belligerent one. Both the Soviet and the American governments have faced internal political and military opposition to arms control, and both have had to deal with the problem of technological developments outpacing actual negotiations.

Before examining Gorbachev's arms control policy and its successes and failures, let us briefly summarise the policy of the Brezhnev administration in the 1970s. This will give us a yardstick to measure the extent to which it has been changed (if at all). The most important dimension of arms control in the 1970s was the negotiations concerning limitations on strategic nuclear weapons which led to SALT I and SALT II. The SALT I agreements include the Treaty on the Limitation of Anti-Ballistic Missile Systems, which restricted both countries to 200 anti-ballistic missiles. As we noted in Chapter 1, this can be argued to express the principles of MAD. The other SALT I agreement, the Interim Offensive Arms Agreement, limits both sides to the number of ICBMs and SLBMs they possessed in the summer of 1972 (Payne, 1980, p. 2). The 1979 SALT II Treaty provided for a number of ceilings — for the overall number of strategic nuclear weapons of all kinds (initially 2,400 to be lowered to 2,250 after 1 January 1981), with a 'sub-limit of 1,320 imposed upon each party for the combined number of launchers of ICBMs and SLBMs equipped with MIRVs, ASBMs equipped with MIRVs and aeroplanes equipped for long-range (over 600 km) cruise missiles'. Limits were also imposed on the number of re-entry vehicles on each of the above-mentioned types of launcher. The Treaty also included prohibitions of a qualitative kind, for example 'on the testing and deployment of new types of ICBMs, with one exception for each side', and 'on systems for the delivery of nuclear weapons from Earth orbit' (Goldblat, 1982, pp. 33–4). It must be emphasised that the Soviet Union negotiated these agreements only after it had achieved a state of rough parity in strategic nuclear weapons in the late 1960s and early 1970s. (We say 'rough parity' to reflect the somewhat different composition of the nuclear arsenals on each side.) It is clear that, just as this parity was a prerequisite for the SALT negotiations, so also the Soviet leadership must have at the time made a decision not to try to seek superiority, but to negotiate the maintenance of parity. Though there are indications that there was some opposition to this new policy from among the Soviet military (see Payne, 1980, pp. 49–56), it was a policy well suited to Soviet interests and capabilities. Development of new weapons systems, particularly ABMs, would threaten the deterrent value of the Soviet nuclear arsenal, and thus threaten this hard-won parity. It would, then, by necessity involve the Soviet Union in an expensive arms race, which a government committed to continuing improvement in the standard of living, and facing rising popular expectations in this respect, was keen to avoid. Arms control, in the strategic nuclear area in particular, thus became the cornerstone of Soviet détente policy. Parity in strategic weaponry would maintain the state of mutual deterrence and thus provide a framework for peaceful coexistence. The build-up in conventional arms (particularly naval) would then enable the Soviet Union to act as a great power globally, as at least an equal of the United States.

This arms control policy was, however, beginning to run into problems by the second half of the 1970s. The problems arose out of the linked issues of technological development and changing strategic thinking, as well as of the politically deteriorating international scene. The SALT treaties were not altogether successful in preventing qualitative armaments developments which could threaten the established balance of mutual deterrence. The development of new missiles, some more accurate and some faster, was seen as threatening to give one or other side a first-strike capability. The deployment of these new missiles, such as the Soviet SS-20s which replaced the older and less accurate SS-4 and SS-5s, would be reciprocated by the introduction of Pershing II and Cruise missiles into the European theatre by the US, leading to mutual recriminations and increasing mistrust. The dilemma of trying to maintain mutual deterrence under conditions in which technological progress constantly threatened it, eventually led to a shift in strategic thinking away from MAD, particularly on the part of the United States. Reagan's Strategic Defense Initiative (SDI), which purports to shift US defence policy from deterrence based on MAD towards defensive invulnerability founded on antimissile systems based in space, was the culmination of this movement.

The other problems complicating the arms control process were political. Soviet-American relations began to go sour in the late 1970s. More active Soviet military involvement in various regions (the Horn of Africa, Angola, later Afghanistan), and lack of progress on certain aspects of the Helsinki process — human rights, for example — were beginning to create a degree of disillusionment with détente in the USA. The Carter administration began, though not altogether consistently, to link progress in arms control with other aspects of Soviet international behaviour, and ended with the non-ratification of the SALT II Treaty due to the Soviet military intervention in Afghanistan. Under the Reagan administration the process of dismantling détente accelerated. This administration has tended not only to take a much stronger anti-Soviet line on most international issues, but also to be less sanguine about arms control in general. It instigated the move away from MAD, which was felt to be insufficient to cater for American global interests. By creating a strategic stalemate, MAD was seen as leading paradoxically to greater instability at the regional level. What was required was a more extended deterrence, and this was to be provided by acquiring military capabilities to protect American vital interests other than the protection of American soil. The ability to wage war, including the option of undertaking limited nuclear war, was seen as constituting a crucial part of deterrence. The introduction of weapons which would provide this kind of capability — into the European theatre, for example — became crucial to the new policy.

Though this shift in the American position did not mean that the US abandoned arms control altogether, it did mean that 'national security was to be sought less in international co-operation and more in unilateral action' (Smith, 1986, p. 150).

The Soviet response to these developments had largely been articulated before Gorbachev's succession. It was mainly based on the need to avoid an expensive arms race at a time of economic stagnation, and to prevent weapons development and deployment that might threaten Soviet security and its hard-won strategic parity. Under Andropov, the major Soviet concern was with NATO's deployment of new generation land-based medium-range missiles in Western Europe. The very fast Pershing II missiles and the ground-launched Cruise missiles were argued by Moscow to have given NATO a potential pre-emptive strike capability. Reagan's zero option — the non-deployment of these missiles by NATO in exchange for the Soviet dismantling of its SS-20s — was turned down, the Soviet government consistently maintaining that unlike the new NATO missiles, the SS-20s were simply replacements for the older SS-4s and SS-5s, conformed to the SALT framework, and did not threaten the existing balance of forces and stability in Europe. A vigorous public campaign against the deployment was launched, which included specific proposals designed to have some appeal to Western public opinion. The hope that the existing public opposition to these missiles in Western Europe would succeed in preventing their deployment there was, however, to be disappointed.

With the announcement of SDI, the main Soviet arms control effort turned to concentrate on preventing its development, now identified as the biggest threat to the existing military-strategic equilibrium. A good summary of the pre-Gorbachev public Soviet position on SDI can be found in a report by the Committee of Soviet Scientists for Peace Against Nuclear Threat, circulated in the West in January 1985, which concludes that the 'deployment of space-based anti-missile systems would increase the incentive for pre-emptive first strikes, and worsen the danger of wrong decisions in a political crisis'. (Sagdeyev and Kokoshkin, 1985).

Gorbachev's arms control policy closely follows these established lines, and arms control remains at the centre of his approach to East-West relations. Certainly the policy has been pursued with a much greater sensitivity to public opinion at home and abroad, a much greater sense of public relations and better media presentation, increased flexibility in negotiations, and more frequent recourse to unilateral measures (e.g. the moratorium on nuclear testing). But it remains crucially concerned with strategic parity and the prevention of the US SDI programme as the biggest threat to that. The following quotes from Gorbachev's public statements illustrate this line quite graphically.
Re parity:

> . . . we told the President that we would never allow the
> USA to gain military superiority over us . . . Both sides had

better get accustomed to strategic parity as a natural state of Soviet-US relations. What we should discuss is how to lower the level of this parity through joint efforts, that is, ways to carry out real measures to reduce nuclear armaments on a mutual basis. (Gorbachev, 1985b, p. 438)

Re SDI:

> We cannot take in earnest the assertion that the SDI would guarantee invulnerability from nuclear weapons thus leading to the elimination of nuclear weapons. . . . However, even on a much more modest scale, in which the Strategic Defence Initiative can be implemented as an anti-missile defense system of limited capabilities, the SDI is very dangerous. This project will, no doubt, whip up the arms race in all areas, which means that the threat of war will increase. (Gorbachev, 1985c, p. 12)

Re SDI again, this time to the Supreme Soviet of the USSR:

> The possibility of the militarisation of outer space signifies a qualitatively new leap in the arms race which would inevitably result in the disappearance of the very notion of strategic stability — the basis for the preservation of peace in the nuclear age. A situation would develop when fundamentally new decisions, irreversible in their consequences, would in fact be undertaken by computers, without partici-pation of human mind and political will, without taking into account the criteria of ethics and morality. Such a develop-ment of events could result in a universal catastrophe . . . (Gorbachev, 1985d, p. 442)

What kind of parity were the Soviets trying to preserve, and what methods and measure were they using for that purpose? There are some indications that a debate has been going on in the Soviet Union on the meaning of strategic parity, with opinions ranging from those claiming the importance of numerical equality of launchers and warheads to those who maintain that strategic parity does not mean an 'arithmetical, numerical equality' and that 'preponderance in arms and armed forces is of no practical significance' (V. Petrovskii, quoted in Ritherland, 1986, p.8). The various arms control proposals put forward by the Soviet government since Gorbachev's succession reflect the different strands of this debate. For example the well-publicised Soviet offer made in September 1985 to reduce by 50 per cent the nuclear arms capable of reaching the other power's territory was designed to produce an advantage for the Soviet Union. The 50 per cent reduction would apply to launchers and not to warheads, so that it would allow the USSR to retain its substantial numerical advantage in ICBM warheads. More importantly for the US side, all US missiles and bombers stationed in Europe capable of reaching Soviet territory would be included in the calculation, so that the reduction on the US side would effectively be disproportionate. On the other hand, the use of unilateral measures, such as the freeze on the deployment of nuclear missiles in Europe (including the SS-20s and shorter-range missiles in East Germany and Czechoslovakia) in April 1985, and particularly the announcement in August of the same year of a moratorium on nuclear test explosions — since extended several times — reflect a more flexible approach to parity, as well as the recognition that unilateral actions are not necessarily concessions, but indeed help to create political pressures on the other side to reciprocate. On the whole, though, leaving aside detailed disagreements about the numbers of missiles, launchers and warheads each side possesses in their triad, it is clear that the Soviet view of strategic parity is MAD-based:

> . . . we do not think that the ability to respond equally with a blow to a blow against our territory is an imbalance. On the contrary, this is the foundation of supporting equilibrium in nuclear forces, an important factor of maintaining peace and stability. Rough equality is the necessary basis also for the process of nuclear arms limitation. We know that in the United States some people are still dreaming about returning to the situation when an invulnerable 'fortress North America' could threaten any state with nuclear annihilation. But there is no returning to the past. (Akhromeev, 1985, p. 381)

This brings us back to SDI. The maintenance of parity, in the Soviet view, requires that the US abandon SDI. Otherwise the Soviet Union would have to develop a similar system of its own with a consequent dangerous escalation of the arms race:

> . . . an agreement banning the development of strike space

weapons is a key, principled question. If no ban exists, an unchecked arms race will start, both in strategic offensive weapons and space weapons. . . . The Soviet Union cannot show naivety and count only on peaceful assurances by the US leaders, which serve as a cover for developing strike weapons in space. If that is continued, nothing will remain for us but to adopt counter-measures in the field of both offensive and other, not excluding defensive, armaments, including those based in outer space. (Akhromeev, 1985, p. 379)

In pursuit of the objective of maintaining what they perceive as parity in strategic arms, the Moscow government under Gorbachev has displayed an uncharacteristically Soviet flexibility in seeking opportunities for the USSR to take the initiative in the politics of arms control. We can cite the unilateral measures mentioned above, as well as the general proposal for arms control, leading to eventual nuclear disarmament, put forward by Gorbachev on 15 January 1986 (Gorbachev, 1986b). How seriously meant was this latter proposal is difficult to gauge. It certainly had a strong propaganda element, and it is reasonable to assume that like the unilateral measures it was at least partly designed to create an international climate whereby pressure would be put on the US government by public opinion in Western Europe indirectly, and US public opinion directly, to make significant concessions, particularly in the space weapons sphere.

It is, indeed, in the struggle against SDI that Gorbachev has perhaps displayed most flexibility. The initial line established some time before his succession was to make all arms control agreements conditional on the abandoning of SDI. Thus Gorbachev duly claimed in his interview with *Time* magazine:

Without . . . an agreement (on the prevention of an arms race in space) it will not be possible to reach an agreement on the limitation and reduction of nuclear weapons either. The interrelationship between defensive and offensive arms is so obvious as to require no proof. Thus if the present US position on space weapons is its last word, the Geneva negotiations will lose all sense. (Gorbachev, 1985c, p. 12)

As this position was not seen to be yielding the required results, it was somewhat modified soon after. In Paris Gorbachev proclaimed that regarding medium-range nuclear weapons in Europe and with the 'aim of making agreement easier on their speediest mutual reduction, we consider it possible to conclude a corresponding agreement separately, outside of direct connection with the problem of space and strategic weapons' (Gorbachev, 1985a, p. 358). The additional reason for this shift was that the USSR still had an interest in removing or at least limiting the number of Pershing and Cruise missiles in Europe. Meanwhile, the initial blanket opposition to any SDI research whatsoever was modified by Akhromeev, when he accepted a distinction between 'research and studies in laboratory conditions and a (situation) when models and prototypes are created and samples of space arms are tested' (Akhromeev, 1985, p. 380).

Gorbachev has also shown a willingness to engage the USA's European allies, both in the struggle against SDI, and on the other arms control issues. On the positive side, this involved recognition of the legitimacy of the French and British nuclear arsenals, and the offer to negotiate them separately. On the more negative side, West Germany, for example, was warned that its relations with Eastern Europe could suffer if it joined the SDI research programme (Yakhontov, 1985). In June 1986, General N. Chervov of the Soviet General Staff hinted that the Soviet Union no longer set priority on securing a freeze on Britain's nuclear arsenal but was more interested in seeing Britain urge President Reagan to compromise on SDI ('Russia shifts its attitude . . .', 1986).

Significant concessions have been made by the Soviet Union in the inspection and verification sphere. In June 1986 they suggested monitoring long-range missiles as they leave factories, so that a precise count can be kept by the other side. In August the Soviet side agreed to allow foreign inspectors to check its military activities from the air as well as the ground. There has also been some progress in the negotiations on banning chemical weapons.

On the central and most important issue — SDI — the Soviet government has, however, met with failure. In spite of all Moscow's efforts the US government is going ahead. The first space-based test was initiated in early September 1986. At time of writing the future of the Soviet leadership's defence of MAD seems uncertain.

Overall, then, Gorbachev's arms control policy has been very similar in its content to that of his predecessors. In its application he has, however, shown greater energy and flexibility than his predecessors. The results have so far not been very encouraging — Soviet ability to influence a determined US adminstration in this sphere has proved to be limited.

(2) Crisis management and security arrangements

The second major aspect of détente is management of international conflict. Among the measures designed to minimise the danger of escalation of conflicts into full-scale confrontations between the superpowers, or to help to resolve such conflicts, are provisions for speedy communications in crisis situations like the hot line, regional security arrangements and agreements on international norms of behaviour. The Soviet position on the nature of global and regional conflict, and the role of the superpowers in its management and thus in the possibility and usefulness of regional security arrangements in particular, has remained relatively consistent since the early 1970s. It is clear on the need to prevent nuclear war between the superpowers, and thus on the need to agree on measures preventing such a development. On the question of regional conflicts, however, it has remained somewhat ambiguous. On the one hand, it maintains the right of the Soviet Union as a superpower to take part in managing such conflicts — 'there is no international issue of any importance that can be resolved without the participation of the Soviet Union', Gromyko claimed in the mid-1970s (quoted in Bialer and Afferica, 1986, p. 635) — and on the other it proclaims the right to help 'progressive forces' in such conflicts. The former aspect is potentially conducive to some mutual arrangement with the USA but the latter is not. Thus the Soviet Union has sought to play a superpower role in the management of the Middle Eastern conflict (unsuccessfully), whilst intervening directly or indirectly in Angola, Ethiopia and Afghanistan. It is not surprising, therefore, that attempts to agree on common rules of behaviour have not been very successful. The Declaration on Basic Principles of Relations between the USA and the USSR of 1972, for example, did not have much of an impact. In Europe alone, the importance of the region to both superpowers, and the consequent dangers of direct confrontation between them, made it possible to conclude a regional security agreement (Helsinki). Apart from Helsinki there are no agreed principles governing the limits of intervention by the superpowers in regional conflicts.

Under Gorbachev the tension in the Soviet position regarding regional conflict has not been resolved. That position is based on (a) recognition of national interest as the principal and guiding force in international relations:

> When I was in Britain last December, I recalled a phrase of Palmerston's . . . (He) said that Britain had no eternal enemies or eternal friends, but only eternal interests. I told Margaret Thatcher just then that I agreed with that judgement . . . When about two hundred states are involved in the international arena, each of them strives to promote its own interests. But to what extent are those interests promoted. It depends on the taking into account of the interests of others in the course of cooperation. (Gorbachev, 1985b, p. 439);

(b) emphasis on the special role and responsibility of the superpowers in international relations:

> The Soviet Union and the United States are two mighty powers with their own global interests and with their own allies and friends. They have their priorities in their foreign policies. Yet the Soviet leadership regards it not as a source of confrontation but rather as an origin of a special, greater responsibility for the destinies of peace shouldered by the Soviet Union and the United States, and their leaders . . . (and therefore the acceptance of the principle of) discussing any particular regional problems to find ways of promoting their settlement. (Gorbachev, 1985b, p. 439);

this leads on to (c) assertion of the right of the USSR to participate in the solution of all regional conflicts, e.g. in the Middle East:

> There are those who have no interest in the participation of the Soviet Union. But the presence of the Soviet Union in the Middle East is an objective factor and we do not forsake our role. We stand for collective efforts . . . (Gorbachev, 1985e, p. 364);

(d) recognition of Europe as the crucial region;
(e) rejection of the 'spheres of interest' approach and recognition of 'the right of every people to freedom and independence':

The United States which is used to thinking in terms of 'spheres of interests', reduces these problems (regional conflicts) to East-West rivalry. But these days it is an anachronism, a relapse of imperial thinking which denies the right of a majority of nations to think and take decisions independently. . . We have been and remain on the sides of peoples upholding their independence. (Gorbachev, 1985d, p. 442)

This last point is used to justify Soviet intervention in Afghanistan, Ethiopia, and Angola.

It is clear that the practical application of these principles could lead to inconsistencies. The first two principles stand for super-power parity and reciprocity and the last one goes against that, and indeed against the traditional Soviet position on *global* security, as in practice it underpins Soviet support for movements which the USA is likely to see as threatening its interests. Of course, the principle would be somewhat modified in relation to Eastern Europe, cf. the Brezhnev Doctrine.

Soviet policy since Gorbachev's succession reflects this complex pattern. Thus the Soviet government has been willing to discuss various regional conflicts with the USA (at the Geneva Summit, for example): it has tried to enhance its role in the Middle East by seeking to normalise its relations with the conservative Arab states, e.g. through establishing diplomatic relations with Oman and the United Arab Emirates, as well as by trying to re-establish some links with Israel. On the other hand Soviet involvement in Afghanistan continues (though some policy changes have taken place — see final section).

(3) Co-operation measures

The third aspect of détente covered international co-operation in various fields including trade, technology transfer, scientific and cultural matters, exchange of information and humanitarian concerns. The Gorbachev leadership has put a great deal of emphasis on measures of this kind, particularly in the European context, and has repeatedly called for improvements in this area.

(i) Trade and economic co-operation

. . . economic ties engender mutual dependence. This

mutual dependence is then reflected in the solutions of political problems. I think it would be both to the advantage of the Soviet Union and the United States of America to continue furthering economic ties. (Gorbachev, 1985b, p. 441)

On his visit to Paris Gorbachev talked about the advantages for both sides of an 'effective utilisation of the international division of labour' and advocated more businesslike relations between Comecon and the EEC. There is little doubt that the Soviet Union has something to gain from trade and technology transfers. However, there are serious limitations on the development of such exchanges, as we saw in chapter 5. The economic consequences of Helsinki, for instance, were not very great. Though the flow of trade between the USSR and the developed capitalist states increased in volume after 1975, the rate of growth of that trade declined (Hanson, 1985). As to technology transfer, the Gorbachev government has made it very plain that it is counting on 'accelerating scientific and technological progress not through "transfer of technology" from the US to the USSR but through "transfusions" from Soviet science' to Soviet industry and agriculture. Scientific and technological co-operation would only provide additional (non-essential) advantages (Gorbachev, 1985c, p. 13).

(ii) Humanitarian concerns

Gorbachev's public line on international (particularly European) co-operation in the humanitarian sphere has not differed from that of his predecessors. Whilst proclaiming that 'the Soviet Union attaches the most serious importance to ensuring human rights', he insists that it is 'necessary to free this problem from hypocrisy and speculations, from attempts at interference in the internal affairs of other countries' (Gorbachev, 1985a, p. 359). The Soviet position on international concern with and legislation on human rights has consistently maintained that international agreements provide standards to be implemented by states, but that the implementation itself and the enforcement of that legislation is a matter for the internal jurisdiction of those states. As the Soviet concept of human rights, based on Marxism-Leninism, differs significantly from the Western liberal-individualistic one, in that it is couched in terms of a relationship between the citizen and the state in which individual rights and interests are subordinated to the good of society, the Soviet government has regarded as unacceptable interference in Soviet affairs any attempt by the West to intervene on behalf of individuals or groups considered in the West to have been denied their rights. The Soviet government has strongly resented attempts to link Soviet performance in the human rights area (the right to emigrate for example) to trade concessions, or even to progress in arms control negotiations. As we saw in Chapter 2, Jewish emigration from the Soviet Union, for instance, has dramatically declined since 1979, and under Gorbachev the annual rate of Jewish emigration is lower than any time since the 1970s (see Edwards, 1985; 'Moscow announces rights commission', 1986).

There have so far been very few signs of a significant evolution in the Soviet conception of human rights, or of attitudes to domestic implementation. Until the Soviet and Western approaches to human rights come closer together, the subject is likely to generate more conflict than co-operation.

. . . . .

Our examination of the three major aspects of détente, in its Soviet interpretation, leads us to conclude that there has not yet been a significant change in the Soviet approach to East-West relations, and that there are substantial obstacles to major changes in that approach.

Soviet-East European relations

The essential problem which Gorbachev has inherited in Eastern Europe is a multifaceted one of legitimacy — the legitimacy of the authority relationships between the Soviet Communist Party and the communist parties of Eastern Europe, between the Soviet government and East European governments, and between Soviet and East European governments and their respective subject populations. While the problem originates from the very nature of the post-war settlement in terms of spheres of influence, it acquired its present complex form only after the death of Stalin in 1953.

If we understand legitimacy to imply that in legitimate political orders the rulers and the ruled are bound together by a shared belief in the rightness of that order, of the rule of the particular authority, then we must further argue that legitimacy should be distinguished from force. Under Stalin, the principle of legitimacy operated in a coherent, if rather Byzantine way. As we have seen, the interests of the world socialist movement were taken to be identical with the interests of the Soviet Union. In line with Stalin's interpretation of the Marxist-Leninist analysis of the relationship between nationalism and internationalism, nationalisms could be ordered hierarchically on the basis of their progressiveness — meaning their positive contribution to the development of international socialism. The fundamental requirement of unity within the socialist bloc of nations, as well as within each of the socialist states, made such ordering easy, for the form of socialism being practised in the USSR was taken to be the most advanced form then existing in the world. Therefore it had to serve initially as a useful, and eventually as a binding, example for all other countries now taking the socialist road. From the late 1940s this, in conjunction with the 'two-camps' theory of world affairs, expressed itself in terms of a starkly monolithic interpretation of Soviet-East European relations. And because this interpretation of the nature of the socialist camp and the international communist movement was based firmly on the principle of the leading role of the Soviet Communist Party in the three types of authority relationship distinguished above, because this in turn implied a strictly hierarchical relationship within the communist world, the Stalinist principle of legitimacy was thus unaffected by the formal distinction between Party and state. None of this is to imply that legitimacy served as a *sufficient* basis for Soviet control in these countries of Eastern Europe. On the contrary, obedience of governments and people alike in Eastern Europe was based as much on systematic and widespread terror as on anything else. But Stalin's idea of legitimacy was at least internally consistent.

This neat system fell apart after the death of the dictator. Stalin's successors were not in a position to ensure obedience through the maintenance of a high degree of terror, whether in relation to the Soviet population, or to the governments and peoples of Eastern Europe. Both Malenkov and Khrushchev in the Soviet Union proclaimed a shift towards 'gulash communism', with the implication that there should be a shift in emphasis within the articulation of authority relations towards considerations of living standards. The introduction of Stalinist central planning in East European countries had done little for the East European consumer. The shift towards incentives or, if you like, bribes, as a basis for political stability, introduced for the first time the issue of 'economic reform' within the Soviet bloc, and implicitly destroyed the idea that the Soviet Union provided the only model for socialist development. Meanwhile, the regularisation of Soviet-East European trading relations, following the gross exploitation of the Stalinist period, introduced for the first time the problem of the international 'socialist division of labour', with all that that implied in terms of a movement away from hierarchy and monolithism towards some kind of 'commonwealth' conception. And while the economic dimension provided an optimistic perspective in welfare terms, it did at the same time result in a general tendency for expectations to rise. Thus while the notion of gulash communism was originally introduced as a substitute for terror, it could not fail to have implications for the most fundamental problem of all — that of legitimacy.

Developments on the purely political side dramatically deepened this impending crisis of legitimacy. Khrushchev, in his 'secret speech' at the XX Congress of the CPSU in 1956, effectively, though unintentionally, created a series of contradictions in the post-Stalin construction of legitimacy. With the debunking of Stalin's personality cult, the demythologising of the charismatic leader, the CPSU found itself searching for a new basis for its authority. The relinking of the Party with the Leninist legacy, coupled with the emergence of the Communist Party apparatus as an important functional social group, made it possible to construct the basis of a new form of legitimacy within the Soviet Union. Internationally, however, matters were very much more complicated.

By admitting that things had gone badly wrong in the past in the Soviet Union, Khrushchev could no longer insist that the Soviet example was in any way binding on the rest of the world communist movement. This broadened out the argument already broached in purely economic terms. The way was therefore opened up for the development of approaches to 'national socialism'. That had obvious implications for states and peoples, but equally important ones for communist parties. With the movement away from hierarchy and monolithism each party emerged as the body best equipped to interpret local conditions and elaborate appropriate paths to socialism. But this implicitly rehabilitated 'local' nationalism as a powerful and 'progressive' social force. That in turn raised all sorts of questions in relation to the interpretation of the interests of the world socialist movement. Because the Soviet Union no longer served as a shorthand for that movement in all its aspects, the possibility of multiple conflicts was introduced — conflicts between the interests of one particular country and that of the socialist commonwealth, and conflicts in the interpretation of national communism by particular parties and of the concept of the world communist movement. And with the Soviet Communist Party losing its monopoly over doctrinal interpretation and therefore its right to play the arbiter in all such conflicts, the system was left with a most serious weakness. If a certain amount of conflict is inevitable, but if conflicts are to be resolved, what is the mechanism for such a resolution? How can any such mechanism be contrived which does not simply sanction the prerogative of the most powerful member of the commonwealth — the Soviet Union — to impose limits to change? The unfolding of the Polish and Hungarian crises in 1956 brought these issues home to the Soviet leadership as immediate and burning issues. The recourse to military force in the Hungarian case represented a failure of the principle of legitimacy in Soviet-East European relations, and a portent of problems to come, as reform movements gained momentum throughout Eastern Europe, and the problem of limits to reform became an increasingly general one.

We can identify Soviet attempts from 1956 onwards to create legitimising platforms by organising conferences of the entire world communist movement, which, it was hoped, would function in a manner basically analogous to that of the national Party Congress. With the progressive disintegration of the world movement from the late 1950s onwards, and in particular with the deepening of the Sino-Soviet conflict, this approach proved unviable. Subsequently, an alternative was sought through the fora of the existing international organisations of the Soviet bloc — the Warsaw Pact and Comecon. As a result there has been a continuous evolution in the functional spheres of these organisations. But because they are regional rather than global organisations (attempts by the USSR to globalise the Warsaw Pact having met with resistance), and because the Soviet Union is the only member which views itself as having a global role, they cannot easily cope with divergence between national and international interests. As discussed in Chapter 5, the record of Comecon in developing an effective socialist division of labour has been a mediocre one. But the persistence of Soviet attempts to achieve a higher level of economic integration with Eastern Europe has underlined the political as well as economic importance the Soviet Union attaches to the matter. More operational has been the role developed for the Warsaw Pact as a vehicle for the expression of the notion of the 'interest and will' of the socialist commonwealth.

In practice this has meant that the Warsaw Pact has been used as a cover for forcibly stopping reforms in Eastern European countries, if they are deemed *by the Soviet Union* to be against the interests of the socialist commonwealth, with the interests of the socialist commonwealth again being identified with those of the Soviet state. Thus the Brezhnev Doctrine, which provided the theoretical justification for the 'Warsaw Pact' intervention in Czechoslovakia in 1968, and which would do the same for any other such interventions deemed necessary, is not universalisable. It does not provide any real possibility of East European intervention in the Soviet Union, but only of the reverse. In practice, then, the Brezhnev Doctrine brings us back to something similar, if less complete and coherent, to Stalin's position on the dominant role of the Soviet Union within the communist world. In its formulation, the doctrine reflects the continued search by the Soviet Union for some legitimate basis for its hegemony in Eastern Europe after Stalin.

The 1970s witnessed an acceleration of the rate of divergence between the dimensions of the world communist movement and the socialist commonwealth/Soviet bloc, with the burgeoning polycentrism of the world movement. Within the Soviet bloc, Comecon and the Warsaw Pact have continued to provide platforms for increased consultation between partners, though without any implication of attainment of equal status on the part of the East European members. The basic problem of how to deal with specific cases and differing intensities of national divergence remains, however, unresolved, as the case of Poland in the late 1970s and early 1980s illustrates. The situation inherited by Gorbachev in Eastern Europe can, then, be characterised in terms of the following points: (1) an ongoing, but stuttering trend towards economic integration; (2) a host of unresolved socio-political problems and conflicts which have conspired with economic difficulties to ensure that the pressure for political reform is continuous, however manifold the forms it takes; (3) an array of East European governments which continue to enjoy much lower levels of legitimacy in the eyes of subject populations than does the Soviet government. This makes the authorities in the Soviet Union and the East European countries themselves continuously aware of the danger of destablisation of these regimes. It is not surprising that the most conservative regime in the Eastern bloc today is in Czechoslovakia. The search for legitimising platforms has not been successful enough to establish ways in which common interests and particular interests can be reconciled and limits to reform and change established.

Gorbachev's East European policy has so far not undergone any qualitative changes but has, rather, gone a bit further in the direction established in the 1970s. The emphasis has been placed firmly on accelerating the process of integration of the 'socialist commonwealth'. In the economic area this trend can be traced from the Comprehensive Programme agreed at the July 1971 meeting of Comecon, with its stress on the voluntary co-ordination of national economic policies and plans and joint economic forecasting, to the 'Comprehensive Programme for Scientific and Technical Progress' of December 1985. According to Gorbachev the import of this programme 'lies in the transition of the Comecon countries to a co-ordinated policy in science and technology. The accent is being shifted from primarily commercial relations to specialisation and co-operation of production, particularly in heavy engineering (Gorbachev, 1986a, p. 90). Whether this will solve the problems of relative economic decline, inefficiency and slower technological innovation both in the USSR and the Eastern European countries remains in some doubt (see Chapter 5).

In the political and military areas the trend can be seen in the growth in the functions of the Warsaw Pact throughout the 1970s. The organisation has become a major forum for co-ordinating not just the defence policies but also the foreign policies of the member states. The 1970s saw an increased amount of multilateral consultation, and occasionally some successful opposition to Soviet positions, e.g. Ceausescu's rejection of the Soviet demands for increased defence expenditure and a collective censure of the Chinese in November 1978 (see Hutchings, 1983, p. 138). Gorbachev has dramatically increased the number of summit meetings held (Comecon and Warsaw Pact, as well as meetings of communist leaders). On his return from the Geneva Summit, for instance, he stopped off in Prague to inform the East European leaders about the progress made in Geneva, even before the Soviet Politburo had the chance to discuss the matter. Furthermore Gorbachev has, since his succession, visited all the East European states, some of them more than once. Finally the Warsaw Pact was extended on 26 April 1985 by twenty years, and a further ten years after that unless notice of withdrawal is given a year before expiry.

The increased incidence of consultation and meetings should not, however, be taken to mean that the socialist commonwealth is now an association of equals. Though the Eastern European countries have on occasion been able to modify the Soviet stance, the Soviet Union retains its dominant role, and can still be expected to set the limits to acceptable reform in Eastern Europe — without being able to control the forces and material developments that give rise to pressures for reform. To date Gorbachev's position on this issue has remained similar to that of his predecessors. Cautious approval of the Hungarian economic reform is not echoed by any recognition of the need for political reform in East Europe. The emphasis is on vitality, efficiency and initiative, and these are linked to the increase in live and broad communication between 'citizens of socialist countries' and the communist parties themselves. *Glasnost'*, rather than structural reform, is the path being followed at present. The underlying problems, principally that of lack of regime legitimacy, remain unresolved. Poland — the most pressing and recalcitrant difficulty facing the Soviet Union in the region — serves as a good illustration. After more than four years of military government, the economic, social and political crisis which led to the rise of Solidarity has not been resolved sufficiently to enable the reconstitution of a more orthodox, civilian-based, communist government. In spite of the damage this does to the Soviet orthodoxy on the leading role of the communist parties in socialist countries, Gorbachev has given his approval to the further strengthening of the military's position in the Polish leadership (another three generals being appointed to the Politburo at the Party Congress held in July 1986). The alternative which proved unacceptable was radical change.

Soviet relations with China

Soviet relations with China have been difficult and full of conflict for almost 30 years now. The sources of this conflict are numerous, and their relative significance has varied. Over the last few years, the Soviet leaders (Andropov and now Gorbachev) have tried to improve relations. These attempts have had some success, due at least partly to a certain cooling off in Sino-American relations, and also due to the reformist changes in China. Gorbachev's report to the Party Congress in February included this almost self-congratulatory passage:

One can say with gratification that there has been a measure of improvement of the Soviet Union's relations with its great neighbour — socialist China. The distinctions in attitudes, in particular to a number of international problems remain. But we also note something else — that in many cases we can work jointly, co-operate on an equal and principled basis, without prejudice to third parties. (Gorbachev, 1986a, p. 90)

The gratification may be justified and the improvement real, but there are still unresolved problems which pose severe limitations on further significant progress. The spirit of improvement is reflected in a number of high-level visits and negotiations, including foreign ministers. Concrete advances, however, have been mainly in the economic area, including that of technical co-operation (in nuclear technology, for instance), with the first Chinese trade fair in the Soviet Union for 33 years opening in Moscow in July 1986. In the political sphere progress has been slower. The Chinese have claimed that there were three major obstacles to significant improvement in this area — Soviet intervention in Afghanistan, Soviet support for the Vietnamese presence in Kampuchea, and the build-up of 50 divisions on the Chinese border. The most signficant development in this connection occured in late July 1986 when the Soviet leader, in a televised address from Vladivostock, appeared to have made some important offers — he proposed to reduce substantially the 60,000-strong Soviet garrison in Mongolia, to withdraw six regiments from Afghanistan (about 6,000 men), whilst repeating the pledge that all Soviet troops would be withdrawn from Afghanistan once the Kabul regime was no longer in danger. He also offered to enter into discussions with China at any time and any level to 'discuss questions of additional measures for creating a good neighbourly atmosphere', and acknowledged that there was a border dispute — something previous Soviet leaders had refused to do. What kind of a breakthrough this adds up to remains to be seen. The concession on Afghanistan is limited, and there is in any case no chance of a more significant Soviet withdrawal in the foreseeable future. Vietnam's presence in Kampuchea remains a problem too. Whether the Soviet government would be willing to pressurise Vietnam into a withdrawal, and if so whether it has the means to insist, is doubtful. But in any case Afghanistan and Kampuchea are symptoms, rather than the causes, of the continuing dispute between China and the Soviet

Union. Their long border, respective strategic and political interests in Asia and long history of mutual conflict, place natural limits on the scope for improvement in their relations.

Soviet-Third World relations

Interpretations of Soviet designs in the Third World vary widely. Some view Soviet policies towards the developing countries as part of a 'grand design' aimed at Soviet global domination (e.g. Lutwak, 1983). Substantial elements in the Reagan administration have held this view. The official Soviet line, shared by some of their supporters, and even some socialist critics in the West, is that the Soviet role is to champion the cause of anti-imperialism throughout the former colonial world. The majority of contemporary academic writers take a more prosaic view. They see an evolution of Soviet attitudes based on three things: the lessons derived from specific involvements from the 1950s onwards; perceived Soviet interests in the Third World and the evolution thereof, and Soviet capacity, military and economic, to pursue these interests. On this basis we can paint a picture of an essentially cautious, but opportunistic, Soviet approach to the developing world, an approach which has tried to avoid major confrontations with the United States, and which has tried to limit the economic costs of involvement.

If we look at the history of Soviet relations with the Third World we can discern elements of continuity as well as of change, as in other areas of foreign policy. Some elements of continuity can be traced back to the second Comintern Congress, held in 1920, and the 'Theses on the National and Colonial Question' which came out of that Congress. The Theses focused on the need to support nationalist, anti-colonialist forces as the best way of weakening world imperialism, in terms of a world view that did not conceive of the possibility of direct transition from tribalism to socialism. With the development of the doctrine of socialism in one country, support for anti-colonial forces, and Soviet policies in the non-Western world in general, came increasingly to be dominated by the perceived interests of the Soviet state. This, in conjunction with severe resource constraints, helps explain Stalin's essentially isolationist stance *vis-à-vis* what is now known as the Third World.

After the death of Stalin the Soviet Union started to pursue a more active role in the Third World. Khrushchev's naive optimism about the outcome of the economic competition between socialism and capitalism, within the framework of peaceful coexistence, made him equally optimistic about the Third World. A Soviet economic system which had proved its superiority to the whole world would provide an attractive model to countries anxious to industrialise, while at the same time providing the USSR with the material basis for more extended involvement throughout the world. This was the background to the launching of the first Soviet aid programmes for non-fraternal countries in 1954. These programmes involved both economic and military elements.

The experience of a more active policy in the period up to the early 1970s taught the Soviets four main lessons. First, aid is a competitive business, with the Americans, West Europeans and even the Chinese featuring as main competitors. Secondly, as brought home by the Cuban experience, it may be difficult to prevent massive escalation of the cost of specific involvements. Thirdly, it is difficult to pursue global policies in the absence of appropriate military capabilities. Fourthly, and flowing partly from the last point, Soviet, or indeed socialist, advances in the Third World are reversible, as witnessed by the Chilean and Egyptian cases. For a combination of military, geographical, economic and political reasons, the Soviets found themselves unable to 'satellitise' Third World countries.

The conservative Brezhnev regime's understanding of détente, which placed primary emphasis on the attainment of global parity, was based on an interpretation of the experience of the 1950s and 1960s which saw Soviet policy move in two specific directions. The first flowed from the desire to project power on a worldwide scale, and to be involved in the management of all regional conflicts. This meant the increased mobilisation of military capabilities — a process begun in the early 1960s. The other, which reflected past failures of 'socialist regimes' in the Third World, was the concentration of Soviet support, particularly in the form of military aid, on countries of 'socialist orientation' with vanguardist parties and military establishments committed to the revolutionary regime. These regimes were viewed as capable of withstanding internal and external pressures alike. This, in conjunction with the decision to avoid confrontation with the US, places in perspective the selective thrust of Soviet activism in the Third World in the 1970s and 1980s, and the increasing importance of arms exports in trading relations with the Third World. The 1970s witnessed for the first time large-scale Soviet military involvement in the developing world. In some cases, notably that of Angola, this was done through Cuban proxies. In Afghanistan, by contrast, we have seen substantial involvement by front-line Soviet troops. The cases of Angola, Ethiopia and Afghanistan have a number of common features. In each case the Soviets intervened to save, or promote, a regime of 'socialist orientation'. In each case Moscow was reasonably certain that intervention would not lead to direct confrontation with the USA. While they clearly miscalculated in the case of Afghanistan, the miscalculation was not a disastrous one, with the American response being limited to an incomplete grain embargo (see Chapter 5), the boycott of the Moscow Olympics, and the non-ratification of the SALT II agreement by the US Congress. Not even the intervention in Afghanistan should be taken to represent the enunciation of some kind of new Brezhnev Doctrine in relation to the Third World. Afghanistan is a border country in a strategically sensitive area, and there is a long history of Russian and Soviet involvement in the country. Failure to intervene would probably have resulted in the establishment of a strongly anti-Soviet Muslim fundamentalist regime in Kabul, with all that that might mean in terms of the destabilisation of Soviet Central Asia. In areas where the USA is known to be highly sensitive — like Central America — the Soviet Union has, by contrast, offered very limited assistance to radical, anti-American regimes. Even Nicaragua, and Grenada under Bishop, have received support only on a relatively small scale. There also does seem to have been a shift in the late 1970s, initially among Soviet academic writers, towards greater scepticism as to the potential for rapid socialist transformation in the countries of 'socialist orientation'. These countries, it was felt, remained part of the capitalist world economically and geostrategically, and there was no guarantee of the irreversibility of their revolutions, particularly in the light of the strength of local politico-cultural factors like Islam (Valkenier, 1986). Thus by the end of the Brezhnev era Soviet policy towards the Third World had been largely reduced to the exercise of 'great-power responsibilities', as implied in the Soviet interpretation of détente. The policy continued to be fundamentally based on military capability, but manifested all the traditional Soviet caution in relation to involvement with specific regimes. Afghanistan remained, and indeed still remains, a partial exception.

Under Gorbachev this policy has not altered radically. The new

Soviet leader has continued with an approach which combines global activism with caution and awareness of Soviet inability — due to the nature of the international political economy and the position of the Soviet economy within it — fundamentally to alter the position of the developing countries and help them achieve rapid socialist transformation. It is an approach based on gradually acquired, but not yet fully assimilated, experience of the difficulties of preventing developments in allied Third World countries threatening either the Soviet position in that country, or the country's very stability. A good recent example of this was the Soviet failure to anticipate and prevent the coup and civil war in South Yemen in January 1986. There were more than faint echoes of the situation in Afghanistan towards the end of 1979. Soviet relations with Libya illustrate well the cautiousness of Soviet policy, and the extent to which radical Third World regimes are *not* supported simply on the basis of how anti-American they are. At the height of the crisis in American-Libyan relations in March and April 1986 Moscow's public pledges of support for the Libyans were unaccompanied by any indications that this support might take on real practical substance.

It is, however, the case of Afghanistan that illustrates best the difficulties of and limitations on Soviet involvement in the Third World, even though that case is to some extent exceptional, insofar as Afghanistan is the only Third World country in which the USSR has intervened militarily on a large scale. By the time of Gorbachev's succession, the war in Afghanistan had been going on for several years. The Soviet had something in the region of 120,000 troops in Afghanistan. They were doing most of the fighting against the *mujahadin,* the Afghan regime's army being unreliable and prone to desertions. All Soviet attempts to defeat the guerrillas decisively had come to nought, and the war was proving expensive, not just in terms of hardware and human casualties, but also in terms of international political costs (the effect on East-West relations, Sino-Soviet relations, relations with other Third World countries, etc.). The Gorbachev government gradually introduced certain changes in their Afghan policy:

(a) Presentation

In his report to the Congress in February Gorbachev referred to Afghanistan thus:

. . . counter-revolution and imperialism have turned Afghanistan into a bleeding wound. The USSR supports that country's efforts to defend its sovereignty. We should like, in the nearest future, to withdraw the Soviet troops stationed in Afghanistan at the request of its government. Moreover, we have agreed with the Afghan side on the schedule for their phased withdrawal as soon as a political settlement is reached that ensures an actual cessation and dependably guarantees the non-resumption of foreign armed interference in the internal affairs of the Democratic Republic of Afghanistan. It is in our vital, national interest that the USSR should always have good and peaceful relations with all its neighbours. (Gorbachev, 1986a, pp. 89–90)

What is new here is the 'bleeding-wound' reference, suggesting something into which you have been drawn reluctantly, but from which it is not easy to withdraw. Under Gorbachev the war did become much more public in the Soviet Union, the Soviet media beginning to offer a much more extensive coverage of it, in the spirit of *glasnost'*. But some of this coverage took a very nationalistic approach, at times going as far as celebrating the virtues of war (see Prokhanov, 1985).

(b) Policy of the Afghan government

On 21 December 1985 *Pravda* published an article on the inside page indicating a shift in the Soviet position regarding Afghanistan. The article acknowledged 'mistakes in the first stage of the revolution: getting carried away by revolutionary phrases, introducing social reforms by force without due consideration of the reality of the situation, the social and national characteristic features of the country' and called for the creation of a 'climate conducive to a positive dialogue between social and political forces, including those who for the time being adhere to a stance hostile to the revolution, for the sake of the national rebirth of Afghanistan' ('Za rasshirenie sotsial'noi bazy . . .', 1985, quoted in Khovanski, 1986, p. 3). This call for a widening of the social basis of the revolution has been repeated, and the issue proved to be one of the factors behind Babrak Karmal's replacement by Dr M. Najibullah (the other being a desire to appease President Zia of Pakistan, who had refused to negotiate with Karmal).

(c) Withdrawal of troops

Repeated statements have been made by Soviet leaders about the phased withdrawal of Soviet troops from Afghanistan. But until now the only specific unilateral withdrawal announced has been that involving six regiments made by Gorbachev in his Vladivostok speech. The eventual total withdrawal of the Soviet army from Afghanistan is still dependent, in the view of the Soviet government, on securing a settlement which would preserve a pro-Soviet regime in power. The chances of achieving such a settlement without prior decisive military victory — at least as long as President Zia remains in power in Pakistan — are slim.

The essential problem the Soviet Union faces in Afghanistan is that it is in a situation of military stalemate, in which there is very little common political ground between the two Afghan sides, so that the chances of a negotiated settlement acceptable to the Soviet government as well as the *mujahadin* are for the foreseeable future non-existent. As the installation of an anti-Soviet Muslim government in Kabul is the worst alternative for the Soviets, Gorbachev might have to be prepared for a long Soviet military presence in Afghanistan.

Conclusion

We suggest that though Gorbachev has taken a number of initiatives in the foreign policy sphere, and has pursued them energetically, with a sense of style and with quite a lot of subtlety, his foreign policy remains, as far as approach, content and achievement are concerned, very similar to that of his predecessors. It is a policy still shaped by the doctrine of socialism in one country: 'We, the Soviet Communists, are well aware that every advance we make in building socialism is an advance of the entire movement' (Gorbachev, 1986a, p. 90) and by the availability of the resources required for the furthering of the interests of the Soviet state in the international arena. It is a policy which prioritises domestic concerns. Regarding the relationship between reform and foreign policy/international relations, we have witnessed the emergence of a different question from the one originally asked — does the current state of international relations in general, and the policies of other states towards the Soviet Union in particular, encourage or inhibit domestic reform?

Appendix I

Soviet arms control measures and proposals, April 1985 to September 1986

7/4/1985   Freeze on the deployment of Soviet nuclear missiles in Europe. Halt to further Soviet deployment of SS 20s as well as of shorter-range nuclear missiles in East Germany and Czechoslovakia.

April 1985   Offer to reduce nuclear arsenal by 25 per cent.

12/7/1985   General Chervov clarifies the April offer by stating that the 25 per cent reduction meant warheads as well as missiles.

1/8/1985   Soviet announcement of the decision to stop all nuclear explosions unilaterally from 6 August (since then extended).

End of Sept. 1985 Proposal (clarified by Gorbachev in his speech to the French parliament on 3/10) including the following:

1. Total prohibition of space weapons.
2. Reduction by the USSR and the US of all nuclear arms capable of reaching each other's territory by 50 per cent.
3. Offer of separate talks to France and Britain regarding their nuclear arsenals.
4. Moratorium on the deployment of SS 20s. (The number of SS 20s on standby alert in the European zone was 243 as of June 1984.) All SS 20s that were deployed after June 1984 have been withdrawn from standby alert, and the stationary installations for housing these missiles are to be dismantled.
5. Suggestion that an agreement on medium-range nuclear missiles in Europe is possible separately, and without direct regard to the problem of space and strategic arms.

15/1/1986   Proposal by Gorbachev for a three-stage programme to eliminate all nuclear weapons by 1999.

Stage I

Within the next 5–8 years the USSR and the

USA should reduce by one half the nuclear arms that can reach each other's territory. On the remaining delivery vehicles of this kind each side would retain no more than 6,000 warheads. Plus:

Renouncement by both countries of the development, testing and deployment of space strike weapons; the complete elimination of Soviet and American intermediate-range nuclear missiles, both ballistic and Cruise missiles, in Europe; both countries to agree to stop all nuclear explosions.

Stage II

Should start no later than 1990 and last 5–7 years. The other nuclear powers would pledge to freeze all their nuclear arms and not to deploy them in the territories of other countries.

The USSR and the USA would go on with the reductions agreed upon in the first stage, and carry out further measures designed to eliminate their medium-range nuclear weapons and freeze their tactical nuclear systems.

Upon the completion by the USSR and the USA of the 50 per cent reduction in arms that can reach each other's territory, all nuclear powers should eliminate their tactical nuclear arms, i.e. weapons having a range of up to 1,000 km.

Plus:

The prohibition of space strike weapons to become multilateral, with the mandatory participation of major industrial powers; all nuclear powers to stop nuclear weapons tests; ban on the development of non-nuclear weapons based on new principles with destructive capacity close to that of nuclear weapons or other weapons of mass destruction.

Stage III

To begin no later than 1995 and to be completed by 1999. All remaining nuclear weapons to be eliminated.

As the first practical step, the Soviet Union extends by three months the unilateral moratorium on any nuclear explosions, and calls upon the USA to join this moratorium, which could then lead to the complete and general prohibition of nuclear weapons tests.

18/4/1986   Proposal for 'substantial reductions' in conventional forces and tactical air fighter units throughout Europe 'from the Atlantic to the Urals'.

26/5/1986   Offer that the Soviet Union would match any cut in Britain's nuclear weapons with comparable reductions in Soviet arsenals.

11/6/1986   Warsaw Pact proposal includes the following points:

1. Within the next year or two NATO and the Warsaw pact should withdraw between 100,000 and 150,000 troops each from Europe.
2. The Warsaw Pact is ready to reduce the size of its land and tactical air forces in Europe by 25 per cent by the early 1990s, if NATO would do the same.
3. There should be an accompanying cut in tactical nuclear weapons in Europe.

June 1986   (1st, 16th) Limited laboratory research on SDI would be accepted, while both sides would limit their strategic arsenals. (1,600 launchers and 8,000 warheads.) Both sides should agree not to withdraw from the 1972 Anti-Ballistic Missile Treaty for 15 years from 1986.

September 1986 The Stockholm Security Conference on confidence-building measures concluded with a general commitment to 'the principle of peaceful settlement of disputes', and a specific agreement on notification and inspection of military manoeuvres involving more than 13,000 troops or 300 tanks. The Soviet Union agreed to inspection on site as well as from the air.

Appendix II

Estimates of the USSR/US strategic balance

Table 6.1: American view of the US/USSR strategic balance, 1985

	US	USSR
Warheads on ICBMs	2,130	6,300
ICBMs	1,045	1,398
Warheads on SLBMs	5,700	2,077
Ballistic missile throw-weight	4.4 mil. lb	11.8 mil. lb
IRBMs	109	378
Strategic bombers	271	375
ABM forces	Active research program. One EW ABM radar	Active research program. One ABM system deployed around Moscow

Table 6.2: International Institute of Strategic Studies estimate of US/USSR strategic balance in terms of launchers and warheads, mid-1984

	Deployed launchers		Warheads	
	US	USSR	US	USSR
ICBMs	1,037	1,398	2,137	5,230
SLBMs	592	981	5,344	1,874
ICBM/SLBM subtotal	1,629	2,379	7,481	7,104
Bombers	297	143	2,756	286

Source: Jones (1986), p. 45.

References

Akhromeev, S. (1985) 'Washington's contentions and real facts', *Pravda*, 19 October, in *Soviet News*, 23 October

Bialer, S. (ed.) (1981) *The domestic context of Soviet foreign policy*, Croom Helm, London

Bialer, S. and Afferica, S. (1986) 'The genesis of Gorbachev's world', *Foreign Affairs, 64* (3)

Brown, A. (1986) 'Change in the Soviet Union', *Foreign Affairs, 64* (5)

Byrnes, R.F. (ed.) (1983) *After Brezhnev*, Frances Pinter, London

Cassen, R. (ed.) (1985) *Soviet interests in the Third World*, Sage Publications, London

Cohen, S.F. (ed.) (1984) 'The friends and foes of change: reformism and conservatism in the Soviet Union' in E.P. Hoffman and R.F. Laird (eds), *Soviet policy in the modern era*, Aldine Publishing Company, New York

Edwards, G. (1985) 'Human rights and Basket III issues: areas of change and continuity', *International Affairs,* Autumn

Goldblat, J. (1982) *Agreements for arms control: a critical survey,* SIPRI, Taylor and Francis, London

Gorbachev, M.S. (1985a) Speech to the French Parliament, *Soviet News,* 9 October

——— (1985b) Press conference in Geneva 21 November, *Soviet News,* 27 November

——— (1985c) Interview, *Time* (36)

——— (1985d) Report to the Supreme Soviet 27 November, *Soviet News,* 27 November

——— (1985e) Statement at press conference in Paris 4 October, *Soviet News,* 9 October

——— (1986a) Report to the XXVII Congress of the CPSU 25 February, *Soviet News,* 26 February

——— (1986b) Statement made 15 January, *Soviet News,* 22 January

Hanson, P. (1985) 'Economic aspects of Helsinki', *International Affairs,* Autumn

Heller, A. (1985) 'No more Mr Nice Guy', *New Socialist,* December

Hough, J.F. (1985) 'Gorbachev's strategy', *Foreign Affairs, 64* (1)

Hutchings, R.L. (1983) *Soviet-East European relations: consolidation and conflict 1968-1980,* The Wisconsin Press, Wisconsin and London

Jahn, E. (ed.) (1978) *Soviet foreign policy,* Allison and Busby, London

Jones, C.D. (1981) *Soviet influence in Eastern Europe,* Praeger, New York

Jones, D.R. (ed.) (1986) *Soviet armed forces review annual 9,* Academic International Press, Gulf Breeze

Kaldor, M. (1982) *The baroque arsenal,* Abacus, Sphere Books, London

Kanet, R.E. (ed.) (1982) *Soviet foreign policy in the 1980s,* Praeger, New York

Khovanski, S. (1986) 'Afghanistan: the bleeding wound', *Detente,* Spring

Lutwak, E.N. (1983) *The grand design of the Soviet Union,* St Martin's Press, New York

Menon, R. (1986) *Soviet power and the Third World,* Yale University Press, New Haven and London

'Moscow announces rights commission' (1986) *The Guardian,* 1 August, p. 7

Payne, S.B. (1980) *The Soviet Union and SALT,* The MIT Press, Massachusetts

Prokhanov, A. (1985) 'Zapiski na brone', *Literaturnaya Gazeta,* 28 August, p. 14

Ritherland, P. (1986) 'Nuclear arms: a one-horse race?', *Detente,* Spring

'Russia shifts its attitude to a British arms freeze' (1986) *The Guardian,* 8 July, p. 6

Sagdeyev, R.Z. and Kokoshkin, A.A. (eds.) (1985) 'Report on Star Wars', reported in *Nature, 313,* 17 January, p. 170

Smith, R.K. (1986) 'The separation of arms control talks: the Reagan redefinition of arms control and strategy', *Journal of International Studies, 15* (2)

Steele, J. (1983) *World power: Soviet foreign policy under Brezhnev and Andropov,* Michael Joseph, London

——— and Abraham, E. (1983) *Andropov in power,* Martin Robertson, Oxford

Valkenier, E.K. (1986) 'Revolutionary change in the Third World: recent Soviet assessments', *World Politics, 38* (3)

Yakhontov, Yu. (1985) 'Kuda dreiftuet FRG?', *Pravda*, 5 April, p. 4

'Za rasshirenie sotsial'noi bazy afganskoi revolyutsii' (1985) *Pravda*, 21 December, p. 4

7

Conclusions

David A. Dyker

Our main conclusions are as follows:

(1) We closed Chapter 1 with a reference to Gorbachev's impeccable Party apparatus pedigree. Nothing has happened since Gorbachev became General Secretary to suggest that he intends to attack, or even question, any of the main assumptions of Party rule. As Iain Elliot points out, the new leader's sweeping personnel changes were overdue and biologically inevitable, and reversed a trend to absolute security of tenure which had only developed under Brezhnev. Gorbachev's new men are all from an apparatus or technocratic background — there are no 'outsiders' — and all have been nominated to their positions in that peculiarly Bolshevik (perhaps we should say Stalinist) way which seems to reflect so faithfully the tradition of authoritarian arbitrariness. The intimation of a more open approach to leadership changes which Khrushchev's ouster in 1964 brought has found as little response in the Gorbachev era as it did during the Brezhnev era.

We may have to modify this general conclusion to a degree under two headings:

(2) The policy of *glasnost'* — media openness — must be taken seriously, and it does represent a real break with the past. The period in which news of great disasters circulated in the Soviet Union through the media of rumour and gossip may have ended for ever. But the Chernobyl' and Daniloff cases illustrate that there are definite limits to this new media openness. And as Iain Elliot emphasises, there are no signs that *media* openness is going to shade into, or even facilitate, *political* openness.

(3) Gorbachev is more pragmatic about private enterprise than perhaps any of his predecessors have been. We can see this in the

history of Stavropol' province under his prefecture, and we can see it in the agricultural policies enshrined in recent documents. The implicit notion of developing the collective contract idea as a bridge between private and socialist agricultural sectors is genuinely radical, and indeed goes right against two basic principles of the traditional Bolshevik approach — the condemnation of private enterprise and the power of arbitrary command. As we saw in Chapter 4, there are plenty of obstacles, political and administrative, to be overcome before the new line on private subsidiary agriculture can really come through. Outside of agriculture, Gorbachev's less jaundiced view of private enterprise is likely to mean the legalisation of part of the grey economy, with the *shabashniki*, particularly those involved in house maintenance, being encouraged to come out into the open. But the fact that Gorbachev is more enlightened about private enterprise in subsidiary areas does *not* mean that he is in favour of market socialism within the state and collective sectors.

(4) Rather his approach to the planning problems of Soviet industry and collective/state farming alike is that of a *rationaliser* and *disciplinarian*. He perceives that productivity is the biggest weakness of the Soviet economy as a whole, and seeks to attack that problem in two main ways: by following Andropov's example in clamping down on slackness, poor time-keeping and drunkenness at the place of work; and by seeking to ensure that the Soviet worker is much better equipped than he has been in the past. There can be no doubt that he means business on both those counts. Over the first half of 1986 output of alcoholic beverages fell by 35 per cent, while that of non-alcoholic drinks rose by 41 per cent ('Ob itogakh . . .', 1986, p. 5). The unequivocal commitment to the extension of the Sumy experiment and the provisions of the March decree on agriculture underline Gorbachev's determination to turn over a large proportion of medium-scale investment decisions to the enterprises and farms involved, and to insist that they find the finance for these investments from their own profits. The changes in the foreign trade system, actual and projected, described by Alan Smith are clearly intended to underpin this strategy. On the one hand, associations and enterprises are to be allowed more direct contact with foreign suppliers of equipment, to shorten lead-times and ensure that they get the machinery they really want. On the other, production organisations are to be permitted to retain some of their hard-currency earnings from exporting — so that they can

themselves finance the import of machinery.

But there is a problem here. As Andropov saw clearly in his time, behind discipline problems are often to be found planning problems. Uneven supply of inputs means layoffs, and that is when the men start drinking. In conditions where consumer goods are short in supply and poor in quality rubles may be convertible only into vodka, and we can refer back to the key resource-allocation role played by vodka in the village of Zakharovka — how, one may ask, is it *possible* for a tractor driver to stay sober under these circumstances? On the investment side, there is the fundamental problem of marrying up decentralised investment *funds* with centralised investment *supplies*. This was one of the difficulties which wrecked the Kosygin planning reform of 1965, and it could do the same to Gorbachev's reforms.

This brings us on to two key political problems:

(5) Why is it that Soviet leaders, even razor-sharp ones like Gorbachev, seem to find it so difficult to learn from the past? Is it because they perceive, but find it impossible to act? Is it because they see 'reforms' and 'experiments' in purely token terms, and actually feel safer in the knowledge that internal contradictions will inevitably bring them to nought? Such explanations might do for some of the General Secretary's predecessors, but they will not do for a man as energetic and intent at least on *change* as Gorbachev himself. It is hard not to feel that there is something inherent in the political system which ensures that the Soviets, like the Bourbons, never learn anything and never forget anything. Marxist-Leninist modes of thought make it difficult for Soviet policy-makers to think in any other terms except those of a smooth progression — however long it takes — towards Full Communism. Certainly the new Party Programme, which bears a strong personal Gorbachev imprint, breaks fresh ground in admitting that the economic slowdown of the Brezhnev period reflected a general failure to grapple with basic planning problems ('Programma . . . ', 1986, p. 7). But there is still an overwhelming tendency in the Soviet Union to blame past foul-ups on incompetent and/or self-seeking individuals. Gorbachev's new broom policy has done nothing to counter that tendency. Such a political environment cannot but be inimical to the study of recent history as an exercise in 'learning by doing', to the assessment of errors and failures as legitimate pieces of experience, with perhaps more to teach the student than successes and victories. Again, we should

maybe restate the obvious in reminding the reader that very few scholarly works on recent Soviet history are published in the Soviet Union. Soviet Studies as a serious discipline exists only in the West, and its *lingua franca* is English, not Russian. Of course, Soviet leaders do have access to Western materials — even if they have neither the time nor the linguistic accomplishments to use them directly — through the medium of specialised academic units which scan the 'bourgeois Sovietological' output. But if the Soviet authorities are to think more deeply and more systematically about the recent history of government measures in the USSR, they will have to be prompted by their own scholars and think-tanks. Here is one respect in which Gorbachev's *glasnost'* policy, with all its limitations, could make a substantial difference in the long term. But it may be Gorbachev's successor, rather than Gorbachev himself, who benefits from this.

(6) How big a risk is Gorbachev running of becoming critically unpopular with the masses? Iain Elliot draws our attention to the special dangers of a *glasnost'* policy which exposes the incompetence and corruption of individuals, always Party members and often Party administrators, but does not allow anyone from outside the Party to become involved in bringing these individuals to book. Philip Hanson remarks, tongue in cheek, but with a serious purpose, that 'the . . . danger for Gorbachev is that on one of his Western style walkabouts he might get lynched . . . by an alcoholics' revolt' (EIU, 1985, pp. 6–7). Again to underline one of Iain Elliot's key points, the campaign against corruption and unearned incomes hits primarily the ordinary folk, the outsiders. While many Party activists clearly are corrupt, particularly in the Caucasus and Central Asia, the insider is much less dependent on outright bribery to get what he wants — he can use political influence, political blackmail etc. — in a word *blat.* Now Gorbachev's more pragmatic policies on the private sector are aimed to counter this difficulty and ensure that ordinary folk can get their cars fixed and their parties organised without breaking the law. But of course even if car maintenance *shabashniki* are prevailed upon to come out into the open, there is still the question of where they will obtain oil, spare parts, etc. And an approach which seeks to instil discipline by forcing the workers themselves to pay for the effects of foul-ups, however complex the origins of these foul-ups, is hardly calculated to endear.

Certainly we should not assume that Gorbachev is terribly

concerned to endear. The sustained emphasis on the importance of slimming down workforces, at factory and brigade level, the readiness to introduce a savagely moralistic tone into this policy dimension through the Leningrad experiment, the open discussion at the Congress of the likelihood of 20 million redundancies by the end of the century — all this suggests that Gorbachev is seeking to develop a constituency among top workers, manual and managerial, and is frankly contemptuous of those who fail to make the grade. The new ideology of self-management is surely aimed at the achievers, not the masses. Economically, this makes sense. At the present stage of development, amorphous, unskilled labour is of little use to the Soviet Union. Better, as Ota Šik in his time would have argued, to have a smaller number of highly efficient industrial production units, whatever the implications in terms of unemployment, than a string of overmanned, obsolescent capacities. But politically, it must be a slightly dangerous game. Brezhnev ruled, and survived, by serving the constituencies of the Party apparatus and the Soviet working class at large. The new General Secretary must already have upset at least some sections of the apparatus, and he seems intent on upsetting large sections of the working class. However much Gorbachev may have consolidated his position at the XXVII Congress, he will clearly have to continue to cover his political rear.

(7) To make matters worse, he may find that his industrial and agricultural policies offend and upset, without producing the required results. Picking up the argument laid out under (4) above, on the internal inconsistencies in Gorbachev's productivity strategy, brings us back to one of the most fundamental leitmotifs of this whole work. The Soviet system is grossly overcentralised. In the economic sphere it is that overcentralisation which imposes impossible tasks on the industrial supply system and makes supply breakdowns inevitable. It is because successive Soviet governments have not been prepared to bite the bullet and marketise large sectors of investment supply that the strategy of increasing the role of decentralised investment has never worked. All of this brings us back to the theme of wholesale trade in the means of production. As we saw in Chapter 3, Gorbachev has still not really got beyond the stage of making polite noises on that most pressing issue. Of course, he may have plans for the future, but if so he is certainly advancing very cautiously indeed.

The other key technical planning issue is stable norms. The March 1986 decree on agriculture does make some progress in the direction of de-emphasising the output target as the linchpin of the planning system, and thus removing the built-in incentive to capacity concealment and disincentive to innovation which bedevil all attempts to transform the economy into a high-productivity one. In industry, on the other hand, not even the Sumy experiment releases enterprises from the obligation to fulfil output targets. The persistence of output targets does not, of course, necessarily mean that the stable norms principle cannot be maintained in relation to the link between profits and bonus funds. And as East German and Bulgarian experience indicates, output targets in themselves may do little damage — as long as they are slack rather than taut, and subject to a reasonable degree of free negotiation. Now this is precisely the direction that Soviet agricultural planning is moving in, with the general emphasis on the collective contract and the special price provisions of the March 1986 decree. But the analysis of Chapter 4 illustrated just how many problems this approach runs into in practice, and how uncomfortably it lies with a political tradition which has trained the *apparatchiki* to think that when output trends are unfavourable the only proper response is *direct* pressure to improve them.

Finally, Gorbachev's plans to bring the second economy out into the open may backfire. The sharp cutback in state production of alcohol must involve some danger that the moonshine industry, already in a fairly healthy state, will start to develop with renewed vigour. The general emphasis on decentralised investment will certainly produce a lot of pressures for informal procurement — informal wholesale trade in the means of production in fact — which might well outrun cautious steps in the direction of legalising the *shabashnik*. We could end up back in the situation of the early 1970s, with the pushers destabilising central priorities and the *apparatchiki* seizing the opportunity to dig their heels in on all sorts of issues. (8) But things are not so very bad on the domestic economic front. Net Material Product is still officially reported to be growing at around 3 per cent per annum (that probably means about 2 per cent in GDP terms), and the rate may if anything rise a little through 1987 and 1988, as industrial output continues to grow in a fairly buoyant way. Agricultural prospects are less clear, though the 1986 harvest was the best since 1978. But that perennial crisis sector apart, there is nothing in current Soviet production trends to give Mr Gorbachev a big fright. To the extent that this creates complacency, or induces the leadership to think they have all the time in the world to solve their problems, it may be a mixed blessing.

(9) On the international front, by contrast, pressure is building up in a big way. As Alan Smith argues cogently in Chapter 5, the whole pattern of Soviet industrial development has been fundamentally based on the acquisition of foreign machinery and technology, and that is not something that can be changed overnight, whatever Mr Ryzhkov says. But with the collapse in the price of oil, and the likelihood of a need to continue with large-scale food and feed imports, there is no immediate prospect of a recovery in the currently low rate of machinery imports, which could spell technological disaster in a few years' time. Assessment of medium-term prospects must focus on possibilities for increasing Soviet exports, rather than any chance of a sharp recovery in energy prices.

The scenario that Alan Smith alludes to, whereby the input priorities hitherto reserved for the Soviet arms industry might be switched to a new breed of Soviet exporting organisation, must certainly be taken seriously. The Soviets have surely proved, through their Third World arms exports, that they are able to compete in international equipment markets. A number of key individuals have been moved from the defence industry over into civilian industry in recent years, possibly reflecting a desire on the part of the government to 'pep up' civilian industry with some military efficiency. Of course such a strategy would only work if accompanied by far-reaching changes in the domestic economic system. The maintenance of quality standards in the defence industry is crucially dependent on the political muscle of the Ministry of Defence, which ensures that here, at least, the market is not a sellers' one. Export associations constrained to keep up to the exacting quality and technology requirements of the world market would have to be in a position to impose the same standards on their domestic suppliers, and that means having the right to negotiate their own prices and contracts, at least within limits. Taking the argument one step further, and bearing in mind the experience of the Brezhnev period, any new hard-currency flows generated by such an export drive would be to a great extent wasted unless accompanied by measures, rather more far-reaching than those currently envisaged, to ensure that imported technology is assimilated quickly and efficiently.

Still, the economic interest of the Soviet Union in arms control, from the point of view of industrial restructuring, is obvious. Equally obvious is its interest in arms control from the angle of basic macro-economic realities. The Warsaw Pact cannot match the level of GNP

David A. Dyker

of the Atlantic Pact countries, and there is no prospect of it doing so in the foreseeable future. The burden that 'parity' has consequently placed on the Soviet economy is a very heavy one, and the SDI scenario could make it an unbearable one. We have seen in Zdeněk Kavan's chapter how strongly committed to MAD the Soviets are, and we need only add that there is nothing in the idea of balanced arms reduction which goes against the theory of MAD. In principle, an arms limitation deal could allow Moscow to continue to pursue its goal of *political* parity, while substantially reducing the economic pressure that pursuance of that goal currently involves. But there are three major obstacles to such a deal. First, in a situation where the Warsaw Pact enjoys at least numerical supremacy in many areas, the very concept of balanced reduction becomes a difficult one to handle. Secondly, the United States may simply prefer to go for the possibility of breaking the framework of MAD once and for all through SDI, in the knowledge that Soviet technological woes would make it virtually impossible for Moscow to compete. Thirdly, as Zdeněk Kavan argues so forcibly, the human rights dimension is likely to make international co-operation more, not less difficult. The real prospects for change in the international dimension, like the real prospects for reform at home, remain deeply uncertain.

References

EIU (1985) *Quarterly economic Review of USSR* (2)
'Ob itogakh vypolneniya Gosudarstvennogo plana ekonomicheskogo i sotsial'nogo razvitiya SSSR v pervom polugodii 1986 goda' (1986) *Ekonomicheskaya Gazeta* (31), special supplement
'Programma Kommunisticheskoi partii Sovetskogo Soyuza. Novaya redaktsiya' (1986) *Ekonomicheskaya Gazeta* (11), special supplement

Postscript

There were a number of interesting developments touching on our main themes during the period between September 1986 and February 1987. Most of these confirm the general tenor of our conclusions, while at the same time giving us a broader base on which to assess Gorbachev's political and policy style. We take them in turn, following the same sequence as the chapters of the book.

Domestic politics

Gorbachev has continued with his new broom policy in relation to personnel. Ministers are still being regularly sacked, for weakness in the face of corruption, incompetence or insufficient alacrity in the pursuance of new policies. Further up the hierarchy, the veteran Brezhnevite and wheeler-dealer Dinmukhamed Kunaev, dismissed from his post as first secretary of the Kazakh Communist Party in December 1986, subsequently lost his Politburo seat at the January 1987 Plenum of the Central Committee. Kunaev's dismissal, and replacement by an ethnic Russian from metropolitan Russia, Gennadii Kolbin, sparked off riots in Alma-Ata, the capital of Kazakhstan, in which 20 people died. Kolbin is a 100 per cent Gorbachev man, and almost certainly got the Kazakhstan job primarily on the basis of his proven record as a fighter against corruption. This tells us a lot about Gorbachev's priorities, though in the wake of the disturbances Gorbachev may now be reconsidering the political price of ethnic peace. The other main personnel development in the period culminating in the January 1987 Plenum has been the rapid promotion of Aleksandr Yakovlev. Promoted within the Central Committee secretariat to a position of overall responsibility for propaganda and cultural matters at the end of 1986, he was then promoted to candidate Politburo status at the January Plenum. That meeting also produced a number of changes in the secretariat itself, with the retirement of Mikhail Zimyanin and the appointment as full secretaries of Nikolai Slyun'kov, already a candidate member of the Politburo, and Anatolii Luk'yanov. It is fair to say that the extent of personnel changes announced at the January 1987 Plenum was less sweeping than some had expected.

The theme of *glasnost'* has continued to feature strongly. The Alma-Ata riots were reported in the Soviet press in some detail, and without gross distortion. Meanwhile, jamming of the BBC Russian service has ceased. Perhaps most striking of all, the KGB itself began to feel the bracing wind of 'restructuring' right at the end of 1986, with the dismissal of a senior official in the Ukraine for victimisation and unlawful actions. The process set in train by the rehabilitation of Academician Sakharov has gathered momentum, with the release of Irini Ratushinskaya in December 1986, and then the dramatic announcement of an amnesty for 140 political prisoners in February 1987.

The same orientation is evident in Gorbachev's pronouncements on the Soviet political system made at the January 198 Plenum. He set out a series of reforming principles as follows

(1) Party secretaries should be elected by Party committees secret ballot rather than nominated from above.
(2) At factory and farm level foremen, brigadiers and even dire tors should be elected. Open competition should be developed a way of recruiting management personnel.
(3) There should be multiple candidacies for elections to the Supreme Soviet.
(4) More non-Party people, and more women, should be brought into responsible positions.
(5) 'Real democracy does not exist outside or above the law.' A new law to facilitate the pursuance in the courts of complaints against officials is reported to be in preparation.

The implementation of these proposals would, certainly, do less than transform the Soviet political system. It would still be impossible for anyone to be elevated to a responsible position without the positive approval of the Party. Gorbachev immediately qualifies the point about election of Party secretaries with the statement that 'of course it must remain a sacrosanct principle within the Party that decisions of superior organs are binding on all subordinate Party committees, including decisions on jobs and postings.' But the Soviet leader is clearly holding fast to his golden rule that greater openness is a necessary condition for a greater sense of responsibility, just as the latter is the key condition for increased efficiency. He may also perceive the potential of more democratic procedures in breaking up 'family circles' of apparatus men with little appetite for reform.

Domestic economic policy

Further developments have confirmed the status of the Sumy system as Gorbachev's favourite experiment. On 1 January 1987 it was extended throughout a number of industrial ministries, including the Ministries of Chemical and Oil Machine Building and Vehicle Production. The system being generalised to these two ministries specifically follows the Sumy model, rather than the similar but slightly more radical VAZ experiment, in that deductions from profits into the state budget are *planned*, rather than being a pure residual. Beyond that, early reports of the extension of the experiment contain familiar complaints about continued 'petty tutelage'. So what has happened to 'wholesale trade in the means of production'? In an article in *Voprosy Ekonomiki* (No. 10, 1986, p. 19) Petr Bunich tells us that 'non-planned wholesale trade' is to be introduced for 10,000 user-organisations in 1987. It is, of course, unclear exactly what this phrase means. The official line, as expressed by Professor Aganbegyan, is still as clear on the prospective role of the market mechanism within the consumer goods industries as it is vague on its role in relations between core industrial enterprises. At the same time Academician A. Rumyantsev and Yu. Goland have argued in the pages of *Ekonomicheskaya Gazeta* (No. 4, 1987, pp. 14–15) that 'directive planning could be restricted to the production of just a narrow range of key products with stable demand. That means mainly fuel and energy resources, the most important types of raw materials, and custom-built pieces of equipment.' They go on to suggest that industrial enterprises should normally be allowed to devote part of their production capacity to the satisfaction of specific orders coming through the dimension of wholesale trade, with no plan targets as such involved at all. Rumyantsev and Goland lay great stress on the importance of customer power, and talk about the need to develop the forces of competition. This is clearly not the official line, but the fact that it has been published in a key newspaper tells us a good deal about what *glasnost'* can mean in the field of economic policy discussion.

What, then, is the official line? One of the more bizarre developments at the end of 1986/beginning of 1987 was the introduction of the system of *Gospriemka*, a new approach to quality control. A whole new inspectorate has been put together whose task it is to travel the country, descending on selected enterprises, going through their entire production range looking for defects — and generally putting the fear of death into everyone. The new system has three striking characteristics. First, it overlaps with the existing system of quality control. Secondly, it places little reliance on the market mechanism, the most obvious instrument of quality control. Thirdly, and not unconnectedly, the whole campaign has been characterised by a very high Party profile. There is a strong hint of a return to the traditional trouble-shooting role of the Party apparatus in the *Gospriemka* campaign, and that is all the more odd in the light of Gorbachev's statements at the January 1987 Plenum. The Party apparatus, he argued, must stop meddling in economic affairs, and get back to its proper job as educator and inspirer of the people. Indeed at one point in his speech he says that 'we have got to sort out the jumble of checkings and inspections which literally snow under enterprises and other organisations. The benefit we get from these is practically nil.' Elsewhere in the speech, however, he stresses the importance of *Gospriemka*, while at the same time emphasising the difficulties it faces. So what does the Soviet leader really think of *Gospriemka*? Is he, perhaps, allowing the initiative to proceed on the basis that it is as well to keep the apparatus busy while more important things are afoot, and that the inevitable failure of the campaign will strengthen his case for a more thoroughgoing approach?

We are on much more solid ground with the new wage system announced in October 1986. True to the philosophy of incentives and discipline, the wage tariff arrangements have been revamped so as to create bigger differentials for higher skill and responsibility levels, and more automatic penalties for indiscipline. Already a number of enterprises have taken full advantage of the new system to widen the range of wage rates to the maximum and create redundancies on a large scale. Even here, however, full development of the initiative has run up against general systemic difficulties. Some enterprises want to use redundant workers to staff wholly new departments. But the regulations do not allow them to set up wholly new departments. Thus the theme of the incompatibility of partial reform and general immobilism continues to pervade the Soviet economic scene.

Agricultural policy has developed very much along the lines marked out in the early part of 1986. The link is still in fashion, the family link especially so, and farm managements are still being criticised for obstructing the introduction of radically decentralised work-team systems. In line with the new legislation of November 1986 aimed at increasing the role of individual and co-operative labour in the Soviet economy as a whole, there have also been encouraging noises about the private subsidiary agricultural sector. But there is still a hint that the authorities would like to bring that sector under closer control.

External economic relations

We now have more details on exactly how the new foreign trade system is going to operate. The salient points are as follows

(1) A new State Commission for External Economic Affairs has been created. It will exercise general supervisory authority over all organisations involved in foreign trade, and will decide which associations and enterprises are to be allowed to operate directly in import-export matters.
(2) Direct access to the international economy is to be largely limited to machinery and equipment sectors, but will also be extended to some transport and food branches. Fuel exports, accounting for some 80 per cent of total exports, will remain the monopoly of the Ministry of Foreign Trade, as will grain imports. It is expected that in 1987 the new system will cover some 20 per cent of total import-export activity, but as much as 40 per cent of the trade in machinery.
(3) Organisations operating under the new regime will be set targets for hard-currency earnings, and will be allowed considerable autonomy in pursuing these targets. It appears that they will be permitted to agree their own prices with foreign firms, and to negotiate their own contracts with their Soviet suppliers. They will be allowed a definite retention quota of foreign exchange, and will be able to spend this freely. They will also be able to take out hard-currency loans from the Foreign Trade Bank with repayment periods of up to four years.

We should certainly not exaggerate the importance of these measures. They give Soviet organisations real autonomy in relation to imports only to the extent that they can export manufactures, not something the Soviets have found easy to do in the past. But it is striking that the privileged group of enterprises are to be given an unusual degree of freedom to fix their own prices and contracts. If this turned out to be the thin end of the wedge for the Soviet economy as a whole it could be of substantial importance.

Foreign policy

Not a great deal happened on this dimension in the months following the failure of the Reykjavik summit in October 1986. But the Geneva talks have reconvened, and the replacement as chief Soviet negotiator of Viktor Karpov by the more senior Yulii Vorontsov is clearly meant as a signal that the Soviets are still very keen to reach an arms reduction deal. This impression was strongly confirmed in January 1987 when British Foreign Office Minister of State, Timothy Renton visited Moscow. The Soviet announcement that it has withdrawn all its intermediate-range missiles from the Kola peninsula, in the Arctic, is of little military significance, and has been greeted cautiously by the Scandinavian countries. Moscow's statement that while it no longer recognises SALT II limits it does not plan to match US breaches of those limits has to be set against American claims that the Soviets have already gone beyond the SALT II quotas. Meanwhile the Americans seem set on forging ahead with the development of SDI. The declaration of a unilateral cease-fire by the Kabul government on 15 January 1987, coupled with conciliatory statements made by Mr Shevardnadze during his early January visit to Afghanistan, suggest that the Soviet leadership is serious in its attempts to find a solution to the Afghanistan problem. Whether such a solution can be found within the limits of what is acceptable to the Soviet side is another matter.

David A. Dyker

Glossary

ABM	Anti-Ballistic Missile
agitprop	propaganda and agitation
apparatchik (pl. -i)	professional Communist Party administrator
ASBM	Air-to-Surface Ballistic Missile
blat	political back-scratching, who-you-know, string-pulling, etc.
CMEA	Council for Mutual Economic Assistance — Comecon
edinonachalie	one-man management
FTA	foreign trade association
GKES	State Committee for Foreign Economic Relations
glasnost'	media openness
Gosagroprom	State Agro-Industrial Committee
Gosplan	State Planning Commission
Gossnab	State Supply Committee
gostorg	under NEP, organisation which acted as intermediary between foreign organisations and domestic enterprises
ICBM	Inter-Continental Ballistic Missile
khozraschet	business/economic accounting
kolkhoz (pl. -y)	collective farm
kolkhoznik (pl. -i)	collective farmer
kollektivnyi podryad	collective contract
Komsomol	Young Communist League
krai	province
kraikom	provincial Communist Party committee
kulak	rich peasant
MAD	Mutually Assured Destruction
MGU	Moscow State University
Minvodkhoz	Ministry for Drainage and Irrigation
MIRV	Multiple Independently-targetable Re-entry Vehicle
MTS	machine tractor station
NEP	New Economic Policy

NIC	newly industrialising country
oblast'	province
obkom	provincial Communist Party committee
Politburo	Communist Party cabinet
RAPO	district agro-industrial association
RSFSR	Russian Soviet Federal Socialist Republic
SALT	strategic arms limitation treaty
samizdat	illegal duplication and circulation of documents
samoupravlenie	self-management
SDI	Strategic Defense Initiative — 'Star Wars'
Sel'khoztekhnika	industrial supplies to agriculture organisation
shabashnik (pl. -i)	moonlighter, 'lump' worker
SLBM	Submarine-Launched Ballistic Missile
snabsbyt	local supply depot
sovkhoz (pl. -y)	state farm
sovkhoznik (pl. -i)	state farmer
tolkach	'pusher' — unofficial procurement agent
zveno	link — small, autonomous workteam in agriculture

Index

Index

Nikonov, V. 30, 38, 39
non-Black Earth Programme 95

OECD 146
Oman 183
O'Neill, T. 25

Pares, B. 22
Paris 171, 179–80, 184
participation rate 4
People's Commissariat for
Foreign Trade *see* Ministry
for Foreign Trade
permanent production
conference 66
Peter the Great 22, 161
Poland 11–14, 54, 154, 166,
188, 189, 191
Politburo 7, 19, 24, 28–37, 39,
48, 50, 52, 55, 68, 169
Ponomarev, B. 40, 168
Popov, G. 81
population 4, 6
Poznanski, K. 146
Prague Spring 10, 171
prices
agricultural 6–7, 99–102,
107–11, 114, 116–18, 119
in general 58, 61, 69–71, 76,
81–2, 84, 86, 88, 129,
133, 136, 139–42, 142–6,
152–5, 158, 159
priorities 4, 148, 165
private enterprise outside
agriculture 23, 206
private subsidiary agriculture 7,
15, 23, 95–7, 99, 107–10,
115–16
procurement quotas 3, 4, 98,
99, 109–10, 116–18, 121–2
production development fund
60, 63, 70–3, 75
productivity 4, 5, 30, 46, 60,
63–7, 75–87, 95–6, 127,
130–1, 148, 150
Promyslov, V. 49
purges 7, 47, 48, 129
pushers 62

quality 12, 30, 45, 59–62,
69–70, 73, 81–2, 106, 120,
131, 140–50, 156, 158, 211
Quigley, J. 134

RAPO 99, 103, 106, 108–9,
116–20, 122
Rashidov, S. 40, 47
ratchet principle 59, 62, 65, 68,
89, 129
raw materials endowment 4
Razumovskii, G. 38, 41
Reagan, President 14, 41,
167–8, 175–6, 180, 193
redundancy 60, 63–5, 67,
77–80, 103, 106–11, 145
reform, concept of 1–2, 22–3,
164–5
religion 1
rent 101, 109, 118
returns to scale, increasing or
decreasing 115, 129, 157
river diversion project 52
Romania 11, 154
Romanov, G. 28, 31
Rostov 27
Rusakov, K. 168
Ryzhkov, N. 28, 30–2, 35, 39,
41, 79, 87–8, 130, 148–51,
156

Sakharov, A. 53, 54
SALT 13, 169, 173–6, 195
Samotlor 5
savings deposits 17
Schmidt-Häuer, C. 22
SDI 16, 168, 175–81, 201
second economy 17, 63, 71, 89,
113–16, 121, 210
Second World War 6
secret police 7, 26–31, 39, 49,
52–3
self-management 66–8, 77–80
Sel'khoztekhnika 106, 119–20
Sergeev, A. 81
Shcharanskii, A. 53, 54
Shchekino experiment 60, 63–6,
68
Shchelokov, N. 27, 49

225